RAJASTHAN – A ...

describes the surprises of a great twentieth-century Asian capital and its complex past, the pleasures expected and unexpected of Agra, with its Taj Mahal and I'timad ad-Daula, Red Fort and teeming bazaars. The bulk of Philip Ward's travel guide is devoted to the Country of the Princes: Rajasthan, with its nature reserves of Sariska, Bharatpur and Ranthambore as well as great historic cities such as Amber-Jaipur and Ahar-Udaipur, the frescoed havelis of Shekhavati, the desert cities of Bikaner and Jaisalmer, and the sacred sites of Osiyan, Ranakpur, Nathdwara, Eklingji, Deshnok and Mount Abu. Here are the familiar destinations such as Jodhpur and Pushkar as well as jewels off the beaten track such as Kishangarh, Dig, Kumbhalgarh, Bundi, Kota, and Chittor.

Intended for first-time visitors as well as experienced travellers who want to understand the background to the vision, *Rajasthan, Agra, Delhi* provides a sympathetic and thoughtful companion to India's main attractions.

PHILIP WARD, FRGS, ALA, FRSA, has spent much of his life in Asia and Africa, from Morocco to the Philippines, including eight years in Libya and nearly two in Indonesia. Because of his sympathy with Indian spiritual values, he is an ideal companion to the Mughal and Rajput lands of northern and western India, with their background of Hinduism and Islam. His previous travel books include *Japanese Capitals*, *Bangkok*, *Touring Iran*, *Tripoli*, *Travels in Oman*, *Ha'il, Oasis City of Saudi Arabia* and most recently *Finnish Cities* and *Polish Cities*. *The Times* described his novel on the conquest of Mexico, *Forgotten Games*, as 'brilliant in concept, written in prose as spare, lush and pointed as a cactus garden, as powerful and evocative as a rational nightmare, a logical daydream'. His meditations on the heart of Rajasthan, beginning in Delhi and continuing to Agra, will enthral and amuse the armchair traveller and become essential reading for any Westerner intending to explore the intricacies of art, architecture and everyday life in modern north-west India.

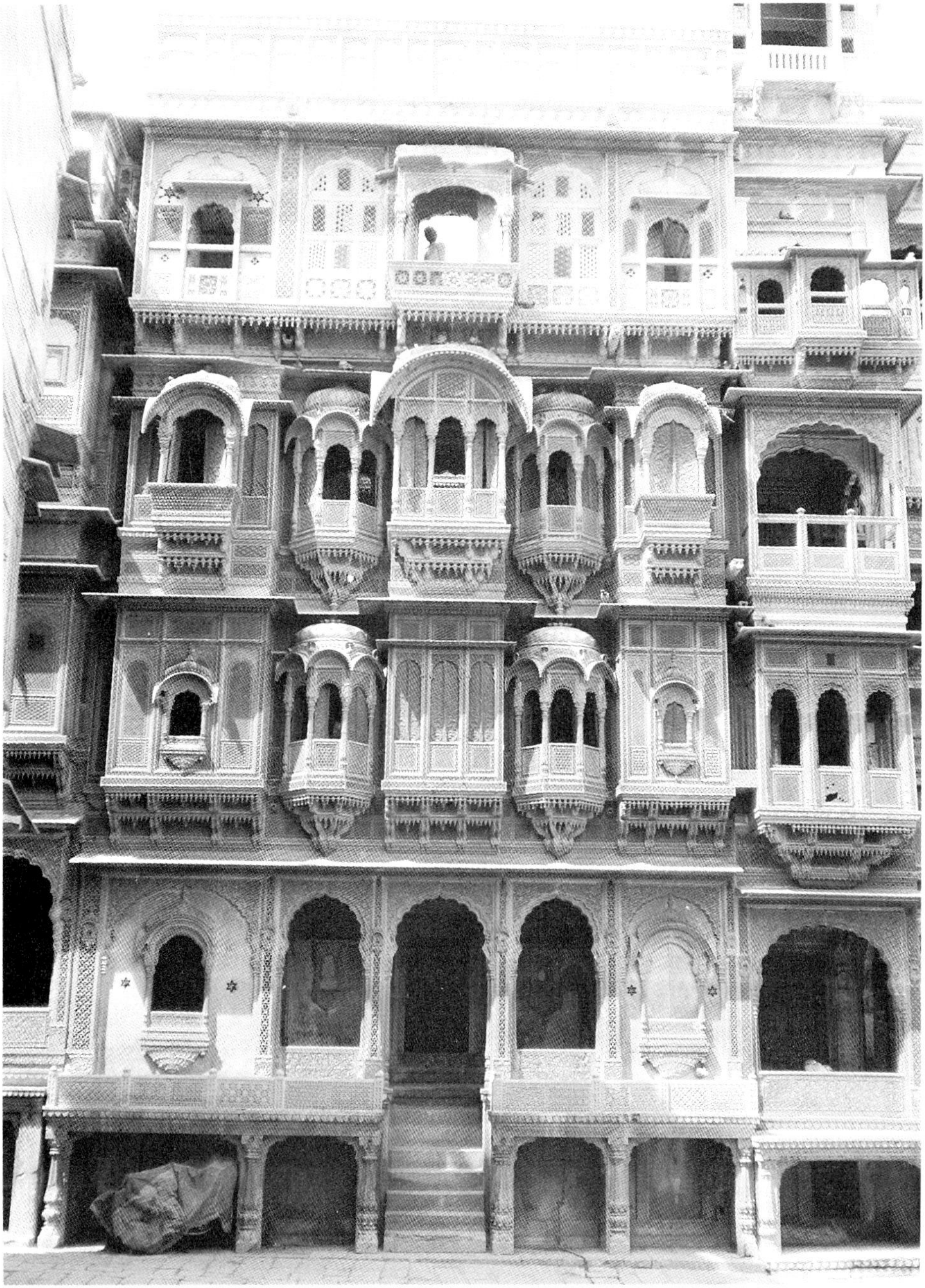

RAJASTHAN AGRA DELHI

A Travel Guide

Philip Ward

Oleander

The Oleander Press
17 Stansgate Avenue
Cambridge CB2 2QZ
England

The Oleander Press
210 Fifth Avenue
New York N.Y. 10010
U.S.A.

© 1989 Philip Ward
and The Oleander Press

British Library Cataloguing in Publication Data

Ward, Philip, 1938-
Rajasthan, Agra, Delhi: a travel guide.–
(Oleander travel books; 15).
1. India (Republic). Agra – Visitors' guides
2. India (Republic). Rajasthan – Visitors' guides
3. India (Republic). Delhi – Visitors' guides
I. Title
915.4'2

ISBN 0-906672-44-9

Printed and bound in Great Britain

Contents

Acknowledgements   vi

Introduction   vii

List of Illustrations   ix

1 **Delhi**   1

2 **Agra**   35
   Mathura – Sikandra – Agra – Fatehpur Sikri

3 **Jaipur**   66
   Bharatpur – Dig – Alwar – Sariska – Amber – Jaipur – Ranthambore – Ajmer – Pushkar – Kishangarh

4 **Shekhavati**   101
   Nawalgarh – Mandawa – Fatehpur Shekhavati

5 **Bikaner**   116
   Bikaner – Gajner – Holi at Bikaner – Deshnok

6 **Jaisalmer**   136
   Pokaran – Jaisalmer – Lodruva

7 **Jodhpur**   159
   Osiyan – Jodhpur – Mandore

8 **Udaipur**   182
   Ranakpur – Kumbhalgarh – Nathdwara – Eklingji – Ahar – Udaipur – Chittor – Bundi – Kota – Mount Abu

Useful Information   223
   When to Come; How to Come; Accommodation; Passports and Visas; Customs and Currency; Health; Clothing; Speaking the Languages; Holidays and Festivals; Books and Maps

Appendix: Salute States of Rajasthan in Local Order of Precedence (1931)   235

Index   236

Acknowledgements

I left England one cold February morning as 'a sudden violent snow storm caused chaos for rush-hour motorists throughout southern Britain' and an astronomer at the University of California disclosed that Jupiter's Great Red Spot, which had baffled scientists since its discovery in 1831, was finally revealed to be not a mountain top, as had commonly been believed, but a swirling 'blob' of gas about thirty thousand miles long and eight thousand miles wide, held in place by winds of more than 360,000 miles per hour.

Somehow my Thai International flight from Heathrow seemed miraculously smooth and comfortable in these circumstances, and I feel I should thank my favourite airline for such a good start. Indian friends and acquaintances made the whole experience unforgettable, and those who have left travelling in India till later in life can be reassured by the fact that I coped adequately with the press of vivid emotions and frequent travel on my first visit to India, at the age of fifty.

My friend Birendra Singh Tanwar's name can stand for all the hundreds of those Indians from all walks of life who, by their enchanting complexity and diversity, made my life so very complicated that even now I have been able to unravel comparatively little, and have cheerfully given up all hope of ever eradicating the wonder of India from my imagination. I thank Giles Tillotson for his personal assistance and indispensable architectural guide to *The Rajput Palaces*.

Veena Chopra taught me the Hindi I wanted for everyday use, and for this gift I shall always be grateful.

My wife, Audrey, and my daughters Carolyn and Angela, have yet again proved that an author is only as thoughtful as his family will allow. To all who made the adventure and its chronicle possible: *bahut bahut dhanyavad!*

PHILIP WARD

Introduction

The aim of the present book is to persuade the reader to travel in Rajasthan, for such a journey is likely to change the reader's life as it changed mine, and wholly (I hope) for the better, replacing vague stereotypes with unforgettably clear images of places he already knows at second hand, like the Palace of the Winds in Jaipur, and revelations of places he is unlikely to have come across even in extensive reading, like *havelis* in Shekhavati, or the Desert National Park near the golden city of Jaisalmer. To reach Bikaner and Osiyan, Jodhpur and Mandore, Udaipur and Kota, it is usual to begin at Delhi, a world capital five years younger, in its present reincarnation, than my father. And customary to stop en route at the fabulous city of Agra, amply worth all the superlatives bestowed upon it not only for Taj Mahal itself, but for the exquisite I'timad ad-Daula, Agra Fort, and nearby Sikandra.

Like Odilon Redon or Kafka, Paul Klee and Adam Mickiewicz, I am a man derelict from his time, confused in the strange contortions that the politicians call 'real life'. I cannot comprehend why I was not born within a cobra's skin, or that of a mongoose, of a Rajput warrior or 'unclean' *harijan*. It is a game of genes and environments, a mystery in which I unwittingly take the rôle of a seven of hearts in someone else's hand.

In the course of a lifetime's eager travel, nothing has disappointed me yet, but I had grave doubts about the ability of India to stand up to the barrage of hyperbole that its visitors have remorselessly hurled at us. It was Mark Twain who remarked in 1896 that 'nothing has been left undone, either by man or Nature, to make India the most extraordinary country that the sun visits on his round'. The scale of contrasts has elongated now that India has become a nuclear power, for aboriginal tribes in jungles and mountains have at least in some part remained as untainted by the follies of inappropriate technology as they were in Akbar's time, or Aurangzeb's.

Let me reassure anybody wanting the 'truth about India' that I cannot suggest what it might be. It could be the 'area of darkness' or 'wounded civilization' described by V.S. Naipaul, or a museum of 'splendours of the Raj' celebrated in lush coffee-table books. The 'truth' about Calcutta may lie in the pages of Dominique Lapierre, who called it a 'city of joy' or in the caustic pages of Geoffrey Moorhouse, who did not.

Ooty Remembered and suchlike paeans to lazy days in hill-stations must be offset by terrible accounts of violence by Thuggee and famines throughout Rajasthan. Any summary that fails to include the Golden Temple of Amritsar and the Sikh movement for an autonomous Khalistan; the coast of Malabar; the caves of Ajanta and Ellora; Kashmir; shall we agree it is doomed from the start? Yet most writers begin with easy generalisations and the conviction that here at last (travelling by rail third class, travelling by bullock cart in Orissa, travelling on foot in Deccan) is the real India. For wavering moments I thought I had caught it beside the burning ghats, or in films like *Pather Panchali*, or in Bharat Natyam dance. But no: the real India always bobs ahead of you, just beyond the novels of Narayan or the poems of Tagore. It eludes you in temples, mosques, and museums. Squatting in Delhi's Chandni Chowk, you thought you had caught it like a butterfly in your net, but no. There is nothing of it in Shah Jahan's Taj Mahal, or in Goa; nothing in the sand flats of the Bay of Bengal (which could be any tropical sand flats) or in Mount Abu Hill Station. Even if you were to begin a summation of all the travellers' accounts, from Ibn Battuta to the latest hippy, by the time you had finished the words would not suffice. Neither would a painter's palette, mixing every hue known to art and artifice. Neither would every scent in a spice bazaar; nor every sound from soft Tamil to a spate of Hindi, from the creak of a water-wheel to the shrieking of dockworkers in Bombay.

There is nothing intentionally or potentially definitive about *Rajasthan, Agra, Delhi*. Its purpose is to persuade you to go there, and to enjoy the experience.

Illustrations

Photographs are by the Author and maps by the Government of India unless otherwise stated. Colour illustrations for the cover were kindly supplied by G.H.R. Tillotson: Qutb Minar (Delhi), a detail from Jahangiri Mahal, Lal Qila (Agra), and a detail from ceiling sculptures in a Jain temple, Dilwara, Mount Abu.
Jaisalmer. Patwon-ki *haveli* (Courtesy of G.H.R. Tillotson)*frontispiece*
Map of Delhi   2-3
Qutb Minar Complex. Sunga iron pillar in archway   7
Humayun's Mausoleum   10
Isa Khan's Mausoleum   11
Map of New Delhi   12-13
Purana Qila. Sher Shah Masjid   16
Lal Qila. Diwan-i-Am   19
Lal Qila. Moti Masjid   20
Chandni Chowk   23
Jantar Mantar   25
Safdarjang's Mausoleum   26
Sikandra. Akbar's Mausoleum   39
Map of Agra   42-43
Agra. Taj Mahal   45
Agra. Lal Qila. Delhi Gate (Courtesy of G.H.R. Tillotson)   50
Agra. Chini-ka Rauza   54
Agra. I'timad ad-Daula   55
Fatehpur Sikri. Jami Masjid   61
Fatehpur Sikri. Jami Masjid. Tomb of Salim Chishti   63
Map of Rajasthan   65
Bharatpur. Entrance to the Fort (Courtesy of G.H.R. Tillotson)   67

Dig. Hardev Bhawan (Courtesy of G.H.R. Tillotson)   70
Amber. Elephant beside the Palace Wall   74
Amber. Palace and town from Jaigarh   77
Map of Jaipur   80
Jaipur. City Palace. Entrance to Mor Chowk (Courtesy of G.H.R. Tillotson)   85
Jaipur. City Palace. Peacock Gate (Courtesy of G.H.R. Tillotson)   87
Jaipur. City Palace. Chandra Mahal in background   88
Kishangarh. Fort Palace (Courtesy of G.H.R. Tillotson)   100
Ringas. Waiting at the level crossing   103
Nawalgarh. Well (Courtesy of G.H.R. Tillotson)   104
Nawalgarh. Street scene with performing *bhopa* (Courtesy of Colin Scott Mackenzie)   105
Nawalgarh. Frescoed *haveli*   106
Mandawa. Maharajah Keshri Singh in his palace   108
Mandawa. Ladhuram Tarkeshwar Goenka *haveli*, from the gateway   110
Mandawa. Ladhuram Tarkeshwar Goenka *haveli*, showing frescoes   111
Prosopis cineraria in sand dunes   114
Map of Bikaner   117
Bikaner. Junagarh (Courtesy of Government of Rajasthan)   119
Bikaner. Lallgarh   122
Gajner. Palace   126
Gajner. Vultures in a *pipal*   128
Bikaner. Selling powders during Holi   130
Nomads on the road to Deshnok after seven years of drought   132
Deshnok. The silver gates of Karni Mata Temple   134
Bap. Women at the salt-pans   137
Pokaran. Fort   139
Map of Jaisalmer   142

Jaisalmer. A *haveli* in the fort (Courtesy of G.H.R. Tillotson)   145
Jaisalmer. Salim Singh *haveli* (Courtesy of G.H.R. Tillotson)   148
Jaisalmer. Vegetable market near Famous Tailor   150
Jaisalmer. Woman cooking inside a *haveli*   152
A village near Jaisalmer (Courtesy of Government of Rajasthan)   155
Jaisalmer. The hill city seen from *chhatris* at dusk   157
Walled village near Agolai   160
Map of Jodhpur   162
Jodhpur. Meherangarh from below   163
Jodhpur. A city view from Meherangarh   164
Jodhpur. Meherangarh. Khabka Mahal (Courtesy of G.H.R. Tillotson)   167
Jodhpur. Meherangarh. Phul Mahal   169
Jodhpur. Bazaar. Women and girls in procession   171
Mandore. *Chhatris* (Courtesy of Government of Rajasthan)   173
Jodhpur. Jewellers and bookshop   178
Ranakpur. Jain temple interior (Courtesy of G.H.R. Tillotson)   184
Ahar. *Chhatris* (Courtesy of G.H.R. Tillotson)   190
Udaipur. Jag Niwas (Courtesy of G.H.R. Tillotson)   192
Map of Udaipur   194
Udaipur. City Palace. East front   195
Udaipur. City Palace. Mor Chowk (Courtesy of G.H.R. Tillotson)   199
Udaipur. City Palace. *Zenana* (Courtesy of G.H.R. Tillotson)   201
Udaipur. Bazaar (Courtesy of G.H.R. Tillotson)   204
Chittor. Rana Kumbha's Palace (Courtesy of G.H.R. Tillotson)   210
Bundi. Fort Palace (Courtesy of G.H.R. Tillotson)   214
Kota. Fort Palace (Courtesy of G.H.R. Tillotson)   217
Map of Mount Abu   221

1: DELHI

It is one of the paradoxes of travel that if you were to ask someone which world capital they would choose to visit first, you might hear Paris, Rome, Peking or Vienna, but you would never hear a firm 'Delhi'. This is remarkable, for India's capital has everything to enchant the historically-minded, from Qutb Minar in the south to the Shahjanabad complex of Red Fort, bazaars and Friday Mosque in the north. The spacious, dignified New Delhi designed by Lutyens and Baker appeals to any connoisseur of modern town-planning. Delhi is not desperately overcrowded: it is no hectic Bombay or chaotic Calcutta, and its environs include the model city of Chandigarh, Agra with its unforgettable Taj Mahal, and Fatehpur Sikri: a sixteenth-century deserted city created by Akbar in barely fifteen years. Delhi is also the departure point for Rajasthan, with excellent road, rail and air communications.

India is a free democracy, and there are few restrictions on travel anywhere in the country. Fares are absurdly cheap by Western European standards, and hotels and restaurants equally reasonable, unless you opt for de luxe treatment. Indians are friendly, communicative, and English is spoken so widely that in the north my attempts to speak Hindi found little sympathy because everyone I met was determined to practise English and to show how well they could speak it. From late October well into March Delhi enjoys crisp nights and bright clear days with temperatures up to the high seventies. It is different in May or June, when blinding oven-heat and dust storms transform Delhi into a furnace from which everyone is anxious to escape, and indeed the designers of New Delhi always intended that the Government should be transferred annually between April and October to Simla, thus building the new administrative capital, in Calcutta until 1911, with a view to withstanding only winters.

Because Delhi extends over so large an area, in practice you do not see the city chronologically, for it did not grow vertically in strata, one level above the next, but in a manner strikingly Indian: by abandoning one ruler's city and beginning again elsewhere. This accounts for the fact that Jaipur succeeded Amber, and that Ahar (near Udaipur) was abandoned and not built over. Delhi has existed on at least nine separate sites: the Indraprastha or 'Indra's Abode' obliterated beneath Purana Qila; the Chauhan or early Pathan city dominated by the superb

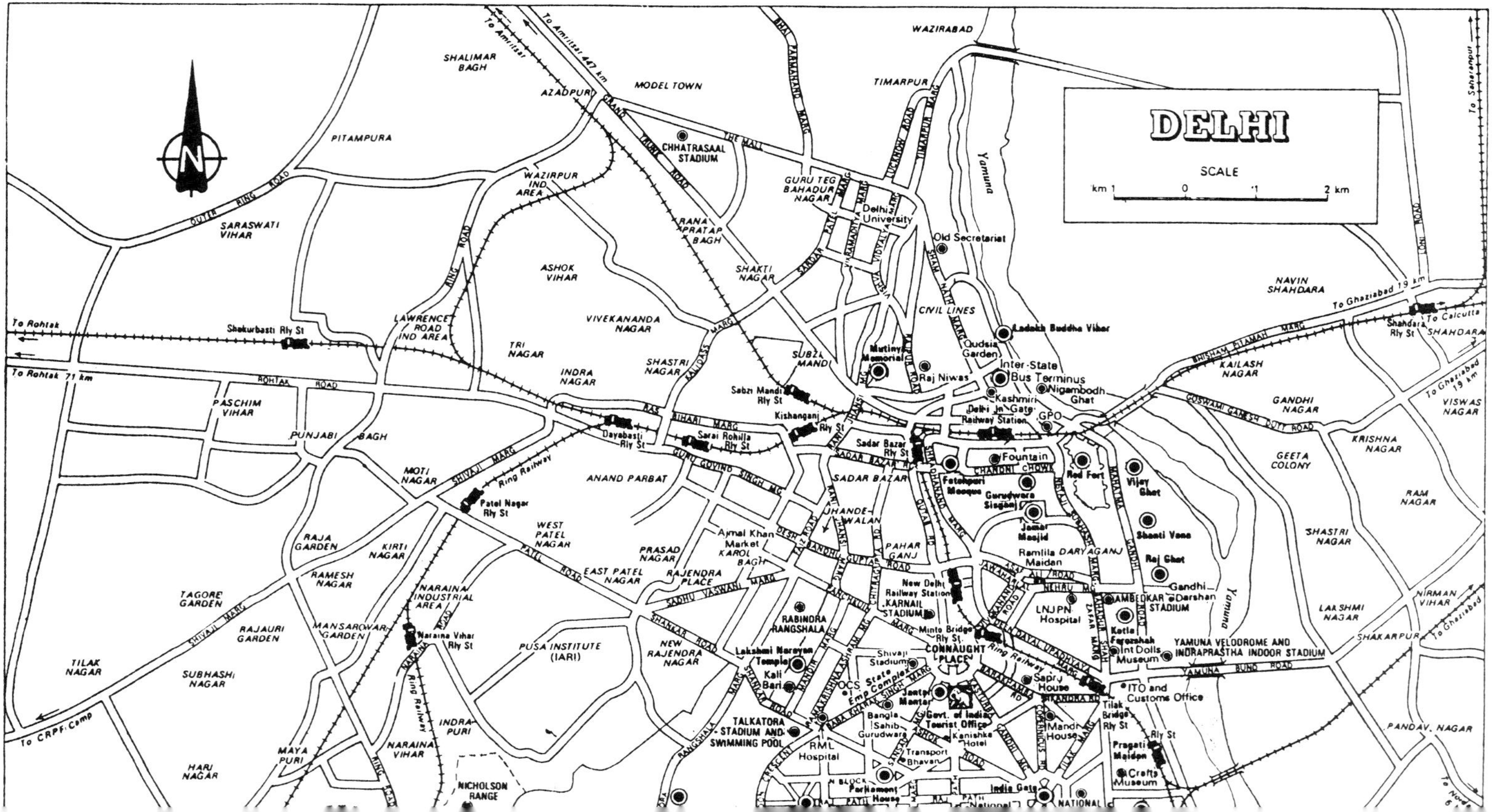
DELHI
SCALE
km 1 0 1 2 km
N
WAZIRABAD
TIMARPUR
MODEL TOWN
SHALIMAR BAGH
AZADPUR
PITAMPURA
CHHATRASAAL STADIUM
GURU TEG BAHADUR NAGAR
Delhi University
Old Secretariat
Yamuna
NAVIN SHAHDARA
To Ghaziabad 19 km
Shahdara Rly St
To Calcutta
SHAHDARA
To Saharanpur
LONI ROAD
To Amritsar 447 km
To Amritsar
To Rohtak
To Rohtak 71 km
To CRPF Camp
SARASWATI VIHAR
OUTER RING ROAD
WAZIRPUR IND AREA
RANA PRATAP BAGH
SHAKTI NAGAR
ASHOK VIHAR
VIVEKANANDA NAGAR
CIVIL LINES
Ladakh Buddha Vihar
LAWRENCE ROAD IND AREA
Shakurbasti Rly St
TRI NAGAR
INDRA NAGAR
SHASTRI NAGAR
SUBZI MANDI
Mutiny Memorial
Raj Niwas
Qudsia Garden
Inter-State Bus Terminus
Nigambodh Ghat
Kashmiri Gate
Delhi Jn Railway Station
GPO
Sabzi Mandi Rly St
Kishanganj Rly St
Sadar Bazar Rly St
Sarai Rohilla Rly St
Dayabasti Rly St
PASCHIM VIHAR
PUNJABI BAGH
ROHTAK ROAD
RAS BIHARI MARG
KAILASH NAGAR
GANDHI NAGAR
GOSWAMI GANESH DUTT ROAD
BHISHAM PITAMAH MARG
VISWAS NAGAR
To Ghaziabad 19 km
KRISHNA NAGAR
GEETA COLONY
RAM NAGAR
SHASTRI NAGAR
Fountain
CHANDNI CHOWK
Red Fort
Vijay Ghat
Fatehpuri Mosque
Gurudwara Sisganj
Jama Masjid
Shanti Vana
Raj Ghat
Ramlila Maidan
DARYAGANJ
Gandhi Darshan
AMBEDKAR STADIUM
Kotla Ferozshah
Int Dolls Museum
YAMUNA VELODROME AND INDRAPRASTHA INDOOR STADIUM
YAMUNA BUND ROAD
ITO and Customs Office
LAKSHMI NAGAR
NIRMAN VIHAR
SHAKARPUR
To Ghaziabad
PANDAV NAGAR
MOTI NAGAR
SHIVAJI MARG
Ring Railway
Patel Nagar Rly St
ANAND PARBAT
GURU GOVIND SINGH MG
SADAR BAZAR
JHANDEWALAN
WEST PATEL NAGAR
PATEL ROAD
Ajmal Khan Market
KAROL BAGH
PAHAR GANJ
New Delhi Railway Station
KARNAIL STADIUM
LNJPN Hospital
RAJA GARDEN
KIRTI NAGAR
PRASAD NAGAR
EAST PATEL NAGAR
RAJENDRA PLACE
SADHU VASWANI MARG
RABINDRA RANGSHALA
Minto Bridge Rly St
CONNAUGHT PLACE
Ring Railway
Sapru House
TAGORE GARDEN
RAMESH NAGAR
NARAINA INDUSTRIAL AREA
Naraina Vihar Rly St
MANSAROVAR GARDEN
RAJAURI GARDEN
PUSA INSTITUTE (IARI)
NEW RAJENDRA NAGAR
SHANKAR ROAD
Lakshmi Narayan Temple
Kali Bari
Shivaji Stadium
OCS State Emp Complex
Jantar Mantar
Govt. of India Tourist Office
Mandi House
Tilak Bridge Rly St
Pragati Maidan
Crafts Museum
TILAK NAGAR
SUBHASHI NAGAR
HARI NAGAR
MAYA PURI
NARAINA VIHAR
INDRA PURI
NICHOLSON RANGE
TALKATORA STADIUM AND SWIMMING POOL
RML Hospital
Bangla Sahib Gurudwara
Kanishka Hotel
Transport Bhavan
Parliament House
N BLOCK
India Gate
NATIONAL
RANGSHALA
CRESCENT

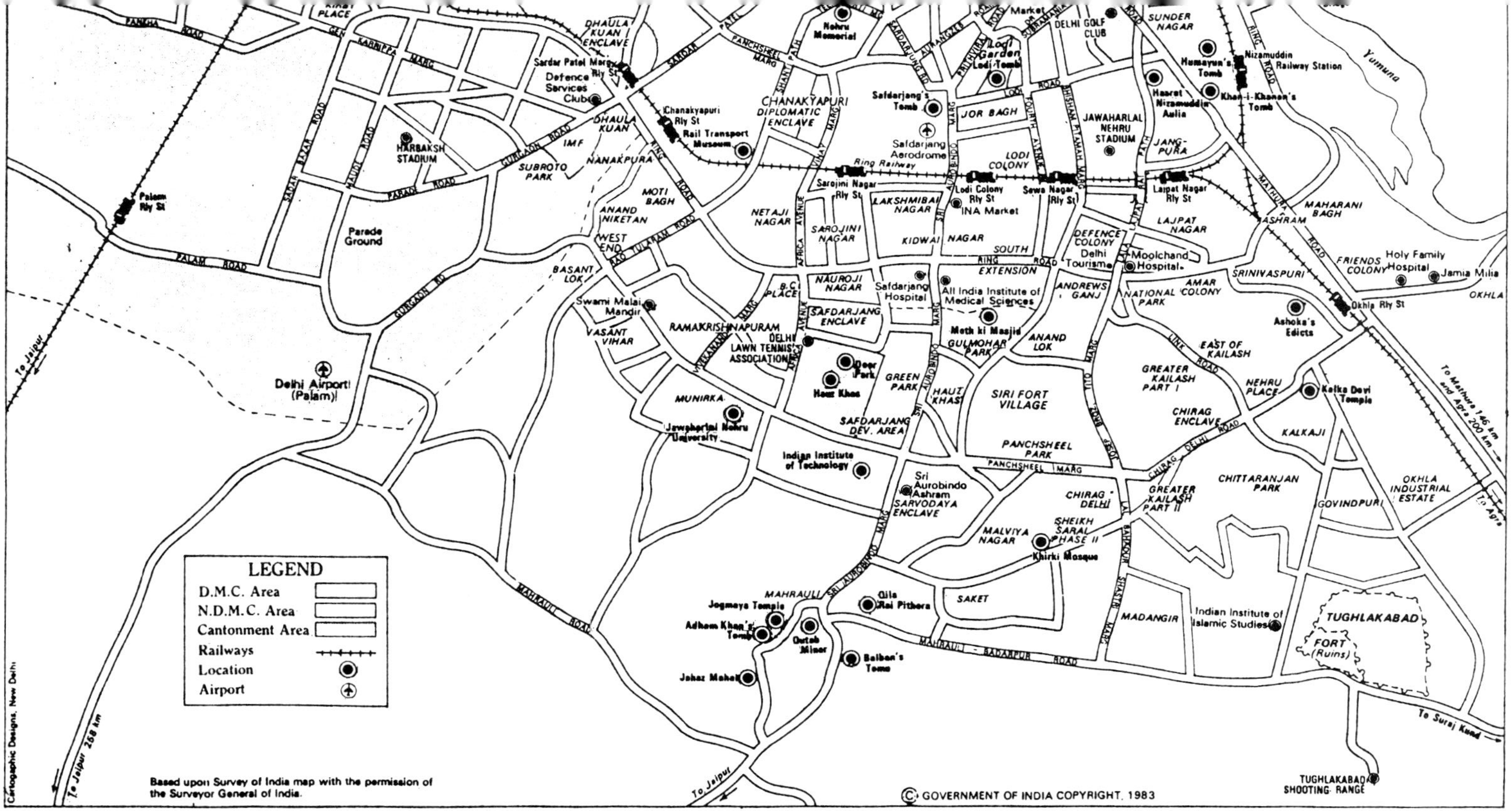

DHAULA KUAN ENCLAVE
Sardar Patel Marg Rly St
Defence Services Club
HARBAKSH STADIUM
DHAULA KUAN
IMF
SUBROTO PARK
NANAKPURA
Chanakyapuri Rly St
Rail Transport Museum
CHANAKYAPURI DIPLOMATIC ENCLAVE
Nehru Memorial
Safdarjang's Tomb
Safdarjang Aerodrome
Ring Railway
JOR BAGH
Lodi Garden Lodi Tomb
DELHI GOLF CLUB
LODI COLONY
JAWAHARLAL NEHRU STADIUM
SUNDER NAGAR
Humayun's Tomb
Hazrat Nizamuddin Aulia
Khan-i-Khanan's Tomb
Nizamuddin Railway Station
Yumuna
JANG-PURA
Palam Rly St
Parade Ground
MOTI BAGH
ANAND NIKETAN
WEST END
NETAJI NAGAR
Sarojini Nagar Rly St
SAROJINI NAGAR
LAKSHMIBAI NAGAR
Lodi Colony Rly St
INA Market
Sewa Nagar Rly St
Lajpat Nagar Rly St
LAJPAT NAGAR
MAHARANI BAGH
KIDWAI NAGAR
SOUTH EXTENSION
DEFENCE COLONY
Delhi Tourism
Moolchand Hospital
FRIENDS COLONY
Holy Family Hospital
Jamia Milia
OKHLA
BASANT LOK
NAUROJI NAGAR
B.C. PLACE
Safdarjang Hospital
All India Institute of Medical Sciences
ANDREWS GANJ
NATIONAL PARK
AMAR COLONY
SRINIVASPURI
Okhla Rly St
Swami Malai Mandir
RAMAKRISHNAPURAM
SAFDARJANG ENCLAVE
Meth ki Masjid
GULMOHAR PARK
ANAND LOK
Ashoka's Edicts
VASANT VIHAR
DELHI LAWN TENNIS ASSOCIATION
Deer Park
Hauz Khas
GREEN PARK
HAUZ KHAS
SIRI FORT VILLAGE
EAST OF KAILASH
GREATER KAILASH PART I
NEHRU PLACE
Kalka Devi Temple
To Mathura 146 km and Agra 200 km
To Jaipur
Delhi Airport (Palam)
MUNIRKA
Jawaharlal Nehru University
SAFDARJANG DEV. AREA
PANCHSHEEL PARK
CHIRAG ENCLAVE
KALKAJI
Indian Institute of Technology
Sri Aurobindo Ashram
SARVODAYA ENCLAVE
CHIRAG DELHI
GREATER KAILASH PART II
CHITTARANJAN PARK
OKHLA INDUSTRIAL ESTATE
GOVINDPURI
To Agra
MALVIYA NAGAR
SHEIKH SARAI PHASE II
Khirki Mosque
LEGEND
D.M.C. Area
N.D.M.C. Area
Cantonment Area
Railways
Location
Airport
MAHRAULI
Jogmaya Temple
Qila Rai Pithora
SAKET
MADANGIR
Indian Institute of Islamic Studies
TUGHLAKABAD
FORT (Ruins)
Adham Khan's Tomb
Qutab Minar
Balban's Tomb
Jahaz Mahal
To Suraj Kund
To Jaipur 258 km
Based upon Survey of India map with the permission of the Surveyor General of India.
To Jaipur
© GOVERNMENT OF INDIA COPYRIGHT, 1983
TUGHLAKABAD SHOOTING RANGE
Cartographic Designs, New Delhi

Qutb Minar, a period from Muhammad Ghuri's victory over the Rajputs in 1192 until the death of Balban in 1287; the Khilji capital called Siri culminating with Ala-ud-Din, who died in 1361; Ghiyas-ud-Din's capital of Tughlaqabad (1320-5), like Siri close to Qutb Minar; Muhammad Tughlaq's capital of Jahanpanah; Ferozabad built by Feroz Shah (1351-88); the Afghan Sher Shah's capital at Purana Qila (1541-5); Shahjahanabad protected by Lal Qila (1638-48) roughly coterminous with Old Delhi, though it did not at that time supersede Agra as the Mughal capital; and New Delhi, the Brasilia-like vision of the British Empire based on the north-south axis of Janpath and the east-west axis of Rajpath, extending from the World War I memorial called India Gate to the Presidential Palace, or Rashtrapati Bhawan.

For those with only one day to spare in Delhi, my advice would be to visit Qutb Minar and its area in the morning followed by the National Museum, and in the afternoon Lal Qila (Red Fort), Shah Jahan's Friday Mosque, and the bazaars nearby, such as Chandni Chowk. A second day could be passed visiting early monuments such as Purana Qila, the Mausoleum of Humayun, Isa Khan's Tomb and those of Nizam-ud-Din, Sikandar Lodi, Khan-i Khanan, Amir Khusraw, Jahanara, Safdarjang and Mubarak Shah. Following Lala Lajpat Rai Path southward, you then come to Siri and Tughlaqabad. In the afternoon you could tour New Delhi, with the Temple of Lakshmi Narayan, Jantar Mantar, Parliament House, and Connaught Place, ending up near the Yamuna to pay respects to Mahatma Gandhi at Raj Ghat. All these monuments are clearly shown on the Archaeological Survey of India's *Map of Delhi, showing important protected monuments*. Visitors limited to a very short stay will find that by far the easiest method of seeing Delhi's historic sites is by regular daily tours covering half a day or a full day. The tours are conducted in English, and save time you would waste fighting your way through the traffic with idiosyncratic taxi-drivers or auto rickshaw-wallahs who may genuinely not understand where you want to go.

Those with more time will hail the first auto rickshaw-wallah and make off into the hazy distance. Opposite flats for single serving officers, near Taj Palace Hotel on Sardar Patel Marg, I hailed auto rickshaw DER 7587, being operated by a chatty, fearless roadhog called Bijay Bhushan Sharma, clearly descended from one of those invading families whose mission in life was to roar down upon defenceless homes and lay them waste with the quickest and noisiest demolition possible. I suggested that we might head for Qutb Minar, and he accepted the challenge with the alacrity that Timur the Lame's generals might have demonstrated on being ordered to advance on the next village, devastate, and loot. Past Maitreyi College, along Satya Marg and the

National Rose Garden we threaded our backfiring way down Shanti Path, above the Railway Museum, tackling the Ring Road with conquering fervour. Open-sided, the three-wheeled menace gave me a high level of low-level pollution. Bijay roared past ruins and the tombs of saints and warriors as though he personally took credit for all carnage. Even a dual carriageway of three lanes each did not dampen his fiendish delight in overtaking anything that moved by a mere hair's breadth to show off his prowess. There goes a Montessori School, the modern Church of S. Thomas, the tennis stadium, Sri Aurobindo Ashram, the Indian Handicrafts Emporium, Indian Cottage Industries.

Qutb Minar complex, alive with a hundred species of birds from purple-rumped sunbirds and house crows to blue rock pigeons and house swifts, simmers with springing chipmunks, never still. After the aggressive traffic, these gentle hillocks and grassy slopes come as a welcome restorative. We are standing on an early Hindu city, formerly governed by Prithviraj Chauhan, who also ruled Ajmer in Rajasthan. This Delhi, called Qila-i Rai Pithaura, had been erected by the Tomar Rajputs in the tenth century to defend fortresses of Rajasthan and the Yamuna, with the sacred city of Mathura three days' cavalry march to the south. Mahmud of Ghazni (971-1031) wanted all the spiritual and material wealth of northern India for Allah, and he raided several times as far as Mathura, but skirted Delhi. Muhammad Ghuri invaded India too, being defeated by Prithviraj in 1191 at Tarain. Nursing his wounds, he retreated to his headquarters at Ghazni, then a year later returned with 120,000 horsemen against the 500,000 of the defenders. This time he won, again at Tarain, and sacked not only Kanauj and Ajmer, but also Delhi. On this spot his fearless general Qutb-ud-Din Aibak, a former slave whom he had brought up and promoted, and who became Ghuri's successor in 1206, made his headquarters. Aibak pursued his military ambitions in India until his death in 1210, when the so-called Slave Dynasty produced other great rulers: Iltutmish (1211-36) and Balban (1266-87).

Qutb-ud-Din completed only the lowest storey of the great minaret; it was left to Iltutmish to add three more. Together they drew in Delhi's blue sky a vertical *alif*; initial letters of the Arabic alphabet and of Allah's holy name. When it was damaged by earthquake in 1368, the fourth storey was replaced by two smaller storeys at the command of Sultan Feroz Tughlaq, who left the bottom of the fourth storey in red sandstone like the others, but added white marble for the upper part of the fourth and the whole of the fifth. It hardly seems possible that so harmonious and elegant a minaret could have been completed in different periods. The circular base is more than 15 metres in diameter and each original storey is patterned differently: the lowest with alternative angular and circular flutings, the second with circular, and the third with angular. The fourth is a circular kiosk with windows and was once domed. Each storey is surmounted by a balcony with stalactite pendentive brackets and Kufic script. You can climb to the top of Qutb-ud-Din's minaret if you feel energetic and have a head for heights, at times when scaffolding and 'works' do not bar your progress; the height of 72.5 metres gives you a different perspective of early Delhi. 'Qutb' means 'a pole, axis, or tower', and a Kufic inscription refers to the minaret's 'casting the shadow of Allah over East and West'. The minaret of Ibn Tulun's great mosque in Cairo is an ancestor that could surely not have been known to Qutb-ud-Din or to his Hindu masons, but his armies may well have included Egyptians or pilgrims who had passed through Cairo on the Hajj. To me it resembles nothing more than the contemporary minaret of Jam, northwest of Herat in Afghanistan, which might also have been known to many in the Pathan army for it dates from the reign of Ghiyas, fifth Sultan of Ghur (1163-1203).

Sooner or later a guide will tell you that Quwwat-al-Islam, the 'Power of Islam', dates from 1193-1316 and is thus the first mosque in India. This is wrong, for Mehrdad Shokoohy, in *Bhadreśvar* (Leiden, 1987) has shown that two mosques and a shrine of Ibrahim at Bhadreśvar on the Gulf of Cutch are dated 554 A.H., corresponding to 1159-60 A.D. A characteristic Indo-Muslim architecture existed well before the end of the 12th century, almost half a century before the Islamic conquest of Delhi and about 150 years before the establishment of Sultanate rule in the region. Then one must also take into account the pre-Sultanate mosque of al-Iraji in Junagadh, on the Kathiawar peninsula.

Quwwat-al-Islam is however of extraordinary interest, for it re-uses material from twenty-seven earlier Hindu temples on the site, with their great carved pillars. (We know the number from an inscription over the east gate). Aibak's original Hindu craftsmen must have thought their new Muslim overlord a strange master, asking them to tear down their creations and then reconstruct them with great care, demolishing only those objects, like the Garuda bird, which insulted Allah by attempting to usurp his function as Creator. The Hindus vibrated to the waves of the Absolute which shows itself in a myriad shapes, gladly planting here at Qutb-ud-Din's orders the Sunga iron pillar of the 3rd century robbed from Mathura. In 1199 the Sultan required an arched façade to be added along the Makkah side, along the entire line of the masonry of the shrine, a Persian inspiration nearly three metres thick. Ogee-shaped and with three arches, this screen of red and white stone measures nearly 15 metres high and seven metres wide. In 1230 Sultan Iltutmish, who is buried in the north-west corner, doubled the size of the mosque, altering the main axis to north-south. Ala-ud-Din Khilji enlarged the mosque again from 1296 to 1316, adding gates on the eastern, northern and

Qutb Minar Complex. Sunga iron pillar in archway

southern sides, the last, known as Ala-i Darwaza, being the main entrance to the whole complex. Beside this harmonious gateway you will be able to visit the Lodi-period tomb of Imam Zamin, who died in 1539.

Ala-ud-Din intended to raise a minaret twice the height of the Qutb Minar, and you can still see its base, with a diameter two and half times that of its rival. But he succeeded in reaching barely a third of the height of his predecessor's tower before internecine struggles against the Tughlaqs brought a halt to the project. The idea was not as ludicrous as it might seem in retrospect for Ala-ud-Din planned a city called Siri, divided from Lalkot (as the Qutb Minar complex is sometimes known) by Jahanpanah, which in 1325 would follow the settlement of Tughlaqabad, an area east of Lalkot. Ghiyas-ud-Din Tughlaq defeated the Khilji dynasty in 1320 and in 1321 began the construction of Tughlaqabad, a city visited by the great traveller Ibn Battuta, who arrived on 20 March 1334; his account of Delhi has been translated by H.A.R. Gibb in *The Travels of Ibn Battuta* (vol.3, Hakluyt Society, 1971). All that remains of Siri is a walled area enclosing the modern village of Shahpur. Khilji buildings are the earliest record of life in a zone surrounding the shrine of Nizam-ud-Din Aulia, which is visited with the Tomb of Humayun.

Nizam-ud-Din, who died in 1325, was given a mausoleum by Feroz Tughlaq, but the present building was ordered by Akbar and has been frequently restored, its present dome dating from 1823.

Nizam-ud-Din Aulia was a Chishti mystic who died in 1325. The Chishtiyyah order is named for a village near Herat, in Afghanistan, where the founder of the order, Abu Ishaq of Syria, had settled, Muin-ud-Din Hassan, the Chishti mystic buried at Ajmer, brought the order to India in the 12th century, and made his home at Ajmer into the Chishti centre of India at that time and for long afterwards. Chishtiyyah taught, through masters and text such as al-Hujwiri's *Kashf al-Mahjub* and Suhrawardi's *Awarif al-Ma'arif*, the unity of being, rejection of private possessions, non-violence, rejection of the state, and living for Allah alone in three phases: firstly the love of Allah experienced on conversion to Islam, then its full realization in adult life by strenuous efforts, and finally the mystical phase result from cosmic awareness. As you visit Nizam-ud-Din's shrine, the tank called Dilkusha, and the mosque, it is good to recall the mystical practices of Chishtiyyah, which involve sitting in the position prescribed and reciting the names of Allah, reciting the names silently, regulating one's breathing in a manner that Hindus master in yoga, and spending forty days confined in solitude while absorbed in meditation, a practice Christians will associate with the period that Jesus is said to have spent in the desert.

The great Urdu poet Mirza Asadullah Khan Ghalib (1797-1869), who wrote mostly in Persian during his youth and middle age, is also buried close by. If you don't bring a copy of the *Ghazals* of Ghalib (New York, 1971) to Ghalib's tomb, perhaps you might pause to reflect on this poem I have translated from the Urdu, which at the same time seems to echo preoccupations common to the Chishtiyya:

> *The ecstasy of a droplet: to die in the stream!*
> *Beyond the limits of pain, the pain is a cure.*
>
> *All tears long vanished, only sighing is left.*
> *So it is that water becomes air.*
>
> *Spring clouds float and dry after rain,*
> *Barren of their weight of grief.*
>
> *Polishing green the winds of spring*
> *bring mildew to the mirror.*
>
> *The return of the rose, Ghalib, increases desire.*
> *In every season, whatever the weather, open your eyes!*

Mirza Asadullah sees no fear in relating to the cosmos, to its mysteries beyond all understanding: intangible clouds water the tangible rose, and both die into an awareness at once existent and inexistent, the reality behind appearance.

Nearby the Jama'at Khana Mosque bears a striking resemblance to its predecessor, the Quwwat-al-Islam. South of the enclosure you will come to some important tombs, among them that of the daughter of Shah Jahan, Jahanara; Muhammad Shah (1748); Jahangir, son of Akbar II; and the contemporary of Nizam-ud-Din, Amir Khusraw (though his tomb is 17th-century). Eastward you come to the tomb of Atga Khan, Akbar's foster-father, and a grey marble pavilion, where Atga Khan's son and his family were buried, called Chaunsath Khanbe. South of this beautifully-proportioned pavilion stands the Black Mosque, also called the Sanjar Masjid, with a central courtyard separated by a cross-shaped arcade into four smaller courtyards. The first octagonal tomb in Delhi is that of Khan-i-Jahan Tilangani (d. 1369) in the square fortress or kot, with a verandah and a central dome, and eight charming cupolas. The Tilangani prototype served for the tomb buildings of the 'Sayyid' and Lodi dynasties, which are virtually all that these rulers have left us. These can be seen at Khairpur, Mubarakpur, and Mujahidpur, the best being Sikandar Lodi's tomb of about 1519 in northern Khairpur, within a fortified enclosure.

Humayun's Tomb is in a style we have seen: that of Atga Khan. Its enclosure wall was started in 1563, four years after the death of Humayun, son of Babur and father of Akbar. Humayun was forced to spend part of his reign exiled in Persia and Afghanistan and the first usurper of his power, the Afghan Sher Shah Suri, completed the citadel of Dinpanah, on the ruins of Indraprastha, and his son Islam or Salim Shah created the Salimgarh on the banks of the Yamuna against the feared return of Humayun, who actually recaptured Delhi in 1555. Humayun's Tomb is the first great Mughal building in Delhi, with foundations laid in 1568. Its architect, commissioned by the shah's widow, was the Persian Mirza Ghiyas, and here we see the application of Persian *char-bagh* style: a quartered garden completed in 1573 and singular in that it is the first Mughal garden plan created that still survives without important changes. Causeways about 14 metres wide have narrow water channels in the centre, a feature that we shall see emphasised by broader canals in later Mughal gardens such as Taj Mahal. The original *char-bagh* system is complicated by these causeways into a system of thirty-two smaller lawns separated by such shallow paths that you might envisage it as a painting rather than a three-dimensional creation, especially since the flowing water, colourful blooms, and most of the trees have evaporated from the plan, so that our eyes are drawn away from the rather flat garden pattern to the

Humayun's Mausoleum

intricate play of red sandstone and white Makrana marble on the mausoleum itself. Crows caw to interrupt the muaddin's call to prayer; chipmunks whisk across red sand paths, their tails high. Within are the tombs of his two wives and three children, and covering all is a fine bulbous double dome which presages the dome of Taj Mahal. Each façade of the mausoleum resembles the others, dominated by a central rectangular fronton with a great arch flanked by smaller octagonal wings each with a smaller arch. Beyond the complex is the Nila Gunbad ('Blue Dome') which antedates the tomb of Humayun and therefore cannot possibly be the Tomb of Fahim Khan, who died in 1626, which many guides still repeat. Within the so-called barber's dome or 'Na'i-ka Gunbad', near the south-east corner. And west of the complex you pass through an overgrown area resplendent with the Tomb of Isa Khan Niyazi, a general in the army of Sher Shah Suri. The tomb dates from 1547 and the mosque of grey quartzite and red sandstone on the western side faces the octagon of the tomb's building. Women were carrying on their heads tin bowls full of red sand which they spread over the huge surrounding terrace below the platform of the tomb. This is virtually the swansong of the octagonal tomb in Delhi: the last, in 1561, will be that of Adham Khan southwest of the Quwwat-al-Islam mosque in the Lalkot complex dominated by Qutb Minar.

Isa Khan's Mausoleum

We return in time to Tughlaqabad, 8 km east of Lalkot, at that moment in 1320 when Ghiyas-ud-Din Tughlaq had defeated Nasr-ud-Din, and expelled the Khiljis from Delhi. Virtually nothing remains of that city, but we have the truncated pyramid of Ghiyas's own tomb, set in a former artificial lake, connected to the citadel by a fortified passage on arches. West of this tomb, and reached from Tughlaqabad by causeway, is yet another abandoned city of Delhi, the Adilabad of Ghiyas's son Muhammad from 1325 until he abandoned his city four years on when he decided to move the capital to Daulatabad in the Deccan. It is at this time, while constructing Adilabad, that Muhammad bin Ghiyas bin Tughlaq created the town south of Siri which he called Jahanpanah, or 'refuge from the world', which has almost totally disappeared from the face of the earth.

Muhammad's successor Feroz Shah (1351-88) restored many of the buildings of his predecessors, but his diminishing coffers denied him the more expensive red sandstone and white marble, and rubble with plaster characterise the mosques of the period, such as a mosque at Wazirabad or Timurpur in the *dargah* of Shah Alam or the Begampur mosque in Jahanpanah. His city, Ferozabad, was situated between ancient Indraprastha and 3 km north of Shahjahanabad (modern 'Old Delhi') and south of Old Delhi you can see ruins of his palace or *kotla*, with one

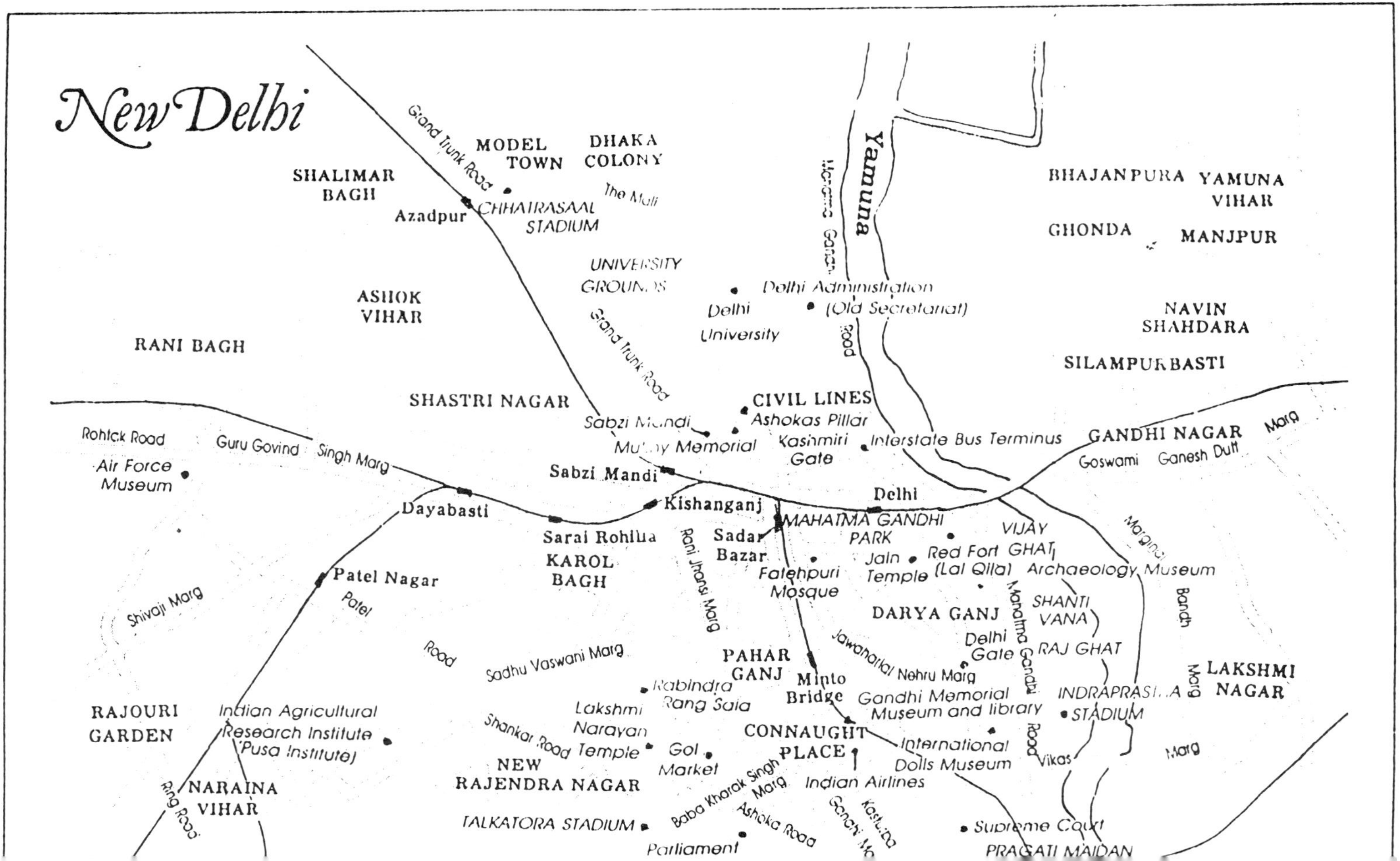

New Delhi
MODEL TOWN
DHAKA COLONY
SHALIMAR BAGH
Grand Trunk Road
The Mall
Azadpur
CHHATRASAAL STADIUM
BHAJANPURA
YAMUNA VIHAR
GHONDA
MANJPUR
Yamuna
Mahatma Gandhi Road
UNIVERSITY GROUNDS
Delhi Administration (Old Secretariat)
Delhi University
ASHOK VIHAR
NAVIN SHAHDARA
RANI BAGH
SILAMPUR BASTI
SHASTRI NAGAR
CIVIL LINES
Ashokas Pillar
Sabzi Mandi
Mutiny Memorial
Kashmiri Gate
Interstate Bus Terminus
GANDHI NAGAR
Marg
Goswami Ganesh Dutt
Rohtak Road
Guru Govind Singh Marg
Air Force Museum
Sabzi Mandi
Kishanganj
Delhi
Dayabasti
MAHATMA GANDHI PARK
VIJAY GHAT
Marginal Bandh
Sarai Rohilla
Sadar Bazar
Red Fort (Lal Qila)
Jain Temple
Archaeology Museum
KAROL BAGH
Rani Jhansi Marg
Fatehpuri Mosque
Patel Nagar
Patel Road
Shivaji Marg
DARYA GANJ
SHANTI VANA
Mahatma Gandhi Road
Delhi Gate
RAJ GHAT
Sadhu Vaswani Marg
PAHAR GANJ
Jawaharlal Nehru Marg
Minto Bridge
LAKSHMI NAGAR
Rabindra Rang Sala
Gandhi Memorial Museum and library
INDRAPRASTHA STADIUM
RAJOURI GARDEN
Indian Agricultural Research Institute (Pusa Institute)
Lakshmi Narayan Temple
Shankar Road
CONNAUGHT PLACE
Gol Market
International Dolls Museum
Vikas Marg
NEW RAJENDRA NAGAR
NARAINA VIHAR
Ring Road
Baba Kharak Singh Marg
Indian Airlines
Kasturba Gandhi Marg
TALKATORA STADIUM
Ashoka Road
Parliament
Supreme Court
PRAGATI MAIDAN

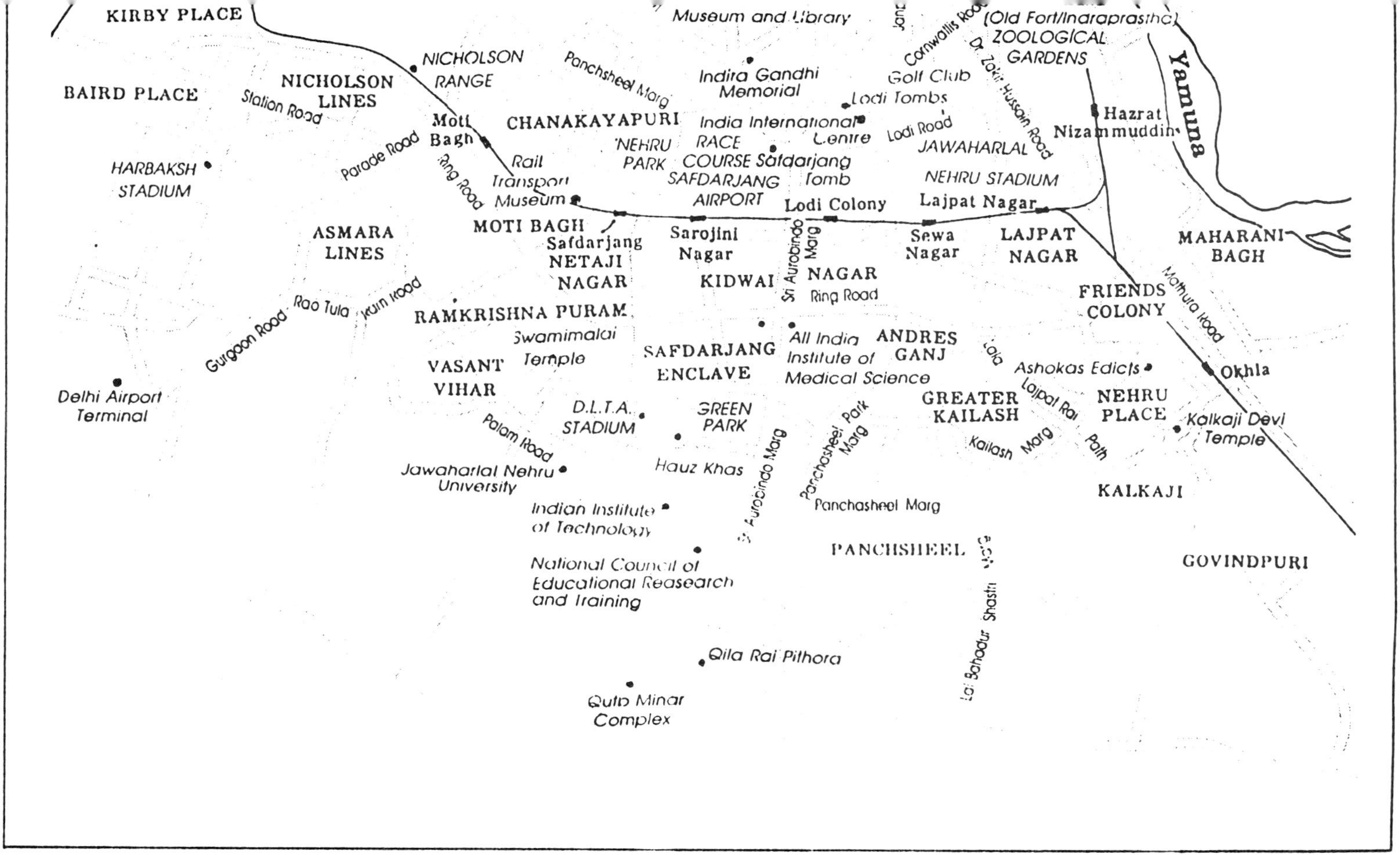
KIRBY PLACE
Museum and Library
(Old Fort/Indraprastha)
ZOOLOGICAL
GARDENS
Yamuna
Cornwallis Road
Dr. Zakir Hussain Road
BAIRD PLACE
NICHOLSON
LINES
Station Road
NICHOLSON
RANGE
Panchsheel Marg
Indira Gandhi
Memorial
Golf Club
Lodi Tombs
Hazrat
Nizammuddin
Moti
Bagh
CHANAKAYAPURI
India International
Centre
Lodi Road
JAWAHARLAL
NEHRU STADIUM
HARBAKSH
STADIUM
Parade Road
Ring Road
Rail
Transport
Museum
NEHRU
PARK
RACE
COURSE
Safdarjang
Tomb
SAFDARJANG
AIRPORT
Lodi Colony
Lajpat Nagar
ASMARA
LINES
MOTI BAGH
Safdarjang
NETAJI
NAGAR
Sarojini
Nagar
Sri Aurobindo
Marg
Sewa
Nagar
LAJPAT
NAGAR
MAHARANI
BAGH
KIDWAI
NAGAR
Ring Road
FRIENDS
COLONY
Mathura Road
Rao Tula
Ram Road
Gurgaon Road
RAMKRISHNA PURAM
Swamimalai
Temple
SAFDARJANG
ENCLAVE
All India
Institute of
Medical Science
ANDRES
GANJ
Lala
Lajpat Rai
Path
Ashokas Edicts
Okhla
Delhi Airport
Terminal
VASANT
VIHAR
D.L.T.A.
STADIUM
GREEN
PARK
Panchsheel Park
Marg
GREATER
KAILASH
Kailash
Marg
NEHRU
PLACE
Kalkaji Devi
Temple
Palam Road
Jawaharlal Nehru
University
Hauz Khas
Sri Aurobindo Marg
Panchasheel Marg
KALKAJI
Indian Institute
of Technology
PANCHSHEEL
GOVINDPURI
National Council of
Educational Reasearch
and Training
Lal Bahadur Shastri Marg
Qila Rai Pithora
Qutb Minar
Complex

of the two Ashoka-period pillars brought to Delhi which has an inscription of 1524 (when the pillar was rediscovered) and a text of 300 B.C. The personality of Feroz can be imagined from his own words which can be translated thus: 'Among the gifts that Allah has bestowed on me, His humble servant, was the wish to provide mosques, colleges and monasteries for scholars and elders, that the pious and holy might worship Allah therein. By His guidance I repaired and rebuilt structures of former kings and ancient nobles which had fallen into decay with the passage of time'. Feroz built canals, set up a marriage bureau and an employment exchange; he paid compensation to the victims of Muhammad bin Ghiyas, and caused a record of these reparations to be placed in Muhammad's tomb so that he could earn credit in the eyes of Allah. We know very little of Ferozabad because so much of it was covered by the later city of Shahjahanabad, but off the modern Palam Marg, north of the Qutb complex, you can see the Hauz-i-Khas complex where Feroz built his own tomb and a religious college or *madrasah*, double-storeyed on the Hauz or lake-side, and single-storeyed behind. The *madrasah* has colonnades of arches joining square-domed halls: the tomb is at the south-east corner. The lake itself had been made by Ala-ud-Din in the 13th century.

The Lodi dynasty which succeeded the local Sayyid dynasty at Delhi in 1451 can be remembered not only in the fine tomb of Isa Khan Niyazi which we have seen in the Humayun complex, but along the Lodi Road which links Humayun's Tomb at the east to Safdarjang's Tomb at the west. Sikandar Lodi's octagonal tomb (1518) was erected by his son and successor Ibrahim in a large fortified enclosure, with an outdoor mihrab on the west wall. The double dome, decorated with polychrome glazed bricks, is one of the earliest of a type afterwards used very widely by the Mughals.

Square Lodi tombs date from the last quarter of the 15th century, but we still do not know whom they commemorated. Near Sikandar Lodi's tomb is the well-preserved Bara Gunbad, or 'Great Dome' (1494) which has lost any tombs it may have had and now appears to be merely a monumental gateway to the mosque and courtyard. Its mosque has fluted pillars alternately round and angular in the style of the bottom storey of Qutb Minar: do not miss the superb plaster decoration in spandrels of the wide central arches of the eastern front. Near here is the exquisitely-proportioned Shish Gunbad, or 'Mirror Dome', with a fortress-like square tomb enlivened with courses of dark blue encaustic tiling.

If your auto rickshaw-wallah roars southwards from Lodi Road, before he comes to the Ring Road he can show you more Lodi-period tombs, including the so-called Bare Khan-ka Gunbad (Dome of the Great Khan), the largest of a complex of three known as Tin Burj

(Three Forts) which seems to possess three storeys from the outside, but when you enter there is only one massive hall, with flapping pigeons. South of the Ring Road is the Moth-ki Masjid (1505), a mosque built by Sikandar Lodi's chief minister. Greatly underrated because of its isolated location north of Siri, the Moth-ki Masjid marks a great aesthetic advance on the mosque we have just seen attached to Bara Gunbad, which suffers from weakly-curved arches and a failure of nerve on the part of the planners which is replaced here by aesthetic confidence, possibly deriving in no small measure from the greater dimensions they were allowed, the sanctuary measuring a good forty metres and more. The façade's five arches curve strongly; its three domes are elegantly spaced; turrets on the rear wall taper gracefully; and two-storeyed towers at the rear corner contribute an almost playful dimension which lifts the spirits in much the same way as the Moorish architects at Granada's Alhambra lifted the spirits of onlookers at much the same period. At the interior squinched arches support a dome above the central chamber, but the side aisles use stalactite pendentives both functional and decorative. Plaster patterns in borders above the arches and in the spandrels were once painted brilliantly, but this feature depends on your imagination for its full effect. Lodi rule was brought to a close at the Battle of Panipat in 1526, but the mosque of Jamali was not finished until ten years later, during the interrupted reign of Humayun; it is located between the dargah of Qutb-ud-Din and the tomb of Balban in the old Hindu walls of Lalkot, south-east of the Quwwat-al-Islam mosque. Its central arch is recessed in a larger arch in a central propylon rising above the level of the façade: the proportions of this smaller arch seem inelegant, vitiating the whole effect.

Sher Shah established the so-called 'Old Fort' or Purana Qila (roughly on the site of Indraprastha) from 1538 to 1545, and we shall see how the design of the Jamali Mosque influences the Sher Shah Masjid, also known as the Qila-i Kuhna Mosque of 1542.

You approach Purana Qila through a massive monumental gateway, but once within the scene is of double desolation: first because the Suri Shah never completed his project of demonstrating his power by a fully functioning citadel, and second because Humayun, on returning to his city after exile in 1550, destroyed all secular edifices such as palaces, chambers and pavilions, and left only the mosque, and a small red sandstone octagon, the Sher Manzil, which he was to use as a library. A two-storeyed pleasure pavilion of 1541, the Sher Manzil stands in a position ideal to survey the Yamuna and the bank on the other side. Purana Qila was moated beyond its ramparts, the moat flowing from the Yamuna on the east. The mosque has five façade bays towards the Yamuna, its external construction being in coursed ashlar, the main façade in red sandstone, much of it finely carved, with white marble and

Purana Qila. Sher Shah Masjid

polychrome encaustic tiling. Within, a double rank of squinches supports the central dome, and at the sides stalactite pendentives support the roof. Roses and pinks flowered between lawns, and chipmunks ran messages for each other under the cloudy sky. Nobody was worshipping in the mosque, but a sharp-eyed woman made sure that I removed my shoes before entering. Bullocks grazed on the grassy ruins, overlooked by the rough rubble masonry. I left by the noble Great Gate, or Bara Darwaza, fashioned of red sandstone and white marble. I took a simple lunch with my auto rickshaw-wallah at the Lovely Tea Stall just outside the Bara Darwaza, and chatted with him and Mr Kanu Bhavsar, an interpreter who recommended the spicy chickpeas and hot sweet milky tea. We sat on rickety chairs, and watched passers-by bringing their picnics to enjoy in this evocative spot, where the history of Delhi may have begun so many centuries ago. A Gaylord ice-cream pushcart stood deserted while the vendor drank tea with us. Young men in smart suits strode purposefully by. Mr Bhavsar was condemning Indian films with the fervour of an Aurangzeb: 'these Bombay movies are trash, for the millions who do not care about the real India: they are all silly romance and nefarious violence dressed up like handsome gangsters, I am telling you'. I riposted with a defence of Satyajit Ray from *Kangchenjunga* (1962) to *Home and the World* (1984), the latter based on Rabindranath Tagore's novel *Ghare Baire* of 1916. Bhavsarji waggled his head in discord. 'We make more than 500 films every year: more than Japan or United States. But do you think these films look like India? Just singing, dancing, fighting.' The film critic Bikram Singh is on record as agreeing that in India 'We produce the most and we produce the worst' and Iqbal Masud sees a great crisis for the 1990s in both distribution and artistic standards. Directors complain that they cannot sell to distributors unless films follow a set pattern – a formula. Distributors complain that they cannot pack houses to see minority films like Ray's *Pather Panchali* (in Bengali). The public is given no choice except in major cities like Delhi, where from time to time you can see classics like M.S. Sathyu's *Garm Hava* (1973), dealing courageously with human issues following partition in 1947; and Adoor Gopalakrishnan's *Elippathayam* (1981), in which a middle-aged feudal landlord fails to adapt to changes in the social fabric and goes mad. Competition with television and video pirates has increased to the point where standards have fallen to appeal to the lowest conceivable level. The actor Naseeruddin Shah tries to persuade writers, directors and distributors to write for him realistic parts with a definite social purpose, but has failed, and denounces soap operas and vacuous family serials as 'rubbish' and 'a disgrace', excepting only the television serial about partition, *Tamas*, partly financed by the Government. Take whatever chance you can to see Indian films in your own country (where subtitles will generally be provided), for in India houses are generally sold out well before showings start, the atmosphere can be very hot and sweaty, and needless to say there is very much more going on outside the cinema than within.

Immediately south of Purana Qila is the Zoological Garden (closed on Fridays); immediately westwards lies India Gate; but we shall travel northward past the kotla of Feroz Shah to Raj Ghat on our way to the Red Fort, Lal Qila. The atmosphere at Mahatma Gandhi's cremation site is reverent – even religious, for 'mahatma' literally means 'great soul', and there is a sense in which Indians of all religious persuasions and castes keenly identify themselves with this patient genius, so cruelly assassinated in 1948. In a beautifully tended park one walks around and above a black marble platform where Gandhi was cremated. Ceremonies take place there each Friday. I saw Hindus proceed through a tunnel, take off their shoes, and make *puja* offerings at the platform; others on a rug within sight of the platform practised manual crafts as Gandhi taught. The former Prime Minister Jawaharlal Nehru was cremated here in 1964.

At Raj Ghat my head reverberated with gently hammering rhythms from Philip Glass's Sanskrit opera about Gandhi, *Satyagraha* (1980), and I mastered only with great difficulty that work's almost unspeakably melancholy view of violence and treachery. How can the meek ever inherit the earth when the cynical majority possess all the weapons and the will to use them?

> *Pre-eminent is he who perceives*
> *in the self-same way*
> *friends, companions, enemies,*
> *the indifferent and the neutral.*

As my auto-rickshaw screamed and braked up Subhah Marg towards Lal Qila, I sniffed the heady smells of a Delhi afternoon, thickened with the whimpering and barking of pi dogs come down in the world, and heated with the intemperate shouting of men without ambition for tomorrow but anxious to eke out the rest of the day before nightfall. Uproar continued through the packed throng entering the Red Fort by the Lahore Gate, so called because it faces another old Mughal capital, now in Pakistan. Shah Jahan began its construction in 1638 to defend his new capital, Shahjahanabad, and it was finished about 1648, at the height of Mughal splendour. The barbican through which you enter is an addition of 1660-66 by Aurangzeb.

The tumult of Old Delhi faded behind me as I passed through Lahore Gate and into a shady vaulted arcade of small shops called Chhatta Chowk selling souvenirs and soft drinks, cigarettes and textiles. I stopped by a stall to refresh myself with a chilled mango drink and a samosa, imagining the scene three hundred years before as court ladies descended in their grace and finery to look at saris and jewels. Now an old woman bent like an 'r' in Devanagari script hobbled from side to side in the dark bazaar.

From here I emerged into a courtyard facing the former Naubat Khana or musicians' gallery, beyond which is the wider quadrangle of the red sandstone Public Audience Hall, or Diwan-i-Am, with fine double columns on the outer sides. The shah would appear on the jewelled peacock throne for state ceremonies, on the raised and canopied niche. Three aisles of columns form the interior, and we should think of them as covered with fine ivory-polished shell plaster contrived by Rajasthani craftsmen to imitate the white marble in the pleasure palaces behind. Above the throne, the alcove walls are designed in *pietra dura*, a small panel at the top being an original example of Florentine inlay depicting Orpheus and his Lute, probably bought or bartered along the trade routes.

Behind the Diwan-i-Am you might expect to find the Diwan-i-Khas, but expectations are foiled, for here instead is Rang Mahal, or 'Painted Palace' built and paved in the finest white marble, with *pietra dura* inlay in the arch-piers. Rang Mahal, with a main central hall and smaller divisions at each end, was considered by a contemporary traveller 'in

Lal Qila. Diwan-i-Am

lustre and colour far superior to the palaces promised in heaven'. The central hall is given a *loggia* effect by the sensitive spacing of ornamental piers, so that fifteen bays are created. One must recreate in the mind's eye its original seclusion, as part of the imperial seraglio, by evoking perforated marble screens between the outside arches, with triple arches of lattice-work along the centre of each side.

The Private Audience Hall, or Diwan-i-Khas, usually contained the great Peacock Throne, which was moved to the Diwan-i-Am only on state occasions. Captured in 1739 by the Persians under Nadir Shah, it was subsequently broken up, but it can be envisaged from miniature paintings of the time. The architecture must even then have impressed visitors more than did the throne, with its shimmering white marble reacting even in degrees of shade to the slightest shift in the sun's brilliance. Thirty metres by twenty-two, the single hall has a five-arched façade, and pillars, walls and ceilings all superbly inlaid with colours at once bright yet subtle. Its polished marble paving reflects the great piers inlaid with floral designs. The side overlooking the Yamuna river has elegant window arches and delicate perforated tracery. The ceiling was once of solid silver, robbed by the Marathas in 1760, but one still fervently echoes the sentiment of the couplet over the fretted arches: 'If there is a paradise on earth, then this is it, this is it, this is it'. In the Diwan-i-Khas in May 1857 the Sepoy rebels declared Bahadur Shah King of Delhi, Emperor of India and here too that after a few months he was tried and exiled to Burma. North of the Diwan-i-Khas you can explore galleries leading to the royal baths, with a channel called 'paradise river' or Nahr-i-Bihisht which led from the river in an aqueduct from 'emperor's castle' or Shah-i-Burj, a vantage point from which the shah and his entourage could watch elephant fights below.

Interestingly, there was no mosque known within Lal Qila until Aurangzeb added the 'pearl mosque' or Moti Masjid in 1662-3. Shah Jahan's great Friday mosque just outside the Red Fort was created in 1648-50, but the devout Aurangzeb required a royal chapel. The marble chosen resembles mother-of-pearl in its polished translucence, and there is no doubt about the richness of the conception, but in proportion to the mosque's size its courtyard seems too small and its three bulbous domes graceless and too large, each of them topped by peculiar spires; the Bengali-style cornice over the central bay again looks out of proportion, and one could have wished Moti Masjid to have been conceived and executed by Shah Jahan rather than by his rebellious son. Aurangzeb's reign was spent in destroying his enemies, such as the Sikh guru Tegh Bahadur; and this restless tide of warfare and fanaticism led

Lal Qila. Moti Masjid

inevitably to a decline in Mughal art and architecture; he himself felt contrition during the last years of his life, as proved by his testament.

Near Moti Masjid stand the relics of a great Mughal water garden called Hayat Baksh, with a pleasure pavilion called Zafar Mahal in a red sandstone bathing pool. Four canals led to two pavilions named for the months of July (Sawan) and August (Bhadon). These pavilions were open to the breezes and rains of the monsoon months at Delhi, when court ladies dallied there, watching the fountains. Mahtab Bagh, or Moonlit Garden, combined with Hayat Baksh to form one luxuriant garden, but the former has been entirely lost, with all its shady trees and colourful flowers.

On the right of the Diwan-i-Am, and as obliterated by time as Mahtab Bagh, were the stables of the Emperor, which Tavernier described in the time of Shah Jahan. The long gallery, elevated six inches above the ground, consisted of porticoes 'full of very fine horses, the least valuable of which has cost 3,000 écus, and some are worth up to 10,000 écus. In front of each stable door hangs a screen made of bamboos woven with twisted silk representing flowers, and the work is very elaborate and requires much patience. These screens serve to prevent flies from tormenting the horses, but that is not deemed sufficient, for two grooms are told off to each horse, one of whom is generally occupied in fanning it. The horses imported from Persia, Arabia or the country of the Uzbeks, undergo a complete change of food, for in India they are given neither hay nor oats. Each receives every morning two or three balls made of wheaten flour and butter, the size of our penny rolls; every evening they receive a measure of chickpeas which the groom has crushed between two stones and steeped in water'.

As you stroll around the perimeter of Delhi's Red Fort, an oblong roughly a thousand metres long and 550 metres wide, think of the inner or private imperial area about 530 metres by 380 concentrated in the centre and rear, with fine views over the river. Visualise cypress-enclosed gardens with crimson and purple in Hayat Baksh, elegant Mughal pavilions glittering with fountains, forty-nine in the central pool alone, and the vivid colours worn by nobles, courtiers and (in the privacy of their *zenana*) the many ladies. While the Emperor gave audience in the Diwan-i-Am, Tavernier notes that music was played: 'sweet and pleasant, making so little sound that it does not disturb those present from the serious occupations in which they are engaged'.

Close to the Red Fort, just inside Chandni Chowk, stands the Parshvanatha Temple of the Jain sect called Digambar. Originally dating to 1526, it has seen numerous additions in four and a half centuries, as the oldest and most convenient centre for Jain worship in Old Delhi.

Just as foreigners coming to England always picture the bookshops of Heffer's in Cambridge or Blackwell's in Oxford, so I wanted to look at the bookshop of Motilal Banarsidass near shops selling handmade paper and perfume on Nai Sarak. I had bought the *Laws of Manu* in the original 'Sacred Books of the East' series edited by the Indophile F. Max Mueller (1886) twenty years before from Heffer's, but Motilal had reprinted this pioneering (if often outdated) series and it was his *Pahlavi Texts* and *Zend-Avesta* that I had acquired in the Orient during the days when I studied comparative religion. Earnest young Indian men were browsing in the books rather than buying, but then the average Indian wage does not permit the purchase of many books. In the end I haggled a twenty per cent discount from Karachi Stationery Mart at 46 Janpath, when buying background books for my travels in Rajasthan, but a dozen other small bookshops, most with similar stock, crowd the little bazaar along Janpath and you might do as well anywhere else. I was offered rupees for my camera, and rupees for my dollars: most rickshaw-wallahs seemed more than keen to supplement their earnings by dealing on the black market.

Not far from here is the Fatehpuri Mosque, named after a wife of Shah Jahan who paid for its construction in 1650. Here, at the western end of Chandni Chowk, I hired a rickshaw to take me back to the Red Fort, for the evening's Son et Lumière, performed nightly in Hindi and, later on, English. Beforehand, I sat on a rusty, rickety tin chair by a wayside stall and devoured a plate of *alu chhole*, a mix of potatoes and spiced chick-peas, and a glass of *lassi*, made with iced water and yoghurt. I closed my eyes against the squealing of brakes, tooting of horns, shouting of men, screaming of women, laughter of children, and the turmoil of traffic, pressing my camera hard on my chest against the pouch of money hanging round my neck and under my shirt to prevent theft. A moment later, I opened my eyes again and everything had changed apart from the wiry little stall-holder in vest and shorts, and the effervescent, all-encompassing noise. Then, allowed in as the first spectator at the English-language show, I found the noise and bright lights diminishing behind me, until the illusion of being alone at night in Mughal Delhi was quite complete.

The religious counterpart of Lal Qila was Shah Jahan's Friday Mosque or Jami Masjid, a truly immense mosque started in 1648 and completed by Aurangzeb after 1660. The largest in India, it is contemporary with the Jami Masjid in Agra and equally refined; it is instructive to relate it to the Fatehpuri Masjid at the western end of Chandni Chowk, with a single dome, as compared with the triple dome of the two massive Friday Mosques. The Jami Masjid, closed to non-Muslims at certain times which must of course be meticulously respected, stands on a high basement storey on an outcrop of an Aravali ridge. I entered by the east gate, which bore this inscription under the heading 'Tears of Blood': 'One more tragedy. Aligarh also made target of shedding blood. May Almighty God destroy the Cruels Killers. Our demands for Aligarh are the same as those for Meerut. The black lowered flags on the rooftops of the Jama Masjid salute with reverence those who met martyrdom from the bullets'. Steep steps lead up to the red sandstone mosque, with white marble facings on the sanctuary and stripes on the two minarets, one at each side of the sanctuary. The three bulbous domes are striped vertically too. The main central arch is flanked on each side by five smaller arches, and I recommend climbing one of the minarets for stupendous views of Delhi, especially the crowded streets and alleys of Shah Jahan's city, and the Red Fort.

I paid off and thanked Bijay, my rickshaw-wallah, and merged with the swaying, chaotic crowds around Chandni Chowk, during Shah Jahan's time a canal-cooled avenue but now a cacophony of a market, pulsating with traffic of all kinds, from porters with tables and refrigerators on their heads to bullock carts and battered taxis surviving on a mixture of string and prayer. 'International Dental Depot' screamed one sign, with flashing teeth. Merchants from Gujarat and Orissa struggled to make their voices heard above the horns and shouting. Punjabi women in long shirts and pyjama trousers carrying

Chandni Chowk

their vegetables were being pedalled by rickshaw. Turbanned Sikhs strode tall between lorries and ambling cattle. Madrasis in dhotis skipped amid the swerving traffic. I found stalls heaped with dusty grapes and shrivelled limes. A roadsweeper thrust a broom comically along the broken pavement in a vain attempt to persuade specks of dirt to change positions with each other: they just flew sadly up into the choked air and came to rest again where they had come from. A moneylender sat in his shop, owl-eyed and stock still. A bullock waded past, weighed down on both flanks by bags of washing, above which a near-naked boy of nine or ten guided his mount nonchalantly through the raucously crowded street. Fidgety chickens in thin wicker cages rattled and squawked their way on the back of a pony cart, between brown crates of crimson and green tomatoes and clattering lengths of aluminium pipe. A palsied *vecchietto* with all Asia's cart-ruts in his ancient countenance pursued the rest of his waning destiny straight as a track, pushing aside figures more sturdy than his own with the force of his ancestry. Two schoolgirls in neat blue uniforms calculated smiles at each other, counting their chittering sparrow-like giggles, not waiting for the other to stop the incessant flow of chatter. A stout Hindu lady swathed like the inside of a laundry-basket scolded her sweating rickshaw-wallah as if he were a lazy donkey. Rummaging in the magical cotton folds on her voluminous lap, she drew out a red handkerchief as if it were a conjuring trick. These scurrying figures, jerking and swerving through the endless hustle, are the heroes and heroines in their own stories and in *nobody else's*: they move like hunted animals in turbulent fear of digressions which might interrupt their transient purposes. If they achieve their aims, they will only start their worries off again tomorrow, adding to the burden of their endless fate. If they fail to achieve their aims, they will take out their irritation on relatives and friends. 'So many months to pay off my creditors at forty rupees per month'. 'If I could only be spotted by a film director, he would at once appreciate my potential'. 'Where can I find the dowry to marry off my orphan niece?'

I, who have lived long years with desert silence and soliloquy, find this pandemonium endlessly distressing, like a wound. Yet it must be endured as an adventure, like the trials of the youngest brother in fairy tales; antithesis to the boredom of the barber who plies his trade with one customer and endures a waiting queue as much as the spectre of poverty without a waiting queue.

South of Chandni Chowk you come to New Delhi Railway Station, then south again to the spacious concentric circles of Connaught Place. Shopping for souvenirs brings you to the Connaught Place area, and the northern end of Janpath. The Central Cottage Industries Emporium opposite the Tourist Office on Janpath displays for sale handicrafts from

Jantar Mantar

all over India, and state emporia are to be found on Baba Kharak Singh Marg at 8 o'clock on the Connaught Place dial from the 6 o'clock of Janpath. At 7 o'clock radiates Sansad Marg or Parliament Street with its astronomical observatory, Jantar Mantar, built in 1725 at the invitation of Muhammad Shah by Maharajah Sawai Jai Singh II. Now incongruous in the proximity of Park Hotel, this is the largest of several observatories built by the Maharajah at five cities, including Benares, Mathura, Ujjain and his own city of Jaipur. One would like to be charitable and accord Sawai Jai Singh high standing in the history of astronomy but, like European astronomers of his time, he was so imbued with ancient astrological superstitions that his motives were primarily to seek auguries and to plan auspicious times and days by planetary conjunctions and movements. The Samrat-Yantra in the centre is a gigantic triangular gnomon with a hypotenuse parallel with the Earth's axis, and measures the time of day correct to half a second, oblivious of the crows that swoop and peck for picnic crumbs around its alien salmon-pink presence.

The last great pre-British monument of Old Delhi is Safdarjang's Tomb, set in Mughal gardens. Started in 1753, it was incomplete at the time of the Afghan invasion of Delhi in 1756 and left unfinished for good when the British captured Bengal in 1757 and set in motion their

Safdarjang's Mausoleum

dominion over the sub-continent. Safdarjang was chief minister to Muhammad Shah (1717-47) and nephew of the first Nawab of Oudh, succeeding his uncle (who had ill-advisedly supported the Persian invader Nadir Shah) in 1739. He died in 1753. The gardens persist, though past their Mughal best, but creative impetus had been lost to some extent, with the hybridisation of certain Oudh features (such as the decorations on the four side pillars). An arcaded terrace about 37 metres long and just over three metres high supports a double-storeyed mausoleum, erected at the initiative of Shah Alamgir II. The elegant dome is a memorable feature, though the roof turrets and kiosks detract from the ensemble. Mughal taste, in the two hundred years since the tomb of Humayun nearby, had declined with the narrowness of the plinth and the exaggerated verticality of the over-fussy mausoleum. To see the progress of Indo-Muslim architecture we should leave Delhi and head eastwards for Lucknow in Uttar Pradesh, governed from 1775-95 by the Nawab Asaf-ud-Daula – but this is another story.

The British took over in New Delhi from 1803, but governed the city from Agra, and only in 1926 was New Delhi inaugurated as complete by the then Viceroy, Lord Irwin. Even if you are convinced that the British had no right to occupy India any more than the Portuguese had any right to take Macão (or Goa, for that matter), there can be no lingering doubt that the movement of capital status from Calcutta to the more central Delhi was inspired, and that the concept of wide roads and ample buildings suited the status of a new capital for a great country. After all, the same concept had inspired the founding of Jaipur two centuries earlier.

Rashtrapati Bhawan (1929) was designed by Sir Edwin Lutyens as the Viceregal Residence, and its hundred and thirty hectares on Raisina Hill now comprise neo-Mughal gardens (based on Kashmir's Shalimar) surrounding the official residence of the President of the Republic. A central dome dominates colonnades. The Secretariat was designed by Sir Herbert Baker, and the Prime Minister's office was incorporated in the north block's west wing. Visiting permits can be arranged by the Government of India Tourist Office at 88 Janpath, which is closed on Sundays. Your embassy in New Delhi, on the other hand, can arrange a permit to visit the Parliament at Sansad Bhawan. Both the Upper House (Rajya Sabha) and the Lower House (Lok Sabha, literally 'House of the People') are based on the British parliamentary system, and similar scenes of reasoned debate and bitter hostility will remind you of the Houses of Lords and Commons beside the Thames. Sansad Bhawan, designed by Sir Herbert Baker, proves a notable architectural success, with its domed central chamber and three semi-circular chambers set grandly but not pompously in a fine colonnaded circular building. Located at the southern end of Sansad Marg, it can be visited at the same time as Rashtrapati Bhawan and the nearby Nehru Memorial Museum in Tin Murti House, Tin Murti Marg, not far from the Ashoka Hotel. A distinguished mansion intended for the Commander-in-Chief during the colonial period, it became the official residence of Pandit Jawaharlal Nehru, Prime Minister from 1948 to 1964, and was turned into the Nehru Memorial Museum on his death. Paradoxically, in a residence created by an occupying power, the home and gardens seem to evoke an atmosphere of self-confidence in Indian Independence, and peace-loving neutrality which Nehru carried off particularly effectively because of his dual appreciation of Indian aspirations and Western development. He set in train the modernisation which slowly built India into a scientific and industrial power respected throughout the world. And just as Gandhi is identified as the father of the idealistic Freedom Movement between 1918 and 1945, so Nehru must be credited with the pragmatic birth of modern India. Annoyed by Gandhi's frequent obscurantism, Nehru nevertheless came to regard Gandhi as political father and religious guru and like Gandhi suffered imprisonment many times: it was in jail that he wrote nearly all his thoughtful books, including *The Discovery of India* and his autobiography. When the time came to elect a leader, the choice lay between the narrow, chauvinistic Vallabhbhai Patel, in shaky health and 72 years old, or the fit 57-year-old suave and westernised Nehru. Gandhi swayed the people inexorably towards his protégé, saying 'Jawaharlal cannot be replaced today. He, a Harrow boy, a Cambridge graduate and a barrister, is wanted to carry on the negotiations with Englishmen.' Nehru's only failure, and that must be shared with the British who departed too quickly for prudence, was the unexpectedly bitter bloodshed caused by Partition. Here too the architect of modern Pakistan, Muhammad Ali Jinnah, must accept part of the responsibility. Nehru's years must otherwise be considered a great blessing for India and the world at large. Rising above sectarian politics as far as he was allowed, he made India a great secular democracy, with an Industrial Policy (since 1948) and five-year plans beginning in 1951. He has been rightly criticised for underestimating the need for birth control, but his Hindu Code became a standard for feminist rights far ahead of its time, legalising divorce, forbidding polygamy, and ensuring property rights to Hindu women. We all know that many Indian women are still badly treated by husbands and the families into which they marry; that most are still illiterate (as are most Indian men); that most women suffer arranged marriages just as before. But things have changed where public opinion and private advantage have permitted, and educated women have now begun to make their voices heard in all branches of central and local government, in industry, in diplomacy, in education.

Because the life of Indian women seems to be hardly better than it was a hundred years ago, I was delighted to have the privilege of meeting in New Delhi a remarkable campaigner from Hyderabad in Andhra Pradesh, Malladi Subbamma. Suffering an arranged marriage at 11, she studied higher school and university examinations with her own children when she was 36, trained in family planning, and with the support of her husband started the Institute for the Advancement of Women, the Cosmopolitan Marriage Bureau, and the Family Counselling Centre and Marriage Guidance Bureau. She has written on the lives and disadvantages of Indian women in novels and social studies, opposing sati or widow-suicide, arranged marriages, the dowry system. She advocates the woman's choice concerning abortion, and intercaste marriages, attacking the powers offering Indian Muslims easy divorce without the obligation to provide maintenance payments for divorced wives. Malladi Subbamma is one of a small number of vocal, determined, and above all forward-looking Indian women, such as Dr Indumati Parikh in Bombay, whose intelligent and sensitive work for women's rights may ultimately help to shape Indian realities beyond virtually meaningless legal protection.

In politics, Nehru's non-alignment played a creative rôle for India exactly as Enver Hoxha's isolationism played a destructive role for Albania. Nehru's dominance in Indian politics was maintained by his only child, Indira, who controlled the Congress Party machine from 1955 to 1959, and in the latter year was elected President of the All-India Congress Committee. On her father's death, Lal Bahadur Shastri became Prime Minister, with Indira appointed Minister of Information but less than two years later, after Shastri died in Tashkent, she became the first woman Prime Minister of India in January 1966. And the Gandhi-Nehru heritage did not die with her but passed to her son Rajiv, again in the sound belief that his family's tradition of pragmatic diplomacy, gradual modernisation, non-alignment and non-sectarian tolerance would prove more deeply beneficial to India, despite his inexperience, than the chauvinistic, obscurantist or superstitious dogmatism of his many rivals. Why has Gandhian socialism mixed with entrepreneurism superseded the early potential of Communism in India? Communists themselves to whom I spoke attributed their failure to take power to a few basic causes: fragmentation into several warring factions; frequent changes in direction giving rise to a loss of credibility among long-term supporters; and lack of the kind of charismatic leadership that has allowed movie stars to dominate politics in Tamil Nadu for long periods. Other opponents of Indira Gandhi were equally divided, lacking mobilised support throughout the whole country. The story of three opponents, told in a sensational journalese style but *published in India* (another incidental testimony to the country's liberalism) can be found in *Decline and Fall of Indira Gandhi* by D.R. and Kamla Mankekar (1977).

As you wander among the photographs and other memorabilia of Pandit Nehru and his family, including the daughter, Indira, to whom Nehru wrote from prison, you can feel the potency of the family's charisma both at home and abroad. A Son et Lumière performance in English is held nightly at 9 in the gardens except between mid-July and mid-September. The house is closed on Mondays. Museums to Gandhi at Raj Ghat and in the Hall of the National Building on Tis January Road are also closed on Mondays.

C.G. Blomfield's Jaipur House, India Gate, now accommodates the National Gallery of Modern Art, which displays the work of the Daniell brothers and other European artists working in and around India in the late 18th and 19th centuries. Heavy-hearted, I must confess that modern Indian art has little to recommend it, as it drifts rudderless among seas of international experimentation and artistic revolution, and even the Daniell aquatints are much more comfortably enjoyed at home in the learned company of Mildred Archer's illustrated book *Early Views of India* (1980), devoted to the journeys of Thomas and William

Daniell. So – as in the Nehru Museum – you will enjoy Jaipur House and garden for the generously-scaled British Raj design. Baroda House too is now open, for it is the railway booking office, and it is also worth looking at W.S. George's S. Stephen's College.

The single most important visit in all New Delhi is the National Museum at 11 Janpath, near the crossroads with Rajpath, with film shows and five free guided tours daily. The museum is closed only on Mondays. The collection originated in Rashtrapati Bhawan in 1949, moving to Janpath in 1960, and, possibly because of the huge quantity of material and its range in time and location, no catalogues of holdings have yet been published. Palaeolithic stone implements of roughly 300,000 B.C. are on show, but Mesolithic paintings on caves and rock-shelters cannot be moved here from their original sites. So the first great period of 'Indian' art, by which I understand the whole sub-continent including present-day Pakistan, Bangladesh, the Himalayan countries and Sri Lanka, is the Indus Valley Civilization of the 3rd millennium B.C. represented by Harappa, Mohenjodaro and Chanhudaro, grouped with pre-Indus sites such as Kalibangan, Nal and Amri. From Harappa for instance we have beads, dice, metalwork, and a red jasper male torso; from Mohenjodaro we have the flirtatious small bronze Dancing Girl (also $c.$ 2500 B.C.) with her head tilted and right arm akimbo, a superbly-detailed tiny yet massive bronze Buffalo, and a splendid terra cotta figurine of a woman (known by the controversial 'Mother Goddess' label) with panniers supported by a double rope-band on her head.

When the Indus Valley tradition petered out about 1500 B.C., sculpture apparently died until the Mauryan age in the 3rd century B.C. represented here by aristocratic objects from Sarnath (Uttar Pradesh) including exquisite small-scale female figures with turbanned heads and a male head with drooping moustache. Dominantly Buddhist in religion, the Mauryas had not yet introduced Buddha or his emblems directly into art: this happened only in the 2nd century B.C. with stone sculpture of the Sungas in northern India, contemporaneously with the Kalingas in eastern India and the Satavahanas in the Deccan. An example of a Sunga Jataka story illustrated in a medallion of a railing post from Bharhut (Madhya Pradesh) shows an elephant and three deer on the obverse and a Yaksha image within Sunga architectural motifs on the reverse.

The 2nd century A.D. saw the rise of the Kushan rulers, who deposed the Greek rulers of Bactria and Gandhara, founding a major school of sculpture: the Kushan art at Mathura and Gandhara, contemporary with the Andhra school at Amaravati stupa in the south exemplified in the British Museum by limestone friezes, pillars and reliefs carved with Buddhist stories obviously influenced by Kushan art of the north.

Gandharan art is best seen in Pakistan, but here in New Delhi outstanding works include a magnificent dark grey schist full-length Buddha with gracefully-flowing robes not half a world away from the Graeco-Roman style that had spread to Roman imperial frontiers (Palmyra from Baalbek) four centuries after Alexander, to whose invasions early art historians had too hastily attributed their influence. Gandharan art soon became indianised, and from the rounded figures and coquetry of the 2nd-century Mathura style evolved into the 5th-6th century Gupta style, which transformed the Graeco-Buddhist hybrid into a new, intimate perfection, repudiating the original Graeco-Roman formality in favour of grace, charm, poise, and spirituality, like a Bodhisattva Avalokiteshvara from Sarnath. The Bodhisattva stands on a lotus pedestal, his fragmentary right hand in *dhyana mudra*, releasing nectar towards two tiny emaciated spirits. Sarnath has also given us the great Gupta Head of Buddha of the 5th century in soft buff sandstone, considered by connoisseurs the peak of achievement for vision *(drsti)*, form *(rupa)*, emotion *(bhava)*, grace *(lavanya)* and idealism *(sadrsya)*, comparable to the great Bodhisattva mural in Cave 1 at Ajanta (early 6th century).

As we are looking at masterpieces, do not miss the elegant Mohini from Karnataka, dated to the 10th century, a miracle of rich carving in black stone showing floral decorations on her *dhoti* and a small attendant below her left thigh. Of the same age is an Early Chola four-headed Brahma from Tamil Nadu. Rajasthan is not very well represented, so it is worth seeking out the white marble Chauhan Saraswati from Pallu near Bikaner, of the 12th century. The Hindu goddess of learning, known to the Jains as Vagdevi, stands on a lotus pedestal and holds in her four hands a vase, rosary, lotus and palm-leaf book. She is contemporary with a Ganga, or personification in stone of the river Ganges, from Mahanada in West Bengal.

Indian bronzes reached their peak of perfection in the south from the Pallava period (7th century) to the Late Chola (12th century) and over a longer period in parts of the north in Chamba, Kashmir, and in neighbouring Nepal. Typifying the former is the Early Chola Shiva Nataraja from Tiruvarangulam, South India, dancing on a defeated demon and performing symbolically five simultaneous actions: creation, protection, destruction, spreading knowledge, and communion with the infinite. From Kashmir we have a complex 9th-century Vishnu with four heads: a human at the front, a boar and a lion at the sides, and a demon at the back.

Terra cottas have always proliferated in the sub-continent, because soft, pliable clay has always been available even to the poorest in most parts of the country, from 7th millennium B.C. figurines found at Mehergarh in Baluchistan to Harappan-period bulls, Mauryan so-called 'mother-goddesses', and 5th-century Gupta terracottas such as the famous Sita from Bhind (M.P.) and the Head of Parvati from Ahichchantra (U.P.). Stuccoists achieved their best surviving works in the Gandharan Man in Agony and Head of Bodhisattva, proving their skill in both secular and religious genres.

Ivories, some of good quality, have been brought from French excavations at Begram, ancient Kapisa, 80 km from Kabul, the summer capital of the Kushan rulers in the 1st-2nd centuries.

Manuscripts in the collection total more than 9,000, major acquisitions including 3,000 in Arabic and Persian from the Nawab of Tonk in Rajasthan, 1,600 Sarada MSS from Shri Brij Kishan, and 500 Sarada MSS from Shri Mohan Kishan Kaul. The Harappans had a script in the 3rd millennium B.C. (not yet deciphered) but the earliest Indian script so far deciphered is the Mauryan script known as Brahmi used by the Emperor Ashoka and, in cursive form, known as Siddhamatrka, which emerged in the 6th and 7th centuries, roughly contemporary with the descendant of Brahmi known as Nagari. From this Nandinagari arose in the south and Devanagari in the north. Devanagari rapidly spread as the vehicle for Sanskrit, Prakrit, Hindi, Gujarati and Rajasthani. The Sarada script is another descendant of the Gupta Brahmi script: it spread in Kashmir, as Gurmukh spread in Punjab and Takari in Jammu. The best MSS here are the outstandingly refined Mughal works: the *Duval-Rani Khizr Khani* (1568) written in a Persian *nasta'liq* script, possibly by Mir Sayyid Ali, for Sultan Bayazit; the Persian *nasta'liq Babur-Nama* (1598) of which other copies can be found in Alwar State Museum, Moscow State Museum of Eastern Cultures, the British Library, and the V & A in London; and the memoirs of Jahangir, *Tuzuk-e Jahangiri* (early 17th century), probably in the Emperor's own hand.

Over fifteen thousand paintings cover the period from the 12th century to the 19th. An unforgettable gem is the *Ragini Vibhasa* (*c.* 1670) from Bundi, in which Raga Megha shoots a floral arrow to delay dawn's arrival so he can enjoy the company of his lover a little while longer. *Krishna the Flute-Player* (late 17th century) is a Bikaneri illustration to Keshava Das' poem *Rasikapriya* signed by Ruknuddin, a court artist influenced by the Mughal style in his refined draughtmanship.

The National Museum's Chamba Room reconstructs a deteriorated collection of murals from Rang Mahal in Chamba, now in Himachal Pradesh, painted in tempera and depicting deities such as Shiva and Parvati, Vishnu and Lakshmi, and the lives of Krishna and Rama, in a style similar to that of Kangra.

A valuable collection of 70,000 coins from India and Sassanid Iran, in particular, extends in period from the silver bent-bar punch-marked series of the 6th century B.C. from Taxila, in present-day Pakistan, up to the present day.

Indian arms and armour held in the National Museum comprise more than 7,000 pieces, dominated by Maratha, Sikh, Rajput, Hindu, Mughal, West Asian and Central Asian specimens. Aurangzeb's sword and armour, Tipu Sultan's sword, Maharana Sangram Singh's shield of 1730, Bahadur Shah Zafar's bow: your readings in Indian history or scenes of warfare in Mughal miniatures will rush back in your memory as you see these famous arms. You might prefer to concentrate on elaborate animal-headed hilts, with ivory, metal or jade horses, elephants, rams and camels. You can learn here to distinguish the curving blade of the *jambia* (Aurangzeb's is here) from the slightly curved, double-edged *khanjar*; and the leaf-shaped *katar* from the *peshqabz* with its pointed single edge.

Decorative arts from the 16th to the 19th centuries are represented by over 7,500 items, mainly from North India, with an emphasis on the Late Mughal period: a late 18th-century mother-of-pearl flagon, a brass astrolabe of 1861, a brocade of 1650, a Mughal jade betel-box of the 17th century, and Orissa ivories of Krishna and Radha also of the 17th century.

Sir Aurel Stein's four expeditions to Central Asian silk roads (for there was a later northern route as well as the more celebrated southern itinerary) resulted in the preservation of thousands of religious curiosities, stuccoes, textiles, and paintings preserved on silk and paper. Fascinating interactions of Bactrian, Sogdian, Indian, Chinese and Graeco-Roman cultures produced an art as infinite in its variety as woman, yet local styles did emerge, at Dunhuang, Miran and Khotan on the southern route, among hundreds of other sites, and at Turfan and elsewhere on the northern route, all areas recently opened to international tourism by the Chinese authorities. Some of these finds can be seen in the British Museum (for example from Dunhuang), in Berlin (from Khocho) and here in the National Museum. A Sassanid-Ajanta hybrid wall-painting from Balawaste, possibly depicting Indra, is dated to the 6th or 7th century, a little earlier than a Chinese-style stucco sculpture Horsewoman from Astana near Turfan; a Hellenistic stucco Head of a Bodhisattva (3rd-4th centuries) contrasts with a vigorous terra cotta Monkey with a Bowl on its Head (4th-5th centuries) from Khotan. In Japan a similar hoard from the Silk Road can be seen (with a letter from your Embassy in Tokyo) at the Shosoin at Nara; in North America the international exhibition *Silk Road — China Ships* (1983-4) circulated throughout Canada and the U.S.A. and its excellent catalogue was published by the Royal Ontario Museum in Toronto. It is extraordinary that these objects have survived (silver spectacles like spoon-bowls to reduce the strain of travelling in sun-scorched deserts; delicate silk Tang paintings) that they merit close and loving examination.

The National Museum has the Heeramaneck Collection of Pre-Columbian Art; Coptic textiles; Luristan bronzes; a range of regional arts from Indian tribes; and jewellery from Mohenjodaro, Taxila, and Mughal pieces from Jaipur, Benares and elsewhere.

Temporary exhibitions are a feature of the National Museum's work, and during my visit 'Russian Icons from Soviet Museums' included a marvellous Christ's Nativity executed by the school of Rublev, a late-15th century Vernicle from Novgorod, and a 15th-century Virgin of the Sign from Pskov, the whole display bathed in the golden background of the icons tinged with the umber tones of the Orthodox liturgy emanating from tape.

If you take a rickshaw 2 km west of Connaught Place, you will come to the Temple of Lakshmi Narayan (Lakshmi being the consort of Vishnu and Narayan the original name under which Vishnu was worshipped), also known as Birla Mandir, or the Temple of Birla, the wealthiest family in India after the Tata family of Jamshedpur. But Raja Baldevdas Birla did not exclude the other Hindu Gods when planning this temple constructed in 1938, with its charming garden on the western side. The inscription over the gateway reads: 'This temple is open to all Hindus (including Harijans), subject to prescribed conditions of cleanliness, full faith, and sincere devotion'. The concept of 'full faith' is difficult for western sceptics to comprehend, because Birla thoughtfully provided shrines within for Sikhs, Jains and Buddhists too, and it may be that Sikhs worshipping within would not have the 'full faith' in Hinduism demanded by R.B. Birla. I watched with quiet wonderment as barefoot Hindu urchins scampered into a menacing stone monster's mouth and then on top of his head in the rock: this is a temple and garden presented to the people with a sense of fun. You too must take off your shoes before entering.

2: AGRA

Mathura — Sikandra — Agra — Fatehpur Sikri

It was my last breakfast in Delhi before leaving for Mathura, Sikandra and Agra. The morning newspapers warned of harder economic days ahead, with an inflation rate of 9.8% (far less damaging than in many African and Latin American countries). 'Bofors probe panel term extended' referred to allegations of corruption in high places. The weather in Delhi (late February) was 9.7° C minimum and 26.6° C maximum. A crisis burgeoned in Hindi-language book publishing, with Hindi books being priced at three times the cost of a similar work in Bengali. 'Verka' pasteurised butter of Chandigarh was advertised: 'The kids simply love it. Ideal supplement to their tiffin goodies'. At Jabalpur, the athletics coach A.K. Kutty had asked the organising committee to hold events on time and in the proper fashion, to which a committee member had retorted: 'We have seen many meets and they all go like this. Don't show me your moustaches and get out'. Unprecedented scenes in the Rajasthan Vidha Sabha were reported as the Opposition protested against the reinduction of Mr Chivcharan Mathur as Chief Minister and the Government's failure to help famine-hit people in the state. A letter from one Moti Lal expressed outrage at several cases of child sacrifice reported in Rajasthan in 1987, concluding: 'The public strongly reacted to the suicide of the three Sahu sisters in Kanpur. But all have remained silent on cases of child sacrifice. It is a sad comment on us.'

My bus wove its haphazard way through bullock-carts, lorries marked 'Public Carrier', and dogged, dusty carts, past the National Board of Examinations, the National Medical Library, World Renewal Spiritual Museum (what can they *display*?), then we reached the border checkpoint between Delhi and Haryana. In Faridabad shops announced 'Bikaner Sweets. Special Arrangements Marriage Parties', 'Usha Galvanised Steel' and 'Indian Aluminium Cables Ltd.' Bullocks hauled carts and furniture. Drought and hardship showed in the thin ribs of cattle. At the town of Ballabgarh, with its huge Goodyear tyre factory, stallholders piled up cabbages, grapes and bananas. An open-air barber clipped away industriously at a customer, while four old men chatted the time away behind them. Eucalyptus trees now began to take over at the roadside, giving shadow while halting sand and dust flows.

Traffic decreased after the town of Palwal, with vultures hovering in the azure above Shyam Rice Mills. A peacock fluttered in alarm in an entirely flat and fertile landscape where bullocks ploughed as they have done for centuries. Single-storey houses, often in compounds, are made of bricks made in a kiln close by. At a wayside restaurant, the Dabchick at Hodal, a little boy tried to pose for a rupee with a sleepy cobra round his neck, and a performing bear shambled in a garden. Ten rupees to ride an elephant, eight for a camel, six for a horse.

Then came the border leading into Uttar Pradesh.

Mathura
I broke my bus journey at the ancient and holy city of Mathura (pronounced 'mutterer') for the same reason that I had interrupted my journey from Jerusalem towards the Dead Sea at Bethlehem: a tale of divine birth. For Mathura claims, albeit with scant likelihood of accuracy, to be the birthplace of the god Krishna, seventh incarnation of the god Vishnu, and the most popular god in the Hindu pantheon.

Located on the banks of the Yamuna, which wends along its leisurely, bendy course to Agra, Mathura has seen the rise and fall of as many civilizations as Jerusalem, Istanbul, or Rome. From 350 B.C. to 465 A.D. it saw the rise and establishment of Buddhism, an ascendancy which did not inhibit the peaceful practice of Hinduism and Jainism and minority or pagan practices. The nomadic Kushan dynasty took Bactria and Gandhara from the Greeks in the early years A.D. and Kadphises II captured Indian territory as far as Mathura, Varanasi (the Hindi form of Benares), and Narbada in the south. Kanishka, reigning until 144, expanded Kushan territory to Kashgar, Khotan and Yarkand, choosing Peshawar in present-day Pakistan as his capital. The invaders assimilated Indian faiths: Kadphises II minted coins with the image of Shiva and Kanishka became a Buddhist but, after the collapse of far-flung Kushan dominance, the Gupta dynasty gradually exerted its influence from the early fourth century to its apogee later in that century under King Samudragupta, at once a scholar-poet and musician, and an energetic military leader, covering most of the northern area of the sub-continent except for Kashmir. The Gupta age was one of Hindu supremacy and the promotion of Sanskrit. Kalidasa wrote his best poetry at the court of Samudragupta's successor Chandragupta II, and Gupta sculpture and architecture reached new heights of refinement. Chinese Buddhist pilgrims to hold places such as Mathura included the chroniclers Fa-Hsien, who in 402 noted the existence of some three thousand monks in twenty monasteries in Mathura, and Hiuen Tsang, who saw Mathura in 643, when Buddhism was already on the decline. In 1071, raids by the Muslim Mahmud of Ghazni, a town south of Kabul, not only looted what he found, but destroyed idols and sacked Hindu temples and Buddhist monasteries, setting the scene for ravages by later Muslim conquerors. Sikandar Lodi humiliated Mathura again in 1500, but Akbar (1556-1605) proved a wiser ruler, recognising the special qualities in India that, despite the occasional sectarian riots and the terrible bloodshed caused by Partition, seems to favour religious pluralism. The Sati Burj (1570) on the bank of the immortal river Yamuna is, as the name indicates, a tower to commemorate the self-sacrifice of a widow, in this case the builder's own mother. A fort on the Yamuna bank was built by Man Singh of Amber (1590-1614), and the present Friday Mosque, 'Jami Masjid' in Arabic, dates from 1661, when it was commissioned by Aurangzeb's governor Abd-un-Nabi ('Slave of the Prophet') to cover the site of the Hindu temple Keshava Deo, itself believed by some to have been built on the site of Krishna's birthplace. A new Keshava temple can be visited, but the most important place in Mathura today, if one excludes marvellous scenes of everyday life at the Yamuna, is the extraordinary Government Museum on Dampier Nagar. The cult of the mother goddess runs like a thread through the early pottery, often black or grey. Early Buddhist sculpture, often in red sandstone, is hieratic and cold, but as the style matures the figures relax, acquiring human properties with which the worshipper can more readily identify. At the Victoria and Albert Museum I had admired Kushan dynasty sandstone female tree-spirits known as *yakshis*, carved in the 2nd century and probably intended as a bracket of an ornamental gateway to a *stupa*. Gandharan art can boast quite a selection of first-rate pieces, but generally speaking the mass-produced Kushan-age sculpture of Mathura seems less than inspired. It is only in exceptional pieces that the quality rises to great power, subtlety, and naturalism, and in the Gupta period we have such masterpieces as the fifth-century Standing Vishnu (SR242) now in Delhi's National Museum. Two red sandstone Standing Buddhas of the same period possess a miraculous inner calm: one in Delhi and the other here in Mathura. Greek-influenced Gandharan sculpture from the Peshawar-Taxila area of contemporary Pakistan has been displayed to offer stylistic comparison. Mediaeval Indian sculpture by contrast loses its originality, its tranquillity, its self-confidence at the moment when Gislebertus is creating his masterpiece at Autun.

If time permits, you might care to visit Brindaban by bus, train, or tempo rickshaws. Ten km away from Mathura, it is connected spiritually by the cult of Krishna, and the Govind Deo Temple, dedicated to him as the Divine Cowherd, dated back to 1590. The fortnight-long fair at Raghunath Temple (closed to non-Hindus) celebrates every February-March the coming of Lord Krishna to Brindaban, and you can see the great procession between the temple and the gardens called Raghunathji-ka Bagicha. August-September is not a good time to be in

Brindaban from the point of view of weather, but it gives you a chance to see the Janmasthami Festival commemorating the birth of Lord Krishna. There are mosques and Jain temples but the thousands of Hindu temples make Brindaban a great source of interest for anyone wanting to see Hindu pilgrims in all their ages, castes, and attitudes. Many temples remain open from sunrise to sunset, but Shah Ji closes between noon and 6 p.m. Because of its sacred character, Brindaban has only vegetarian restaurants. There are no western-style hotels, but you could find accommodation at the Krishna-Balram International Guesthouse, Raman Reti, or at Seth Prem Sukh Das Guest House at Ahta Chowk.

Sikandra

Our road leads to Sikandra, named for Sikandar Lodi, second of the Lodi dynasty founded by Bahlul Lodi (1451-89) and ending with Ibrahim Lodi (1517-26). The Lodis, a dynasty from present-day Afghanistan, had driven out the Sayyid dynasty which ruled the Delhi province as viceroys for Timur, but was to be expelled in its turn by the first Mughal: Babur (1526-30). Though Sikandra was founded in 1492, it is celebrated today mainly for the magnificent mausoleum of Akbar, open from sunrise to sunset. In 1602 Akbar commissioned this himself from red sandstone, but after he died in 1605 it was completed in white marble by his son Jahangir in 1612. One enters by the southern gateway of the four symmetrical entrances, with great symmetrical gardens graced by gazelle and large, lazy amiable monkeys who have no need to go in search of a living because eccentric visitors bring them bananas and other titbits. When in the vicinity of Indian monkeys, stash away anything loose (handbags, cameras, hats) in a pocket, haversack or zippable bag, for their curiosity knows few bounds and, once you lose a possession to their eager, nimble fingers, it will remain lost.

Akbar's Mausoleum fascinates by its quasi-pyramidal structure: you will see at Fatehpur Sikri a similar Panch Mahal or five-storeyed palace owed to Akbar. In a sense one might relate it to a much earlier Mesopotamian *ziggurat* or an Egyptian stepped pyramid, but I suppose that in the minds of its royal designers it remained in the tradition of the tented pavilion, a transfiguration of the nomadic palace which would give them an illusion of reigning wherever they happened to spend the night. As I ascended through gradually diminishing chambers, I came finally to the simulacrum of Akbar's tomb, where an echo of the man's earthly spirit would face the sun, and the sky. The cenotaph is carved with the ninety-nine attributes of Allah, though Akbar himself created (much like Akhnaten in Egypt) a new religion, ecumenically directed to encompass not only Islam and Hinduism, but also Buddhism, Jainism and Christianity. Jews and Zoroastrians are also known to have debated

Sikandra. Akbar's Mausoleum

in the House of Worship founded by Akbar at Fatehpur Sikri. Scholars are divided about the nature of Akbar's new *din-i-Ilahi*, or religion of God, and Michael Brand and Glenn D. Lowry in *Akbar's India* (Asia Society, New York, 1985) assert that Akbar attempted merely to formulate a new code of religious behaviour, but this seems to me special pleading, for Islamic orthodoxy bitterly opposed Akbar's words and deeds, as they apparently undermined the unique divine revelation of the Qur'an al-Karim and thus could not be accepted. The body of Akbar was never placed here, at the summit of his pyramidal mausoleum, but far below, at ground level: its position is shown by marks. In 1761 the Jats of Bharatpur raided Sikandra and looted the remains of Akbar which had rested here in peace since 1613. The walls bear the Islamic invocation 'Allahu Akbar', meaning not only 'God is the Greatest' but also 'God is Akbar', if you ever thought to read it in that way.

Akbar's Mausoleum at Sikandra, like Taj Mahal and a thousand other monuments, is alive and energetic with the scamper of chipmunks. Like any other crazy Englishman, I used to collect bits of unwanted bread from my meal tables in a mucky bag, separated from book bags in my pack for fear of books' worst enemy (grease), and sit down on the grass, like a pallid middle-aged Buddha with spectacles. There I would feed chipmunks crumbs to the endless amusement of passing Indians, who would often confer among themselves to discover whether I could be classified clinically insane, or was merely acting, like a comic mental incompetent in the armies of the Pandavas. Opinion was divided, except among a crowd of neatly-uniformed schoolgirls, who were so terrified of approaching me that they must have unanimously cast me as a suitable case for a straitjacket. I sat down with my mucky bag in front of me at Sikandra, awaiting chipmunks, but because of the presence of curious Indians none approached. I asked a solemn Bengali visitor, 'You have chipmunks here?'. He weighed up this for several seconds, hedging his bets. 'Why you need chipmunks?' 'To eat this bread', I explained. 'Why you can't eat this bread?' 'Because half of it has already been nibbled by chipmunks.' 'No, sir, we don't have chipmunks here', and he waved his hand demonstratively at nearby trees, teeming with beady eyes, bushy tails, and feverishly pumping little grey bodies, leaping from branch to branch. I threw the rest of the bread bits at the foot of a wall, where they were immediately seized and nibbled by chipmunks, gnawing pensively while tense on their strong haunches, then bobbling away like bouncing tennis balls on uneven grass to the next forage.

On the way back I ascended the gateway for an overview of the gardens and mausoleum. On a clear day you can see the Yamuna winding towards the Red Fort and Taj Mahal at Agra in one direction, and in another the towers of Fatehpur Sikri, but I fear that I could discern nothing of the more distant dead city of Akbar.

Agra

You may think of Agra as the city of Taj Mahal, but if an Indian says 'I am going to Agra' the implication is very different, for it has the largest psychiatric hospital in the region and the Indian would open himself to the jocular inference that he is unbalanced mentally and intends applying for treatment. The city has a population exceeding 1.2 million, with a large university and the prestigious Agra College built by the British. Our bus from Sikandra passed the Sikh temple or Gurudwara (literally 'Gate of the Guru, or Teacher'), then the Mental Hospital, and near Delhi Gate we stopped at a level crossing to allow a train to pass. A woman sitting by the road was selling cowdung cakes for fuel at three rupees for five kilos. Beyond the red sandstone S. John's College the bus speeded and braked, our driver hooting and gesticulating, through a maelstrom of rickshaw-wallahs, sacred cows, motor-bikes, buffaloes and cars, past a Baptist Private Secondary School, 'Dixit Retreading Works', 'English Wine Shop with Child Beer', Mall Road Cantonment, Head Post Office and Ashok Hotel, then through officers' quarters built for British officers but now, run-down and untidy, occupied by Indian army officers. I alighted at the former Holiday Inn, now renamed Taj Palace

Hotel and, after special pleading due to surreptitious administration of bakshish, secured a high room overlooking Taj Mahal. If you visit Agra during the winter months, from November to February, you will need warm clothes and there is no need to book an airconditioned room.

Agra must have been in existence long before the Muslim incursions into India, but the first literary reference occurs as late as the first quarter of the 12th century, in a poem by Mas'ud bin Sa'd bin Salman eulogising the Ghaznavid prince Mahmud bin Ibrahim. Masu'd notes the conquest of an ancient fort in Agra by Sultan Mas'ud III (1099-1115), who permitted Rajputs swearing fealty to him to govern the fort. The town remained insignificant until Sikandar Lodi (1489-1517) rebuilt the city from 1505 and chose it as the seat of his government; it retained this position under Ibrahim Lodi (1517-26) and Babur, who razed much of old Agra to create a more worthy capital. Humayun and Sher Shah made it their capital, but spent much of their time away from Agra, which regained pre-eminence only in 1558, the third year of Akbar's reign. But we shall see that Akbar chose to build a new capital at Fatehpur Sikri before returning to his favourite Lahore, and Agra did not resume a glorious rôle until 1598 when Akbar returned. Jahangir was crowned there in 1605 and Shah Jahan in 1628, but neither emperor could stay permanently at Agra for military reasons, and Jahan in any case preferred to create the new capital we have explored at Shahjahanabad, now known as Old Delhi. Agra's importance fluctuated thereafter, but in the 17th century European travellers could compare the city in size and wealth to Paris or London. Raiding Marathas controlled Agra 1758-61, 1770-3, and 1785-1803 and the Jats in 1761-70 and 1773-74. The British seized the city in 1803.

Everyone has a theory about which light suits Taj Mahal best: pink dawn, dazzling noon, gentle dusk, but in my view there is no substitute for seeing it at all hours of the day and, at full moon, during the night as well. For it certainly takes on a new personality like a woman according to the person perceiving and the moment of perception. She can be harsh, dry and strong like alabaster, delicately chaste and fragile like porcelain, noisily populous or quiet and secretive. Like La Scala, Milan, or Great Zimbabwe, Taj Mahal makes one feel more significant as a human being in its space than one feels beyond it: it uplifts and enhances, imbuing us with moments of sublimity that will recur in Strauss' *Der Rosenkavalier* and Turner's visionary empathy with light and colour. We forget that we were ever ordinary. Because nothing is visible behind it but ever-changing sky and scudding clouds, Taj Mahal rises like a mirage in the Takla Makan oasis. It shivers with the excitement of a precipice, of a high waterfall, of the last palm grove before three days across dry dunes. Though dreamed by a man, who had

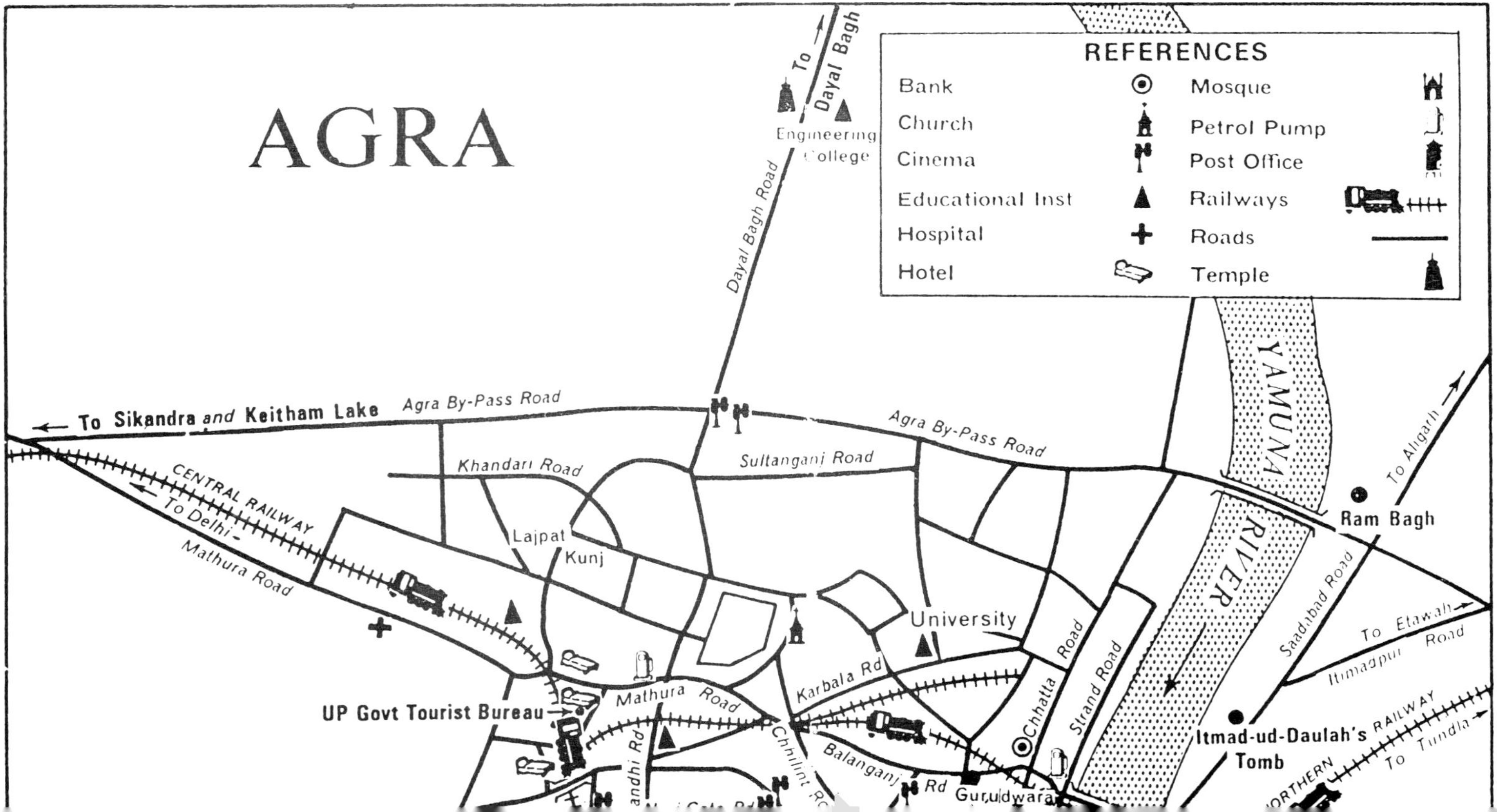
AGRA
REFERENCES
Bank
Church
Cinema
Educational Inst
Hospital
Hotel
Mosque
Petrol Pump
Post Office
Railways
Roads
Temple
To Dayal Bagh
Engineering College
Dayal Bagh Road
To Sikandra and Keitham Lake
Agra By-Pass Road
Agra By-Pass Road
Khandari Road
Sultanganj Road
CENTRAL RAILWAY
To Delhi
Mathura Road
Lajpat Kunj
University
Karbala Rd
Mathura Road
UP Govt Tourist Bureau
Chhilint Rd
Balanganj Rd
Gurudwara
Chhatta Road
Strand Road
YAMUNA RIVER
Ram Bagh
To Aligarh
Saadabad Road
To Etawah
Itimadpur Road
Itmad-ud-Daulah's Tomb
NORTHERN RAILWAY
To Tundla

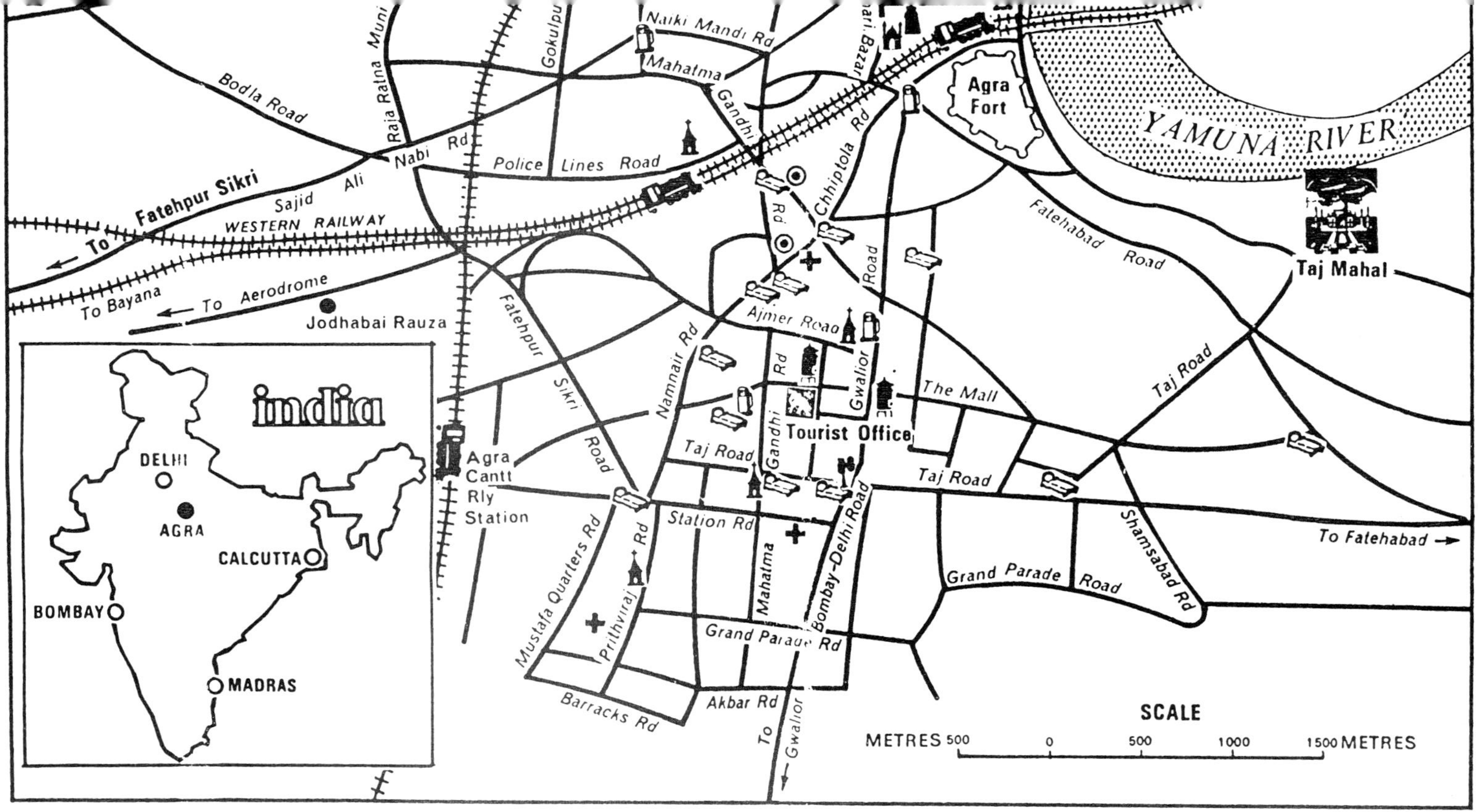
YAMUNA RIVER
Taj Mahal
Agra Fort
Fatehabad Road
Taj Road
The Mall
Tourist Office
Chhiptola Rd
Gwalior Road
Ajmer Road
Gandhi Rd
Mahatma Gandhi Rd
Naiki Mandi Rd
Bazar
Gokulpu
Raja Ratna Muni
Bodla Road
Nabi Rd
Sajid Ali
Police Lines Road
To Fatehpur Sikri
WESTERN RAILWAY
To Bayana
To Aerodrome
Jodhabai Rauza
Fatehpur Sikri Road
Namnair Rd
Agra Cantt Rly Station
Station Rd
Bombay–Delhi Road
Mustafa Quarters Rd
Prithviraj Rd
Grand Parade Rd
Grand Parade Road
Barracks Rd
Akbar Rd
To Gwalior
Shamsabad Rd
To Fatehabad
SCALE
METRES 500 0 500 1000 1500 METRES
india
DELHI
AGRA
CALCUTTA
BOMBAY
MADRAS

fallen in love at first sight when sixteen exactly as I had done, this miracle of human design has assumed a mantle of femininity, in which a married woman, a matron and mother of her monarch's fourteen children has remained forever tantalisingly young and desirable. When Mumtaz Mahal died, giving birth to another child in 1631, the inconsolable Shah Jahan resolved to mark her memory with the greatest celebration of passionate love that the world had ever known, outdoing the mausoleum of his own grandfather Akbar at Sikandra. The Crown of the Palace took nearly twenty-two years to build, employing at times over twenty thousand artisans and labourers (according to Tavernier), though Manrique estimated the number in 1640 at barely a thousand. It is fruitless to speculate on the architect's identity, for historians have been divided on the matter for three centuries and we shall never be sure. Vincent Smith favours Manrique's statement that the original designer and architect was a Venetian called Veroneo, adding that the work was probably concluded by a Persian or Turk called Muhammad bin Isa, though some scholars take him to be a fiction. The truth is that Mughal emperors through their chroniclers, from the time of Babur onwards, were at great pains to stress their own greatness and to minimise the importance of their satellites, omitting all mention of rivals and enemies unless they could be delineated as both evil and defeated by stratagem or combat. You would not expect eulogies of architects, or even perhaps a grudging mention; and you do not find them. But we do know of lesser luminaries in the constellation: the dome-builder Ismail Effendi from Turkey, the calligrapher Amanat Khan from Shiraz, the mosaicist Chiranji Lal from Delhi, the goldsmith Qazim Khan from Lahore.

If you stay at Taj Mahal long enough, and wander at will to observe the gardens and mausoleum from every angle, not forgetting the flowing Yamuna, you will come to a rounded vision very different from the two-dimensional picture of the mausoleum's façade haunting postcards like any truly two-dimensional artefact: Frans Hals's *Laughing Cavalier* or Picasso's *Guernica*. A moment's reflection will remind you that this is not what a building is: it has three dimensions visible and a fourth, that of time, which can be contemplated as one enters living space. We are not really in the 16th-century Lodi capital of India now, but in the new town called Mumtazabad which arose in the 17th century to accommodate the workshops, studios and living quarters of thousands devoting their lives solely to the glorification of Arjumand Banu Begum, called by her royal husband Mumtaz Mahal. Inside the gateway to the compound is a commercial arcade once the financial centre of Mumtazabad, at the end of which you crowd with hundreds (on Fridays thousands) of eager sightseers into a courtyard. Many of these sightseers will be pilgrims, too, for a religious outing to Salim Chishti's tomb at

Agra. Taj Mahal

Fatehpur Sikri will come on to Taj Mahal, and the day will combine merit and refreshment.

Do not rush with them through the main red sandstone gateway, for this constitutes as great a component of the whole as the overture to *The Magic Flute*. The three-storeyed gate stands thirty-three metres high, with a huge archway and many rooms inside. Eleven kiosks surmount the central arch, each above its own tiny matching arch. The southern façade bears calligraphy so ingeniously proportioned around the arch that the size of the characters seems not to vary from top to bottom, as of course it must if each word is to be equally legible. From the gateway gasps of wonder rise in a dozen languages at once: Hindi, Tamil, Bengali, Marathi, French, German, Japanese, Swedish.

A long, slender canal flanked by cypresses extends from the steps below the ornamental gateway to the terrace below the mausoleum, divided only by a small marble platform where eager Indian photographers persuade families and honeymoon couples to pose for posterity. Never forget that Shah Jahan was a figure as remote from daily life as was Louis XIV at Versailles; that he once wore a coat so grandiose, so studded with precious gems that two servants kept him upright while in audience; and that he could command the services, so tradition has it, of five thousand concubines. A man vanishes beneath the weight of legend, and we cannot imagine in these egalitarian days, when leaders seek to impress the populace at large, a man treated like a demi-god, whose word could impose immediate death or sudden preferment. Your eye is captured by the supremely-proportioned dome, whose finial spears the blue sky seventy-three metres from the ground. Like the great tomb below the dome, the platform and minarets (one at each corner of the platform) are created in marble from the quarries at Makrana, near Jaipur. The gardens, immaculately tended by phalanxes of gardeners, resound to birdsong and sparkle with leaping chipmunks. I picked up a feather from a pied myna, which had been preening itself in a quiet corner of a lawn. Such gardens in Mughal India are essentially Persian, for they take as their premise the facts that water is rare (it is commoner in northern India) and that regularity and symmetry are a virtue to be upheld regardless of expense, whereas in India a wilderness is more the norm, and gardens will benefit by a certain idiosyncrasy, as we shall see in Rajasthan. No, for the Persian a garden must be perfect, because it is a mirror on earth of paradise in heaven, *firdaus* in Persian denoting both 'garden' and 'paradise'. Persian taste arrived with Babur, and remained in favour with Akbar and Jahangir, cultivating roses, flowers, carpets, poetry, miniatures of courts and pools. Because in Islam four is the most sacred number, Persian influence decreed a quadriform garden, a *char-bagh*. There are four minarets, four quarters to the garden, each with sixteen flower beds, each with four hundred flowers.

Though one can see Indians squatting to perform their natural functions openly in a busy city street or by the open road, the etiquette is never to speak of it or allude to it but to ignore it as an all-pervasive aspect of life, like sex or death, which is never discussed. This Indian quality of being able to abstract oneself from one's surroundings, so crucial to staying sane amid squalor, is monumentally present in Taj Mahal, and it is no accident that Agra's most celebrated marvel (though by no means the only one) possesses a truly monumental abstraction in its vast tactile presence due partly to its almost infinite whiteness and gradations of whiteness, partly to huge perspective in empty space, and partly to its tacit rejection of all grubby contact with our daily routine, our sweat and poverty, unpunctuality, dishonesty, stupidity and frailty. Whatever affects us daily should not affect us here and now in this stainless stone, a pledge to pure eternity. Timeless and inscrutable, Taj Mahal transforms us from whining infants to potentially mellow sages.

I slowly climbed the steps on to the wide platform and, while others surrendered their sandals to a snatching raid of watchmen, I placed mine in a special plastic bag I carried for my sandals everywhere in India. Each minaret soars some forty-six metres into the piercingly bright sky, and each has an eight-windowed cupola, access to which is denied by thousands of screeching bats congesting each spiral staircase. The minarets are deliberately built to lean, so that if they fell, or were toppled, they would crash away from the mausoleum and off the platform altogether. Within, you may visit the simulacrum of the tomb of Mumtaz Mahal, with her royal husband's tomb set asymmetrically between the centre and the magnificent inlaid octagonal marble screen, the whole subtly illuminated by natural sunlight filtering through marble screens.

In fact, the real tombs are to be visited below, in a hot, dark scrum which I found sweaty and undignified, but a necessary part of my visit. Remarkably, earlier travellers such as François Bernier (*Travels in the Mogul Empire*, 1670) or Jean-Baptiste Tavernier (*Travels in India*, 1676) were forbidden to enter the upper cenotaph chamber, but I could gaze in amazement at inlay in jasper, agate, malachite, cornelian, jade, mother-of-pearl which seems not so much ostentatious as ethereal, when the surface of the marble is so purely, gleamingly white.

Across the river you can just make out the remnants of Mahtab Bagh, the Moonlight Garden. Shah Jahan had intended to build himself a counterpart to Taj Mahal, using black marble, and possibly even a bridge, black marble to the centre from the northern bank, and white marble to the centre from the southern bank. (Other sources suggest the bridge was to have been of solid silver). But Aurangzeb had no time, patience nor money to fulfil his father's great plans and, after eliminating his brothers one by one, imprisoning his son, and executing two grand-nephews, put his father under house arrest in the Red Fort in 1658, thereupon crowning himself as Emperor in succession to Shah Jahan.

I returned to the gardens, turning every few moments to enjoy changing perspectives, changing light, distance, background. At the western side of the mausoleum stands a mosque, in warm red sandstone as a foil to the central white marble. At the eastern side an assembly hall was built as a reply or *jawab*, also with a large central arch, in Persian terms an *iwan*, with a large central dome, and two smaller side domes. Tree-planting by Europeans or in a European style during the 19th century marred the original intention, with parterres full of flowers, as described by Bernier, now lost. I took a quick journey on a ferry-boat to the other bank of the Yamuna, from which the 'back' of Taj Mahal glittered no less brilliantly than the 'front', though all angles are equally effective. I sat on a lawn and watched starlings compete with sparrows for crumbs. I admired the frieze of tulips and irises on the base of the outside walls. At the base of the dome, inlaid jewels flared then died in the extravagance of the setting sun. Exhausted, I trudged out of Shah Jahan's dream, and into the noisy chaos of Agra.

'Hello mister!' Ganeshi Lal intercepted me from a buzz of insistent rickshaw-wallahs. 'You want cinema, good time, marble workshops very cheap?'

'No thanks. What I really want is to see if I can get my photographs developed so that I can see whether I have adjusted the exposure properly for these tricky light conditions.'

Ganeshi Lal didn't know where I could have my photographs developed, so he just pedalled up and down the bazaar, till we stopped outside Agra's Montessori Nursery School. The photographer's opposite was empty except for framed examples of their work: sloe-eyed beauties.

While standing at the counter of Foto Quick Foto First, 4/4/3 B Khan, Market Baluganj, Agra 1, I peeled an orange above the goggling eyes of three, four, seven and eventually twelve, fifteen, and twenty-nine urchins, in turns requesting pen, rupees, orange pieces, rupees, and photo mister. It was a good ten minutes later before the owner of the shop revved his motor-bike and locked it with understandable concentration against a lamp-post before leaping up the step.

I was standing with bits of orange peel in my hand. 'You have rubbish bin?' I enquired diffidently, seeing no such receptacle. 'Yes', he nodded fervently. I gave him the orange peel. Bunched in his right hand, the bits of peel suddenly flew out of the open doorway and into the street, where a pig snuffled at them with gratification. You wait outside a photo shop long enough, and the occupants will feed you orange peel.

'Six o'clock', enunciated the photographer.
'My photos will be ready at six?'
'I bring them to your hotel; you pay me then'. He shook his sorrowfully at the receipt, then handed it to me and I wrote down the name and address of the hotel. 'Not fail', he shouted, as Ganeshi Lal poured me into his tight-fitting back seat, and began to pedal off again, his thin, muscular legs pushing down as he stood upright to gain uphill. Luckily there are not many hills and dales in Agra.

Again I entered Taj Mahal, and again lost myself for hours, as the queues of patient pilgrims had disappeared, leaving the raised platform of the mausoleum ineffably white, as hard as death to bear and bright as paradise, gleaming against the ever-changing sky of scudding clouds and darkling blue. Ganeshi Lal hailed me in the thinning crowds as I emerged, quiet, chastened, and we made off back to my hotel – I silent, he chattering about taking me to one of his many uncles who owned marble shops, carpet shops, you want to look only, I take you, no buying, just looking, we go yes? Like any bumbling, well-meaning fall guy I suffered myself to be taken, almost without complaint, to one emporium after another, for these inlaid marble boxes and tables too are Agra; they derive from the families of the craftsmen who converged on Shah Jahan's Mumtazabad in the 1630s and '40s. I nodded mutely at proffered dhurries and embroidery, brass and copper, marble, jewellery and again marble inlaid with semi-precious stones. The unwritten script required me to praise the merchandise. I praised the workmanship.

The next morning I arranged with Ganeshi Lal to take me to Lal Qila, the Red Fort: not the brick fort of Sikandar Lodi which he ordered after Agra became his capital in 1501, but the red sandstone successor executed under Akbar from 1565. Akbar's son Jahangir is quoted in his *Memoirs* as saying that Sikandar's fort had been 'demolished by my father before my birth. He rebuilt it with red hewn stone, the like of which is not to be seen by any who travel throughout the world. It was finished in the course of fifteen or sixteen years.' Enter the walled fort through the impressive Delhi Gate and walk straight ahead to the Great Audience Hall then continue to the farthest right-hand corner for the earliest building in the great complex.

Akbar's own creation still surviving is the Jahangiri Mahal, designed as its name suggests for the prince his son, in red sandstone, with a superb gateway. The palace's façade is lightened by lines of white marble, necessary in view of the two great inner courtyards with carved brackets that clearly supported a balcony. Take a staircase to the pavilion on the roof for an overview of Lal Qila itself and Taj in the distance.

Jahangir himself had little affection for Agra: as we have seen at Sikandra his most enduring architectural feat was the completion of his

Agra. Lal Qila. Delhi Gate

father's mausoleum. But Shah Jahan transformed Agra into the heart of an Empire, strong in its Red Fort and gentle in its Taj Mahal. Shah Jahan added palaces and mosques within the moated fort, creating a harmonious ensemble of Hindu and Muslim architecture. His private palace or Khas Mahal, a fine marble building adjacent to Jahangir's, overlooks the Yamuna, benefits from the river's breeze, and protects rooms below from the heat of summer. In front of Khas Mahal a formal Mughal garden may once have harboured grape vines to judge from its name: Anguri Bagh. Soil for the garden was brought from Kashmir and a stone pergola once existed. But the grapes in question may have been represented in 'a kind of lattice-work of emeralds and rubies that should have represented grapes when they are green and when they turn red', according to the traveller Tavernier. A mirror palace, that *shish mahal* type which we shall encounter in royal palaces throughout Rajasthan, forms another delicate element in the *zenana* or women's quarters of the palace.

Shah Jahan reconstructed the Public Audience Hall in its present form, In front of it students lazed and laughed at a picnic on the lawns, and I fed bread to leaping, scurrying chipmunks. Up the steps from Diwan-i-Am is the intimate Nagina Masjid, of Gem Mosque, and nearby a little Ladies' Bazaar takes its name from the practice of allowing traders of silks and other finery to display their wares to Mughal noblewomen. Rose-ringed parakeets winged their raucous, chattery way around the octagonal Saman Burj, the jasmine tower beside Mina Masjid, built by Shah Jahan for Mumtaz and ending up as the place of his death in 1666, eight years after he had been deposed by Aurangzeb, his unlikeable son. He spent his last years here in comfortable house arrest, with his daughter Jahanara and his fabulous collection of jewels. From his suite of rooms he could see Taj Mahal, as you can today. I gazed down from the parapet, imagining fights between pairs of elephants goaded by a couple of riders each. Across a mud wall they contended for supremacy, the winning animal being the one who could knock down the wall and chase the loser away. Enraged elephants would frequently toss and maim or massacre one or more of the riders, whose families would be compensated. A winner would be well rewarded.

And imagine the Machhi Bhawan (Fish Building) as it was before the Jats of Bharatpur looted its marble basins and fountains in the 18th century. There are no more sacred fish in Machhi Bhawan.

But the Pearl Mosque, or Moti Masjid, dazzles now as surely as it ever did in 1654, when Shah Jahan created its ineffable whiteness. The only exceptions are a yellow marble inlay on the floor and, over the entrance, a black marble inscription comparing the mosque to a precious pearl, for none other is lined throughout with marble. Once the private chapel of the Court of Emperors, Moti Masjid might be thought of in the context of Lal Qila as S. George's Chapel relates to Windsor Castle. Three rows of arched columns are roofed by finely-proportioned cupolas crowned by three high domes. Cloisters of fifty-eight slim pillars on square bases surround a central tank for ritual ablutions.

Of course you have to populate the palace buildings and courtyards with hundreds of servants, including musicians playing in empty rooms in case the emperor should enter. The Mughal court might reside at Agra, Delhi or Lahore, but contemporary travellers agree that the palaces in Agra's Lal Qila were the most sumptuous of all. We must see Shah Jahan ensconced in his fabulous Peacock Throne, a copy of which was in the possession of the former Shahinshah of Iran. The original is lost, but is well known from texts and from royal portraits such as that by Nadir az-Zaman in the Metropolitan Museum of Art, New York. An elevated rectangular platform bore twelve emerald-studded pillars, whose capitals consisted of two bejewelled peacocks, one on each side of a tree with diamond leaves. A canopy was inlaid with pearls, gold, sapphires and emeralds. Mughal magnificence can be judged from the fact that the emperor used a different throne for every day of the week, and the treasury at Agra contained, *unused by craftsmen*, 750 pounds of pearls, 275 pounds of emeralds, 5,000 gems from Cathay, corals, topazes, 200 daggers, a thousand gold-studded and jewelled saddles, 2 golden thrones, 3 silver thrones, a hundred silver chairs, five golden chairs, 200 precious mirrors, a hundred thousand precious plates and utensils, 50,000 pounds of gold plate... Lahore's treasury was assessed at roughly three times this value.

Today Lal Qila is filled from morning till sunset by hordes of travellers, mainly Indians, of all four generations, the Hindu 'ages of life'.

And everywhere rickshaw-wallahs urged me to visit their uncles, with best marble. The relentless zeal of the courteous shopkeeper and his more desperate touts is such a feature of life in Agra that it forms a sub-culture. In the absence of kings and princes, visitors from America and Europe, Japan and the Middle East are plied with tea or coffee to lure them into shops and workshops. 'We sell at factory prices, dear Sir'. 'You can get here less than ten per cent of cost'. 'Today we are making no profit'. 'This shop is patronised by King of England, look we made replica for you of Taj in pure marble sent to Buckingham'.

I was manhandled out of the clutches of one carpet-seller into the doorway of another by the force of Niagaratic speech and body language combining into a hypnotic power to which most British people have no innate resistance. 'These jewels you are getting genuine only in this emporium. Thrice welcome, Sir.' Hyperbole and wide-eyed flattery have not perished with the end of the Mughal Empire: Mughal poetry was half-eulogy, written and recited in the hope of immediate reward, and this tradition, debased as jerky prose, lives on unabated in Agra and Delhi.

Ganeshi Lal hailed me from the throng emerging through Delhi Gate, and we walked together to his cycle rickshaw. 'You want girl mebbe?'. 'No, thanks, I'm married, Ganeshi Lal. Here's a photo of my wife.' 'You want boy mebbe? In Mal-ka Bazaar we are having many boys for good time.' I declined all offers of sexual gratification and persuaded Ganeshi Lal that I really would rather see Aram Bagh, on the other side of the Yamuna. Traffic on the road bridge seemed even slower and more chaotic than on the streets, which gave me ample time to watch *harijan* ('scheduled caste' is the British euphemism) hitting wet clothes on the dhobi ghats in the trickling Yamuna below. Several years of drought had reduced the flow of the once-mighty river, and I wondered how India would clean its laundry, without washing-machines or lakes or rivers. Black water-buffalo headed absent-mindedly straight towards white cotton sheets drying in the sun on the Yamuna's expanse of dry sand. I averted my eyes...

Covered tongas and a myriad bicycles filled the dusty road towards Aram Bagh and other Mughal gardens on the eastern bank of the Yamuna, between the road and the river. Aram Bagh (Garden of Repose) may have been the earliest of all Mughal gardens in India: scholars dispute its claim with those of the Zahara Bagh next door and the larger Chahar Bagh much farther towards Taj. Whatever the malleable truth, it has certainly been greatly altered over the centuries since it was laid out in the 1520s to the command of Babur. Anyone who has visited Babur's tomb in Kabul will remember how overgrown are its terraces, afflicted with henbane. Aram Bagh, for all its distinguished ancestry, has suffered the same fate. Not only do weeds proliferate: its gardeners are few and apathetic, reflecting the paucity of casual visitors. But Aram Bagh, with its views towards Lal Qila and the never-failing fascinating of Yamuna's waters, links us directly with the very first of those Mughal emperors whose influence at the time of Akbar would extend as far as Orissa and Bengal in the east, and beyond the river Tapti to Berar in the south.

Babur tells us in the *Babur-Nama* (as translated by F.G. Talbot) that he first sank a large well. 'I next fell to work on that piece of ground on which are the tamarind trees, and the octangular tank; I then proceeded to form the large tank and its inclosure; and afterwards the tank and grand hall of audience that are in front of the stone palace. I next finished the garden of the private apartments, and the apartments themselves, after which I completed the baths. In this way, going on, without neatness and without order, in the Hindu fashion, I, however, produced edifices and gardens which possessed considerable regularity.'

Vultures flapped on branches swaying under their weight. Monkeys nonchalantly peered at me between examining each other for fleas. I stood, emperor of a causeway, on a stone platform called a *chabutra* where the emperor might have whiled away a serene hour amid spring blossoms before continuing his campaign to subdue northern India. But by 1530 Babur was dead, and this melancholy garden, misunderstood by later generations who have not cared about restoration, has pitiably few of those admirers who have sought to maintain the splendour of Taj Mahal.

South of Aram Bagh and Zahara Bagh I asked Ganeshi Lal to stop at another mausoleum overlooking the Yamuna, that of a dignitary in the court of Shah Jahan, one Afdhal Khan Shukrallah of Shiraz who died in 1639 and prepared this massive, quasi-royal tomb to receive his earthly remains. Most of the tiles have been removed over the centuries, but enough of their fine blue design remains *in situ* for you to evoke its atmosphere in the 17th century, when it would have been surrounded by neat, regular gardens. The popular name of Afdhal's mausoleum is Chini-ka Rauza (*chini-mitti* are the glazed Chinese-type tiles), and it lies

Agra. Chini-ka Rauza

just to the north of another neglected garden: that of Wazir Khan.

Some way to the south, again on the river side of the road that parallels the Yamuna's eastern curve, stands a magnificent tomb that should really be seen before Taj Mahal, because it is clearly a stylistic predecessor, yet also claims a romantic background. A Tehrani noble, one Mirza Ghiyas Beg, fled with his wife and family to Kandahar but, robbed *en route* of all but two mules, arrived shortly before the Mirza's wife gave birth to a second daughter, Mihr an-Nisa, who eventually married an Afghan noble, one Sher Afghan. Ghiyas Beg obtained a position in the service first of Akbar, and then with Jahangir, who secured the murder of Sher Afghan and in 1611 married Mihr an-Nisa, whom he thereafter called Nur Jahan, Light of the World, honouring her father with the title of I'timad ad-Daula, or 'Trust of the State'. This became literally true when Jahangir slipped further and further into opium addiction, surrendering the government behind the scenes to I'timad ad-Daula, Nur Jahan, and Nur's brother Asaf Khan, father of the lovely Arjumand, who was to become world-renowned as Mumtaz Mahal, and only slightly less so as persecutrix of the Portuguese Catholic

Agra. I'timad ad-Daula

community in India.

Some feel the mausoleum of I'timad ad-Daula is the most beautiful building in Agra, and it certainly possesses intimacy on a human scale to which a visitor may more easily relate than to the Taj, for one thing because there are few other people to distract attention from the square balustraded building with its charming inlay, and a water pavilion you can climb for delightful views both to the river and to the tomb. Dignity is provided by a raised platform, allowing the tomb to dominate the *charbagh* (fourfold garden) from each of the four centrally-placed gates. On the platform the square tomb is enlivened by an octagonal tower at each corner. Within, I'timad ad-Daula's tomb is to be found in the middle chamber, and other tombs in adjacent chambers include those of Asaf Khan and his wife, Mumtaz Mahal's father and mother. Inlaid in the marble are garden motifs composed of semi-precious stones, representing flowers in vases and cypresses. The creamy marble tombs are glimpsed through graceful marble lattice work. I was steeped in the beauty of this place when gently greeted by a softly-spoken Sikh, who introduced himself as Jagjit Singh, an engineer in the Janta Radiator Works in Agra. His smiling wife Rajender was dressed in a full-length brown sari and shawl, and his little son Surabjit swathed in a thick pink pullover. We spoke of the Sikh problems in Punjab, the siege at Amritsar's Golden Temple, and the pride that Sikhs take in their mechanical skills. Jagjit invited me to visit his Gurudwara past the Mental Hospital and to spend the night with his family before leaving for Fatehpur Sikri, and this was not to be the last generous offer of hospitality made by an Indian to a perfect stranger during my stay. I did not say that I came from a city in England where a genius with motor neurone disease is working on a grand unified theory that would relate to each other all the forces of the Universe. Jagjit Singh finds his place in a Sikh community in the larger city of Agra, bringing up his wife and child in the time-honoured customs and rituals of the Sikhs. I could not explain that I had no religion at all, that I should feel uncomfortable in suggesting any mode of conduct to my wife and daughters, relying on their free will, practical good sense, and innate morality to lead a good life unwatched, unscolded, unfettered. A yellow splurge in the treetops attracted little Surabjit's attention. A black-headed oriole perched still, beady-eyed, above our heads and winged off across the Yamuna. I parted from my new Sikh friends.

Ganeshi Lal, catnapping, stood and stretched as I emerged from I'timad ad-Daula, asking the price of my binoculars. Since India is one of those countries (which outnumber the others by some eight to one) where you can ask a total stranger his wages, and receive an answer, even if false, I asked Ganeshi Lal how much he earned and spent a month. His pay as a cycle-rickshaw wallah is low but supplemented by commissions from shops to which he takes tourists; his expenses are low, with one main meal a day, usually in the evenings, and rent of Rs 100 a month (about US$9) for a room occupied by his father and himself. We trundled back from Aligarh Road to the two-level bridge, and along Daresi Road to the Friday Mosque. Shah Jahan's daughter, Jahana Ara Begum, paid for this great mosque, outside Lal Qila's Delhi Gate. Raised between 1644 and 1648, it is contemporary with the Jami Masjid in Delhi. It was 4.40 p.m., and Muslims were praying in one long line on a blue prayer mat facing Makkah al-Mukarrimah. I found wild bees nesting in the squinches, where they remain undisturbed at such a great height. The open courtyard has marble lattices all around. Women sat on raised platforms outside. Large metal fans on the mihrab wall were not working: they were not needed in the cool of the late afternoon. A three-stepped marble minbar was decorated with three domes in relief. Two clocks dustily ticked their trivial lives away: in the abode of eternity, who needs the time? Outside, a red sandstone minbar for the Friday sermon is reached by a functional if inelegant ladder. A central square tank for ritual ablutions formed a locus for conversation. A boy of twelve guzzled greedily from one of the honeycomb terra cotta drinking pots. Only ten per cent of Agra's population is Muslim, following Partition, so the Jami Masjid is no longer crowded to the doors at evening prayer. Nevertheless the atmosphere remains as radically Islamic here as at Akbar's city, Fatehpur Sikri.

Fatehpur Sikri
The best time of day in India is *al alba*, as the Spaniards say, at dawn, beginning the day at the first letter of the alphabet, with a bell's clarity. 'A' begins the Sanskrit alphabet, just as it begins the Spanish and English. My bus rolled out of Agra at 7.40 towards the forty-km drive to Fatehpur Sikri. I noted that the day was Monday, and so auspicious for Shiva. A friend called Pritam Singh talked not so much like a tap flowing: rather like a soda syphon in full gush. He had sold the bicycle for which he had paid Rs 770 and on the black market had acquired a motor scooter for Rs 19,200. You could buy one new for Rs 13,000 if you joined a waiting list, but he needed to travel round quite a lot, so had forged ahead of the queue. By the side of the road a woman in an orange sari was sedulously sweeping fine dust from outside her compound into the road. Traffic roaring past would then whoosh it back to its point of origin: she did not look up, but held her shawl over her face to protect her eyes from the blinding particles. 'These horses are hire for wedding,' announced Pritam Singh, shaking his head at a rake-thin Rocinante, its head bowed in the shade of a mango-tree. 'The groom should sit on horse going to bride's family, marriage always in house, never in temple, then in temple they bless marriage'. I asked

whether the dowry had not been abolished. 'By law, abolish,' answered Pritam Singh, in that declamatory manner used by educated Indians to impart finality to their words, 'by custom, we keep dowry. If not, no girl can get husband.'

Fields of wheat, mustard, pulses, and barley spread out around us, as we hooted very loudly past Ashok Leyland 'public carriers' transporting cattle fodder to Rajasthan's drought-affected regions, past yoked bullock-carts, and vultures feeding off a pig that had wandered carelessly on to the road. At Midhakur by 8.10, I closed my eyes with pity at the sight of two Himalayan black bears performing for a few paise. 'Also many Hindus come to Fatehpur Sikri'. Pritam Singh waved his dark hand at busloads of Muslim pilgrims converging on the deserted Muslim city. A mongoose sniffed the air and padded away, in no great hurry. The city itself starts with a swathe of bougainvillea, but natural delights immediately give way to the same kind of wonder at the ingenuity of man that one experiences at Teotihuacán, Persepolis, or Karnak. A fortress wall some 5 km long forms roughly three sides of a square, while the northwest side was protected by an artificial lake that dried out long ago. The pre-existing village of Sikri had been chosen for his mosque and school by a pious Muslim Shaikh called Salim of the Chishtiyyah sect. The emperor Akbar visited Shaikh Salim in 1568, when the mystic prophesied the birth of a son to Akbar's first Hindu wife, Jodhbai, the daughter of Bihari Mal of Amber. He had married the Amber princess in 1562, but no male heir had survived, so it was to untold relief that in 1569 the prince Salim (to succeed as Jahangir, in 1605) was born and survived. Akbar certainly named Salim after the Shaikh, but his decision to transfer his capital from Agra to the 'City of Victory' or Fatehpur, must also have been based on other factors, such as the wish to immortalise his victory at Ahmedabad, with the subjugation of Gujarat; the sight of Mandu, which he had seen during campaigns to Central India; the recollection of Amber, home of his wife; and the symbolic importance of a hill near Sikri where his grandfather Babur had conquered the Mewari Rana Sanga in 1526. My own view is that Akbar must also have been influenced in his choice of site by the local abundance of red sandstone, which can be seen everywhere except in the elegant small-scale white marble mausoleum of Salim, nestling in one corner of Jami Masjid's great courtyard.

Motives apart, Akbar ordered the construction of a royal capital in 1569, by 1570 work was well under way, and within 7 years much of the city had been completed: a third of the time that Shah Jahan's workmen took over one building, Taj Mahal. By 1585, Akbar had tired of the dry heat and virtually waterless plains surrounding Sikri and abandoned his new capital for the more congenial climate of Lahore. Within a few years, the pomp and bustle of the red sandstone city had vanished forever and yet its regally-inspired construction methods had proved so enduring that today the city, quite uninhabited as regards the Akbarid royal chambers, has scarcely a single derelict room and one expects to see pigeons emerging from the pigeon houses, artists at work in their studios, patients in the first full Indian hospital, trained elephants, and singers, one of whom was reputed so learned in the technique of vibration that his voice could kindle wood. We no longer see the processions of ambassadors, soldiers and guards, and anxious-faced subjects with petitions. After passing through the Naubat Khana, a double gate at which the emperor would be saluted by musicians, we reach the ruined elephant stables near the mint and the treasury.

The Elizabethan traveller Ralph Fitch left Agra (with two English companions) for Fatehpur Sikri in July 1585, anxious to deliver a royal letter to Akbar. Fitch described the road as 'more crowded than a London street', with hostelries and shops for Hindus on one side and Muslims on the other. Travellers used either fine horses or 'two-wheeled carts drawn by little bulls, decorated with silk or fine cloth and used as our coaches in England'. The hovels of the poor and merchants' stores have all disappeared in the course of centuries, leaving only palaces and places of worship.

We enter the Hall of Public Audience, or Diwan-i-Am, where Akbar, illiterate like the vast majority of his countrymen, would have reports and books read to him. The emperor could be approached by anyone with petitions, and a dignitary was appointed to deal with them. Akbar might sit crosslegged on a heap of cushions or perhaps on a throne. Akbar's decisions were recorded by a scribe, sitting near the two openwork screens. A paved courtyard is called Pachisi after one of the games played on the large 'board' laid out on the ground, where Akbar played the game of *chaupar*, using slave-girls as 'pieces'.

The Private Audience Hall, or Diwan-i-Khas, strikes me as one of the most remarkable buildings of this period, when the first playhouses were being put up in London and Sir Francis Drake was about to begin his second circumnavigation. Dating from 1575, the square *diwan* seems simple enough from the outside, but within are two storeys connected by a central octagonal pillar on a square base, both finely carved, blossoming like a lotus or symmetrically branching tree with 36 uniform brackets at the centre, the hub from which a circular stone platform radiates to each of the four sides. Akbar sat in the centre, audible but invisible to those below: his ministers, advisers and generals. One climbs to the first floor, standing in the centre of the pillar as at the navel of the world. A flat terraced roof has corner pillared kiosks, reminiscent of chhatris you will see throughout Rajasthan. At one time the Diwan-i-Khas was assumed to have been the renowned Ibadat Khana, that House of Worship where Akbar debated religious systems with invited proponents. In 1579 he was declared infallible as the highest authority in matters of religion and in 1582 renounced Islam in favour of a more tolerant 'Din al-Ilahi' or 'Religion of God', but this ecumenical authoritarianism disappeared with his death, and the divisions formally to end with Partition were exacerbated by the Muslim zealot Aurangzeb.

The little Ankh Michauli ('Closed Eyes') may well have served as a treasury, with secret recesses referred to as the 'closed eyes' of the title; or it may be that the name of the building, a game similar to our 'blind man's buff', came from one of the many pastimes of the enigmatic emperor, who could be at once profound and flippant, foolhardy in pranks with elephants and sagacious in military strategy which occupied so much of his thoughts.

Sparrows darted through the House of the so-called Turkish Princess: Akbar had only one Turkish wife, whom he may have accommodated here apart from his Hindu *zenana* and Muslim *harem*. In red sandstone, the little room is however decorated with charming Persian-style mural carvings. The private palace (Khas Mahal or Khawabgah) on the southern flank of the paved courtyard is frescoed, including a boat, again with Persian influence. Akbar's position as an art patron follows the Persian tradition, by which painting is considered a sacred discipline since it reveals the poverty of human endeavours to imitate God's handiwork. He not only maintained large studios, inviting masters from Iran and Afghanistan, but even agreed to pose for portraits, a significant step which gave Indian painting one of its most successful and enduring genres.

Your eye will be taken and delighted by the complex tapering forms of the five-storeyed palace, or Panch Mahal, with the bottom floor containing 56 columns, and top floor one single square kiosk. Ascend by a staircase in the southwest corner for a fine view over the surrounding palaces and courts. Each side was probably closed in by openwork stone screens, so the possibility is that Panch Mahal was a ladies' pleasure palace, though it has been mooted that astronomical observations were taken from the roof.

The so-called Palace of Jodhbai is named for a Rajput princess who in 1585 became the first wife of Akbar's son Salim, the future Emperor Jahangir. Total privacy from without is guaranteed by a wall ten metres high. As befits the lady's status, her palace is the grandest of the intimate palaces in Fatehpur Sikri, belonging to the first Imperial period of Hindu-Mughal architecture. Its lintels and balconies are Hindu in derivation, and the baths and domed kiosks Mughal. The lower chambers were heated in winter, and the upper storeys airy in summer, being a Hawa Mahal of the type that will reach its apotheosis in Jaipur.

A similar two-storey arrangement provides interior freedom and seclusion from without for another queen. Tradition assigns the building to Akbar's wife Maryam, mother of Jahangir, but this is less likely than the theory that it was occupied by Babur's grand-daughter Sultana Salima, later another wife of Akbar. Most names assigned to buildings in Fatehpur Sikri are apocryphal; Michael Brand and Glenn D. Lowry in *Akbar's India* are at pains conscientiously to multiply the word 'unidentified' on their plan of the city to most buildings, such as Divan-i-Khas, Panch Mahal, Maryam's House, and they even wonder whether the palace linked with Jodhbai's name might have been Akbar's own private palace.

I thought of the court musician Tansen, and his lasting influence on Indian classical music; of the *Akbarnama* (*c.* 1590) in London's Victoria and Albert Museum, with miniatures showing Akbar's return to Fatehpur Sikri; of the elusive library, which irritated the Jesuit Monserrate by the clamour of its scribes. Babur had loved books, and Abu'l Fazl relates how Humayun considered the rarest manuscripts as his 'real companions' and always kept them with him, even on campaign, strapped in boxes on camelback. Akbar collected and inherited Persian paintings above all, and later on conceived a mania for European paintings, which he collected and exhorted his own artists to copy.

Fatehpur Sikri. Jami Masjid

As I wandered around the silent empty stables north of the so-called Jodhbai Palace, I could hear the neighing of hundreds of stallions; I could see the disgruntled champing of hundreds of camels in between campaigns. A hubbub of stablehands filled the air, and the stench of animals confined in one compound rose to my nostrils.

What a contrast to the religious life of Fatehpur Sikri, so stubbornly active that no imagination whatsoever is required! A bazaar consisting of stall after stall offers every kind of trinket: plastic Taj Mahals, combs, bracelets, bangles, toys such as mass-produced cars, planes and buses, soldiers and dolls. The mosque courtyard is plagued with begging: even teachers at an open-air school offer signed receipts for 'donations'. The Bibi Khanum Mosque in Samarkand (1399-1404) must have been the model, or one of them. The Friday Mosque, begun in 1571 and completed about 1575, must have been one of the largest mosques in India at that time, measuring 168 metres by 144, with a huge inner courtyard. Gateways allowed access originally at east, north and south but only the first of these remains unchanged. The sanctuary blooms in red sandstone with a warmth that changes subtly throughout the day, depending on the sun's angle and brilliance. Birds and chipmunks roam at will throughout the arched and pillared interior, and wild bees cluster in the squinches, adding batlike darkness to sun-faded frescoes. A large rectangular archway and pillared arcades to left and right comprise the façade, with one great central dome and others smaller over the flanks. Kiosks line both wing-parapets, in the manner of the main gateway that will face Taj Mahal in the time of Shah Jahan.

Within, a nave containing the mihrab below a clock is netted to stop birds from nesting below the dome and fouling the interior. From the central part of the sanctuary aisles lead out through archways, each with a chapel to permit long vistas as in any Gothic cathedral; beams and arches interplay in design and balance so that each perspective pleases. The mural decoration, carved, painted or inlaid, is of such a quality that we can safely assume – despite loss – that Akbar's reign saw no more skilful ornamentation outside the miniature painters of its artists.

There is little connection between the Friday Mosque and its monumental gateway, the Sublime Gate or Buland Darwaza, because the latter was an afterthought, replacing the existing southern gate with this magnificent celebration of a military victory: either that over Gujarat in 1573 or that over Khandish (Deccan) in 1601. A flight of steps 14 metres high leads to a gateway rising some 45 metres above the top step, presenting a spectacle, in its splendid isolation, even more grandiose than the Delhi Gate in Agra's Red Fort. The centre of the façade is a high archway leading to a great vestibule with a dome resting on panels like the side panels outside. Akbar caused to be inscribed on the gateway, in lovely Persian calligraphy, an extraordinary reference to

Christian belief in the sense of 'take no thought for the morrow'. The Persian is rendered: 'Jesus, son of Mary, on whom be peace, has said: "The world is a bridge. Pass over it but build no house upon it, for whoever hopes for one hour, hopes for all eternity. The world is one hour. Spend it in prayer, for the rest is unseen".' No more eloquent epitaph to the Mughal Empire – and all other world-encompassing empires – could be imagined.

Recalling the significant part played by the Muslim sage Salim Chishti in the life of Akbar and the fate of Fatehpur Sikri, it is hardly astonishing that his tomb should be distinguished in the courtyard of the Friday Mosque, where a stream of worshippers ties little cords and paper wishes to the screens and indeed to any surface they can find. Originally built of the same red sandstone as every other edifice in the new city, Salim's mausoleum was later reconstructed in the white marble favoured by Shah Jahan. Its intimate character, so utterly different from the grandeur of Buland Darwaza, suits the childless women who come to pray for sons, just as Akbar himself did more than four hundred years ago. If they conceive a son, the credit is given to Salim Chishti, if they fail, the blame is theirs: a neat equation to keep women in their subservient, quaking place. I tried to forget the pathos of anguished women with wrinkled faces, their brown hands raised in supplication

Fatehpur Sikri. Jami Masjid. Tomb of Salim Chishti

like dead twigs within the darkened mausoleum. Aesthetically, the main effect is external, from the refined proportions of the porch, verandah and dome, to the fine pillars and distinctive brackets of serpentine volutes which seem almost ivory in their grace and delicacy and look all the more remarkable when you realise they have no function at all other than their appearance. It is the highest possible note on which to take leave of this most gloriously alive of 'dead' cities.

After Akbar's departure from Fatehpur Sikri, military matters and a concern for dynastic continuity occupied his mind more than religious, artistic or social matters. His son Murad died of alcohol poisoning in 1599, Salim led a five-year revolt and assassinated Akbar's general and administrator Abu'l Fazl, then his third son Daniyal died of alcohol poisoning in 1604, forcing Akbar's hand to agree that Salim, his only surviving son, should accede. Fatehpur Sikri did not die, however, with the departure of Akbar. Jahangir honoured his birthplace by spending seven months there with his son Khurram (later to become Shah Jahan) who himself returned frequently to shoot birds on the lake, and to hunt tigers in the forests.

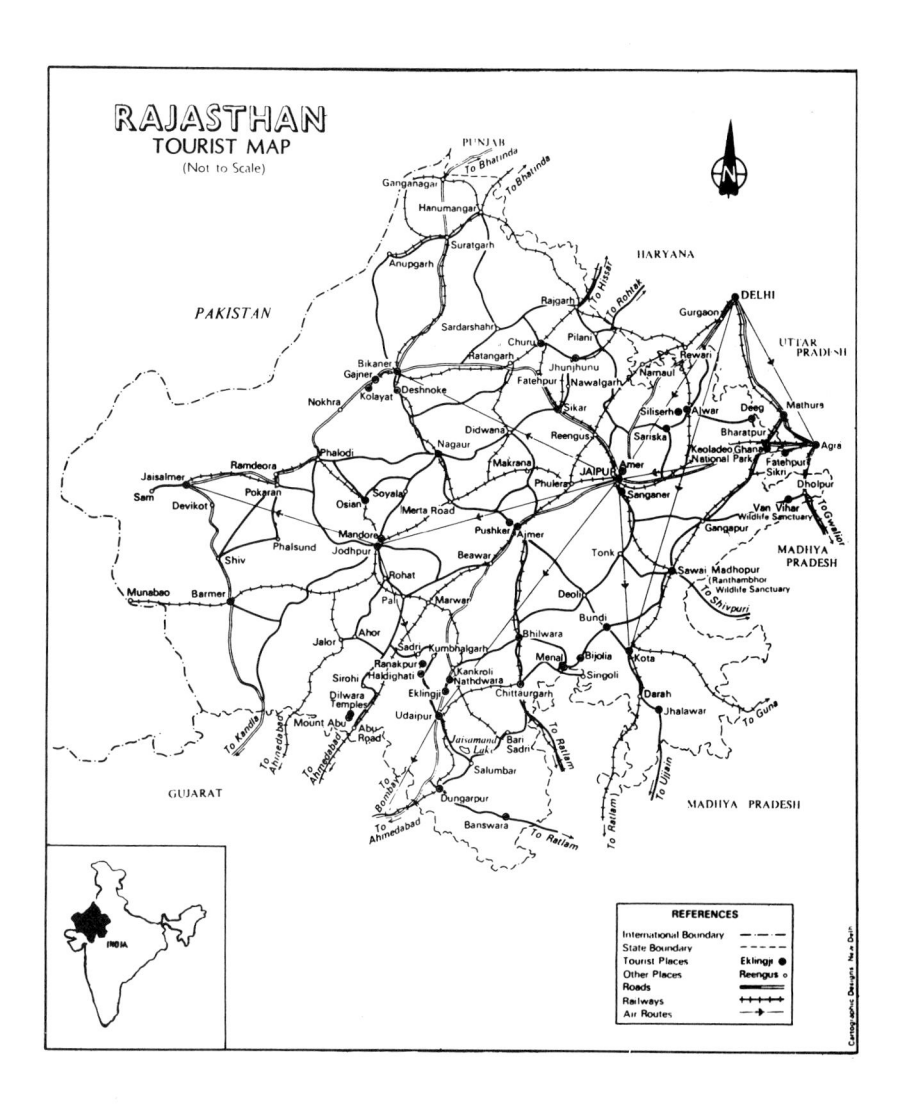

RAJASTHAN
TOURIST MAP
(Not to Scale)

3: JAIPUR

*Bharatpur — Dig — Alwar — Sariska — Amber — Jaipur —
Ranthambore — Ajmer — Pushkar — Kishangarh*

In his *Annals and Antiquities of Rajasthan*, James Tod describes how the Hindu Jats, reduced from their original status among the 'Thirty-Six Royal Races', nevertheless fought dourly for their independence from the disunited Muslim successors to Aurangzeb, building castles in Sinsini and Thun, villages near Bharatpur, and raiding the countryside far and near, to the anger of the ruling Mughals.

That violence was caused by the iconoclasm of the fanatical Muslim Aurangzeb, an Ayatollah Khomeini of the 17th century, who began to suppress Hinduism in 1669 with the destruction of temples, and reinforced his bitter campaign in 1679 by imposing taxes on non-Muslim worship. After Aurangzeb decreed the destruction of the great Kesava Deo temple in the nearby city of Mathura, the Jats openly rebelled, then in 1691 desecrated the tomb of Akbar himself.

Bharatpur

Under the Cincinnatus-like Churaman, who left his peaceful farming labours to lead them, the Jats withstood in 1716 twelve months siege outside Sinsini and Thun by the royal astronomer Jai Singh of Amber, founder of Jaipur. Churaman's younger brother, Badan Singh, was liberated from Churaman's prison and in 1722 joined Jai Singh in attacking Thun, which finally fell six months later, though Churaman escaped. Jai Singh now installed the victorious Badan Singh as his client Rajah in the town of Dig, 35 km north-west of Bharatpur, with a palace used as a summer residence for the Maharajah of Bharatpur in later years. Badan Singh abdicated in favour of his eldest son Suraj Mal who seized Bharatpur from a relative and in 1761 succeeding in capturing Agra itself, a city the Jats held for thirteen years, until ousted by the Marathas. A later ruler, Ranjit Singh, fended off Colonel Lake's siege of Bharatpur in 1804-5, but British invaders finally took the town in 1826, suffering heavy losses.

The Iron Fort of Bharatpur was begun by Suraj Mal in 1732 though not completed till late in the century. Its strength determined the peace and security of Bharatpur when so many lesser forts gave way more

Bharatpur. Entrance to the Fort

easily, so the town enjoyed stability throughout the period from 1826 to Independence. A moat surrounds earthen ramparts, surmounted by great outer mud walls (demolished in 1826) and inner mud walls, parts of which survive, as does a single cannon.

At the highest point within the Iron Fort rises the palace of Badan Singh, created around 1733, but amplified in succeeding generations as happened invariably in Rajasthani palaces. You enter the fort by the tiny gateway flanked by elephant murals, at the end of a causeway over a moat. Two towers commemorate victories: Jawahar Burj (1765) recalls an attack in Delhi and Fateh Burj a victory over the besieging British in 1805. Look for an iron pillar about 30 cm in diameter recording an optimistic genealogy of the rulers' names beginning with Lord Krishna himself. The State Archaeological Museum (1944), closed on Fridays, is devoted to finds in eastern Rajasthan, chiefly sculpture. I liked best the simple terra cotta toys dated to the Kushan culture of the early centuries A.D., and a tenth-century Ganesha. The palace itself has work by descendants of craftsmen working within the Rajput tradition, as at Dig. Both are constructed around two courtyards, and thus rectangular. The Badal Singh Palace, the oldest, is laid out as part of the museum, while the Kamra Palace to the west once housed the armoury and treasury. The eastern Mahal Khas incorporates the royal apartments added by Maharajah Balwant Singh (1826-53) and contrasts oddly with the rest of the fort in its wall paintings.

The bus station is situated southwest of the fort, with buses from Delhi, Mathura, Agra, Gwalior and Jaipur. You can also take a bus to Dig and Alwar. By rail, you can get direct to Delhi or Bombay, and on a metre-gauge line to Agra and Jaipur.

You can hire a cycle or a cycle-rickshaw up to and within the Keoladeo National Park; a few de luxe buses enter the sanctuary as far as the India Tourist Development Corporation hotel called Bharatpur Forest Lodge, which is 8 km from the rail station, 4 km from the bus station, and 5 km from the bazaar. But beware! You *must* make advance reservations here between September and March, and often also during April. The off-season, from May to August, is less congested. Alternative accommodation can be found at the Golbagh Palace Hotel (Agra Road), Saras Tourist Bungalow (Fatehpur Sikri Road), and Circuit House (Agra Road). One of the more bloodcurdling photographs I have ever seen shows the silent, sullen durbar of the Maharajah of Bharatpur in about 1865, taken by Shepherd and Robertson, and reprinted by Naveen Patnaik in *A Second Paradise* (1985). Weapons are not actually brandished and throats not actually slit, but the implications of a warlike community strike one as forcibly as in a samurai film with Toshiro Mifune, or the fabled exploits of Charlemagne and his knights. One shudders at the memory of duck shoots organised by the Maharajah of Bharatpur at his specially-created fresh-water marshland near the confluence of the rivers Banganga and Ruparel. That Maharajah invited Lord Kitchener and Lord Curzon to his inaugural massacre of wild birds in 1902, but the most obscene violence took place in 1938, when the Viceroy Lord Linlithgow became guest of honour at the destruction of no fewer than 4,273 birds. Those times are gone forever in Bharatpur. In 1956 Keoladeo National Park was created, to protect three hundred and fifty-odd species belonging to fifty-six families. From December to March you can see rare Siberian cranes. Four hundred pelicans remain about a month, and in winter you can hardly avoid seeing some of the ten thousand coot, three thousand greylag geese, teal, pintail and widgeon. On one side egrets, cormorants, and grey herons; on the other weaver-birds and Saras cranes. Embankments between the waters permit jeeps and cycle-rickshaws to roam the marshes, while boats ripple gently through the reeds and along banks. Dry land is home to ring-doves and parrakeets, quail and partridge. Sambhar and blackbuck, nilgai and pig, blue bulls and chital might be glimpsed by the walker with guide, the latter stalking by scent or footprint, sound or the identification of droppings. As I watched by an isolated creek, a flash of kingfisher darted past. I distinguished ruddy shelduck, red wattled lapwing, Saras crane, grey heron and purple heron, green bee-eater, bulbul, purple moorhen and ring-tailed fish eagle. Take a sweater for a vigil at dawn or dusk, binoculars, and watch out for pythons! Spotted deer and hyena made my safari exceptionally interesting, but no matter what you see, at whatever time of year, Keoladeo must be one of the most magical sanctuaries in the world, with bar-headed geese from China and greylag geese from Siberia.

There are charges for entry, guiding, and for still or movie photography, for boating and for cycle-rickshaws.

Dig

Take a bus 35 km to Dig (pronounced 'Deeg'), the summer resort of the royal family of Bharatpur. You can stay at the P.W.D. Dak Bungalow at Dig, or go on to Alwar. Dig Fort has twelve great towers, the largest being Lakla Burj, retaining its cannon. Entry to the fort is from the northern side. Do not miss the Suraj Mal *haveli*, decked with the spectacular domes so typical of Dig, called *bangaldar*, originally based on a Bengali bamboo curved roof. The best account of Dig's palaces and pavilions is in Giles Tillotson's *The Rajput Palaces* (1987), which also covers in detail the palatial architecture of Chittor, Gwalior, Orchha and Datia, Amber and Udaipur, Jaisalmer, Bikaner and Jodhpur, Dungarpur, Bundi and Kota, and Jaipur: one could construct a fascinating itinerary simply from this sequence, though it would of course leave out the life of the vast majority of Indians.

The mid-eighteenth century summer palace of the Maharajahs of Bharatpur is Dig's foremost attraction, and it is worth drawing attention to its connection with the monsoon season, so eagerly awaited throughout Rajasthan, and so bitterly disappointing in its sparseness in recent years up to 1988. Two lesser pavilions flanking the major Gopal Bhawan are named after the monsoon months (Sawan means the July-August month and Bhadon the equivalent to our August-September) and the Kesav Bhawan opposite once possessed picturesque monsoon effects, such as invisible stone balls above your head which could be rattled by piped water to mimic thunder, and spouts around the eaves which could crash as sheets of rain on all sides of the open pavilion.

A marble-framed swing, now pitiably lacking its ropes, which stands on the terrace near Gopal Bhawan reminds us again of the fecundating monsoon, when Rajasthani girls celebrate the festival of Chhoti Tij, on the third of Sawan, and sing songs while swinging on the colourfully decorated *jhulas* or swings. The sexual symbolism of swinging will not be lost on any Freudian. Hindu legend tells how Lord Krishna's *gopis* had their clothes made at Dig, and the sensuality of the atmosphere surely

Dig. Hardev Bhawan

cannot be all in my romantic imagination? The Hindu gardens of Dig look back to Muslim antecedents, but there are no parterres such as are often found in many Muslim gardens, leading one to visualise a denser, more riotous display of colour and foliage reminiscent of some Rajput miniatures, though most are set in the wilderness of the hunt rather than in the intimacy of a walled haven.

Gopal Bhawan retains much of its original furnishings and fittings and, as Dig is off the familiar trek of mass tourism, quietness adds its own nostalgic flavour to the magic of the day. Southwest of the main complex stands the white marble Suraj Bhawan, completed by Suraj Mal's son Jawahar Singh (1764-8), and in the southwest corner the Hardev Bhawan has *jali* screens revealing its former use as the *zenana*, or harem.

Alwar

Dig lies 38 km west of the holy city of Mathura, and 90 km east of the beautiful city of Alwar, accessible from Dig by bus or train, and two hours from Delhi on the Pink City Express to Jaipur. On arrival, you should visit the Superintendent of Police to obtain permission to visit the 300-metre high Bal Qila, a fort accessible only by four-wheel-drive vehicles, or by a steep footpath. It is the earliest surviving monument of Alwar, dating from the epoch of the Nikhumba Rajputs. The city itself split off from suzerainty under Jaipur in the 1770s, following which the usual temples, gardens, lakes and palaces were constructed in the green Aravali Hills, with that key to any successful Rajasthani city: a perennial water supply.

Alwar's finest palace, Vinai Vilas Mahal or the City Palace, dates from the mid-nineteenth century, a period which in Europe saw Ruskin's *Modern Painters*, Mendelssohn's *Elijah*, and Dumas père's *Three Musketeers*. How far in spirit it still seems, this last echo of Rajput palatial building style! Today, the local government occupies the treasury, armoury and palace library, converting into the quotidian and ordinary the palace of the Prince of Alwar who, exalting himself with the Ruler of Jaipur, let himself be known as Sawai Maharajah, or a 'Maharajah and a Quarter'. The *zenana* of Alwar Palace is the setting for the performance of Shakespeare's *Antony and Cleopatra* that you may have seen in the evocative Merchant-Ivory film *Shakespeare Wallah*. Some of the treasures of Alwar remain with the former royal family (the durbar room may be seen only by permission of the former Maharajah at Alwar House in Delhi), but many may be seen at the museum, occupying a part of the City Palace, accessible throughout the day except on Fridays and public holidays. Seven thousand fine manuscripts adorn this exceptional museum, with some splendid miniature paintings of the Alwar School and others, including Bundi (regrettably uncaptioned). From the armoury come superb gem-encrusted weapons dating from the times of Ali, son-in-law of the Prophet Muhammad (salla Allahu 'alyhi wa sallam), and from the treasury precious ivories and jades, an elaborate silver table with *trompe l'oeil* fishes swimming across it. The view from the upper storey of the palace encompasses a reservoir, temples and *chhatris* below the sweep of the Aravalis. Alwar's great man, who shook off the sovereignty of Jaipur, was Pratap Singh; he conquered the Jat city of Alwar and defeated the Marathas, while obtaining authority from the Mughal emperor himself. Pratap's successor was Bakhtawar Singh, whose cenotaph was erected by Maharajah Vinai Singh in 1815: its arches and roof derive from the elegant Bengali style. If you take a cycle rickshaw from the City Palace, passing through Sarafa Bazaar and Bajaja Bazaar, and crossing Hope Circus, the charming Company Garden, renamed Purjan Vihar, is approached to the right off Mangal Marg. After a meal in the restaurant opposite Company Garden, you can explore the fine precincts laid out in 1868 by Maharajah Shiv Dan Singh. For a few rupees you can ask the attendants to permit the fountains a brief renascence of their former glory. The Simla fernery, discreetly neglected to allow one the illusion of a hill-station (far from the nearest actual hill-station, Mount Abu), remains doggedly cool and fresh during the heat and dust of a Rajasthani summer. Both Company Bagh and Vinai Vilas Mahal were once watered by an aqueduct from the Siliserh Sagar or reservoir, about 10 km from the city, an aqueduct sadly no longer functioning. Siliserh Palace, a hunting lodge created by Maharajah Vinai Singh in 1845, overlooks the reservoir and the *chhatris* on its embankment and has been converted into a comfortable hotel with ten rooms.

If you stay in Alwar, the Phool Bagh Hotel in the south of the city opposite the stadium on Raghu Marg has air-conditioned rooms. You can take an auto-rickshaw to Vijay Mandir Mahal, the royal home built in 1918 by Maharajah Jai Singh, about 9 km from Alwar. Its beautiful setting beside Vijay Sagar (Victory Reservoir) explains why the former royal family still live there, in preference to the Italianate palace called Yashwant Niwas which Jai Singh had built a little earlier. Parts of the palace may possibly be visited, but this is discretionary, and must not be expected as a right. The drive there is in any case amply worth the small sum you will spend on transport, with changing views of the fort, palaces, the distant town, and the countryside around Vijay Sagar. Deciduous trees claw their roots into steep hills and the palace suddenly emerges like a ship resting at anchor below a flawless azure sky.

Sariska
Two roads lead south from Alwar: due south 35 km to Rajgarh, the former capital of Alwar – what Amber is to Jaipur – and one southwest to Sariska Tiger Reserve. Ideally, one might visit Rajgarh first, and carry on to Sariska if one is heading for Jaipur. Rajgarh itself postdates the Gujar-Pratihara capital of Rajorgarh, of about the third century A.D. Pratap Singh built his redoubtable fortress on the ruins of a Gujar-Pratihara stronghold in the eighteenth century, and you might explore the old mansions and fertile gardens, after investigating the royal fort which gives the town its mighty name.

At just over 800 square km, Sariska is nearly twice the size of Ranthambore Tiger Reserve, which lies 14 km from Sawai Madhopur on the main railway line from Bombay to Delhi. Sariska is easily accessible on the regular bus route between Alwar and Jaipur. You can view the reserve by buses, but since these are inevitably noisy, and the animals avoid the regular routes, your best chance of enjoying them will be from concealed hides at dawn and dusk. No: to answer the immediate question, there is little chance of seeing tigers in this sanctuary, founded in 1955, and made more significant by Project Tiger since 1979. The dry deciduous forests offer four distinct viewing seasons. In spring, the jagged hills soften with flame-trees and a kaleidoscope of blossom and blooms. Summer scours the land dry and brown again, but monsoon rains invigorate the land, which reverts to brilliant green. Winter turns the scene cold and windy, but migrating birds from Siberia and northern China find a respite from sub-zero lands. Forest authorities have augmented sparse natural lakes and pools with extra water-holes sited along roads which tourist vehicles traverse. From your Sariska Palace Hotel, facing Baran Tal Gate and built by Maharajah Jai Singh in 1902 to accommodate hunting parties ensconced on elephants, you can take advantage of early morning and twilight sightings. Predators include the leopard and jungle cat; scavengers the hyena and jackal, and their prey nilgai, sambhar, chital and chinkara. You might see wild boars scampering through the thorn bushes, or rhesus monkeys and langurs skipping effortlessly through protective tree cover. Hundreds of peafowl congregate daily by the waterhole called Kalighati; at Salupka waterhole you might catch sight of a nilgai from your hide, but patience is as usual of the essence in such a sanctuary. From the mediaeval hilltop fort of Kankwari, a redoubt throughout Mughal times, you may well see eagles and Egyptian vultures in flight, but then you will see many a vulture by the wayside in Rajasthan, where sick animals are left to die, and be picked clean. Skeletons of camels, mules and horses beside these roads have often struck the casual visitor as famine victims, being photographed for sensational magazines and newspapers as examples of the plight of rural India.

Amber
The story of Jaipur begins eleven km away, at Amber (locally pronounced 'Amer'), a hilly area possibly once dedicated to the fertility goddess, and earth mother, Amba, a form of Durga, and occupied since the tenth century by the Minas, a tribe who continued to enjoy certain ceremonial posts (such as guardians of their treasure) long after their defeat by the Kachchwaha about 1150. The name Amber might also derive from Ambarisha, a King of Ayodhya, one of the seven sacred cities of ancient India; or from Ambikishwara, another name for Shiva. But whatever the origin of its name, there can be no doubting its majesty, as the eye sweeps upward from the town in the valley, to the great seventeenth-century palace dating back to the time of Man Singh (1592-1615), and finally to the fort of Jaigarh dominating the skyline.

The temptation to ascend as far as Amber Palace at once seems overwhelming but, as usual, I resisted it in favour of a stroll through the local bazaar. Little children played the begging game, then wandered off when I ignored them. Women sauntered past frankly adorable in jangling bangles and bright saris. An old spice-merchant on his haunches waved vaguely at his pungent sacks: I can never pass spices without closing my eyes and trying to distinguish them by smell, but these sacks were too closely packed to allow such distinctions. Grotesque ginger filled one basket like deformed, shrivelled dolls; paprika another. We smiled at each other, accomplices in the freemasonry of spices, like Magalhães, Vasco da Gama and Columbus: all of them spice-hunters. A bus to Jaipur was filling up with an incredibabble of sprawling passengers paying one rupee for their eleven-kilometre ride, roughly one-twentieth of a similar fare in Britain. A toothless lady who might have been fifty sprayed betel juice from her crimson mouth into what might loosely be considered a gutter, though there was in fact no difference between the road and the 'pavement': all was potholed and uneven, spotted with cowpats that would shortly be prised up for fuel. I found a café with table and chairs where I could watch the cavalcade: bullocks and sacred cows, horse-drawn carts and tempos, cycle rickshaws and men of burden carrying on their head and back such cargo as a refrigerator and a chest of drawers. The racket of shouts and motorhorns was describable: Indian. I was fifty years old, beatifically happy, in Amber at last.

Four willing hands thrust me up from a wide platform on to an elephant howdah and the bar locking me safely in was clapped shut by an attendant. A turbanned musician played the *ravanhattha*, a folk spike fiddle allegedly invented by the Hindu demon Ravana. My caparisoned

Amber. Elephant beside the Palace Wall

elephant rolled gently like a bed in a mild earthquake below me, and at a contemplative amble padded silently up the winding slope through one gateway, then a second, third, fourth, fifth, sixth and seventh until the extraordinary great courtyard is eventually reached. By then you have devoured each changing vista, down to the minarets and domes of Amber town, up to the mediaeval fort's arrogant acropolis and the serene blue sky.

The majestic two-storey ceremonial gate is called Ganesh Pol after the elephant-headed god of wisdom and remover of obstacles. It dates from the reign of Sawai Jai Singh II (1699-1744), at least in its present form, according to Giles Tillotson who follows Rousselet against the earlier date of 1639 put forward by Fergusson and Rushbrook Williams. The great courtyard called Jaleb Chowk is even now a bustling arena, for riding elephants, postcard-sellers, trinket-vendors, and drinks stalls. Ganesh Pol divides the private palace from the public in their (once) milling thousands, though of course now Amber is scarcely more than a small town.

From Singh Pol (Lion Gate) I ascended the steps to the Temple of Kali, goddess of war, here worshipped in her aspect as Shila Mata. The temple is open from 9 to 4.30, except during *puja*. To enter, one has to doff not only weapons, shoes and socks, umbrellas and cameras, but every leather article whatsoever, so in the interests of modesty combined with enterprise, I suggest that if you wear a belt in India and intend to visit temples, you choose a plastic belt. The private temple was built by Man Singh in 1604 and remains family property. *Puja* takes place with a fearsome racket of drumming and bellringing that scares even the local pigeons out of their inconsiderable minds. In the confined space I turned deaf for half a minute amid a forest of Carrara marble pillars painted green. Man Singh II added the solid silver doors in 1939 as a votive offering to Shila Mata after surviving an aeroplane accident.

Respecting the chronological point of view, I made my way through Ganesh Pol and across the succeeding courtyard to look at the earliest courtyard of Amber Palace, surrounded by a palace in its own right, and subsequently the women's palace or *zenana*. It dates from the time of Man Singh (1592-1615) but it was converted by raising balcony parapets to close in the balconies as corridors invisible from without. Two more courts were added by Mirza Raja Jai Singh (1623-68), and it is to the earliest years of his rule that the great Diwan-i-Am dates. The open hypostyle hall derives its appearance from the public audience halls of Chittor and Udaipur, but is more impressive than either, leading Shah Jahangir to express so much pleasure at its proportions that it struck fear and apprehension into the heart of Jai Singh, according to Louis Rousselet's *India and its Native Princes* (1876). This Diwan-i-Am stands in the north-east corner facing Ganesh Pol, and its column bases show influence from the Shalimar Bagh pavilions of Kashmir, a subtle compliment to their builder, Jahangir.

Between Ganesh Pol and the Zenana Mahal the middle courtyard is flanked by Sukh Niwas (Pleasure Palace), adjoining a small formal garden, and the Jai Mandir ('Hall of Victory') giving way to the Jas Mandir upstairs, the 'Hall of Glory', with floor-level views down to Lake Maota, the Dilaram Garden, and the saffron garden. In Jas Mandir an ingenious air-conditioning system consisted of pricking holes in copper pipes so that running water might drip through and provide a moist atmosphere throughout long, hot, dry summer days. Both these levels have a *shish mahal* or hall of mirrors, with tiny winking glass mosaic set at all angles, especially evocative when the doors are closed and candles are lit to allow the ceiling its accurate imitation of the night sky with a thousand glittering stars. Jai Mandir reveals the splendour of Jai Singh's personal taste, with murals of the hunt and the battle, exquisite flowers and tall cypresses gleaming even today because of the glossy coat incorporating eggshell, powdered marble and powdered pearl. Niches now empty once flickered with candles, or were filled with freshly-cut flowers or cult images.

Sukh Niwas was called the Hall of Pleasure because of its clever air-conditioning, allowing the royal family to relax in shade and cool air no matter how hot the day. Here the technique depended on the erection of four parallel walls to face the mountain breezes, each higher than the next, thus compressing and cooling the air till it passes through three high windows where it came into contact with perfumed water, cooling down still farther as it penetrates the marble filigree directed in two ways so that air is not only dispersed, but fills the whole area on each side of the rippling channel.

Spurning the prospect of paying an outrageous 125 rupees to be driven by jeep up the minor road to Jaigarh ('Victory Fort'), which nestles like a sleeping lion, tawny on the skyline above Amber, I sauntered up slowly, with the company of playful monkeys anxious to snatch food, hat, camera, bag, anything that might merit eating or careful examination. Constructed in its present incarnation by Jai Singh II in 1726, Jaigarh boasts (perhaps somewhat unwisely) 'the world's largest cannon on wheels, which will fill your heart with a sense of wonder', but I have seen larger cannon made for Süleyman the Magnificent's armies. You can see a royal treasury, an armoury, and the temples of Ram Hari and Kel Bhairava, once past the derelict stepped gateway. A motley museum includes a souvenir programme of the visit to Jaipur by Bulganin and Khrushchev in the 1950s, a tenth-century camel-hide oil container, a photograph of Sawai Man Singh II as Indian Ambassador to Franco's Spain, spittoons, old locks, silver-coins containers for journeys, and portraits of Sawai Madho Singh

Amber. Palace and town from Jaigarh

(1880-1922) and Sawai Bhawani Singh, decorated for gallantry during the Indo-Pak War of 1971. The armoury mounts a parade of famous named cannon: the Budh of 1599 cast for Man Singh, the Banjari of 1600, the Bhairavi of 1723, the Naharmukhi of 1675. Pigeons cooed within these warlike walls, where bows and arrows collect dust alongside spears, swords, battle-axes, muskets and rifles. Nobody interrupted my study of these outdated weapons; with India at peace, what interest can they possibly have? The answer is that history is the fabric of Amber, even more than of the eighteenth-century city of Jaipur a few leagues away. There are no warriors in Subhat Niwas now: no commanders in the simple Khilbati Niwas, but the echo of musket fire will never finally die away. I puzzled in vain over the notice 'Smoking of Cigarettes, Bidies and Spitting in the Palace Complex is strictly prohibited', and even after all this time I cannot work out whether I carried on my person illicit 'bidies', for I know not what they are. Almost deserted except for an occasional soldier, Jaigarh must nevertheless be enjoyed for unsurpassed views of the town far down in the valley, the great palace we have just visited, and the abandoned palace of 1036 within its successor's shadow.

Back down in Amber village I wandered around the gardens and temples, visiting in the gardens of Dilaram the little archaeological museum, with pottery from the ancient city of Bairat (on the Alwar road northwards), and some interesting Indo-Greek coins. Bihari Mal built the Vaishnavite temple of Shri Jagath Shiromani distinguished by its marble gateway, called *toran* in the religious context, protected by stone elephants, and within a Garuda shrine.

Jaipur

A bus from Amber will bring you to Hawa Mahal, the Palace of the Winds celebrated in a thousand photographs: Jaipur's equivalent to Agra's Taj Mahal. Built on the outside of the City Palace wall, near the crossing of Tripolia Bazaar with Siri Deorhi Bazaar, Hawa Mahal was built in 1799 by Pratap Singh (1778-1803) for Krishna and Radha. Seemingly a mere façade of five pink filigree storeys with over nine hundred niches and windows, the Palace of Winds is in fact a real palace, with residential quarters and two courtyards. Aesthetically, you might find the eastern façade fussy in its elaboration; towering into a brilliant blue sky, its fantasy of white, pink and red strikes me as gracefully witty, function apart. But surprisingly enough Hawa Mahal's eastern façade was functional to the last decree. Firstly, it acted as a purdah screen for women of the *zenana*, through which the great events and festivals of Jaipur could be glimpsed. Secondly, its countless niches allowed a constant flow of air to cool the ladies and the palace interior while restraining the effects of long sunny hours. Within, a museum of Jaipur craftmanship is open daily, and the view from the top is amply worth the climb. One is gratified that the descendants of Pratap's architect, Lalchand Usta, remain tax-exempt to this day in honour of their ancestor's prowess, for these walls have stayed aloft so long despite being barely 25 cm thick!

Near the entrance to Hawa Mahal, by Jaipur Saree Emporium, I stood bewitched as the extraordinary street scenes of Jaipur filled my horizons with the kind of teeming colour and incident that Hollywood mimics in its efforts to provide Kipling's tales of India with exotic realism. Peasants still wear pink headgear, Brahmins yellow, Rajputs saffron. An elephant plods steadily along advertising the latest Bombay musical movie from its hand-painted sandwich-boards. A rally, demonstration and procession organised by the Congress Party hoots noisily past, with its cycle rickshaws, auto-rickshaws, brass band, and firework specialists, letting off rockets in the middle of the road under the benevolent or absent gaze of be-truncheoned policemen. As I strolled towards Ram Niwas Garden for the zoo and the Albert Hall Museum, I noted the Maharajah's High School, Sarfaj Boot House, and the Jaipur Computer Horoscope, an emporium devoted to the profitable technology of backwardness. A lady from the north of England, trapped in the bazaar like a bee in a circus tent, hazarded the comforting guess to her Widnes-sounding companion that the bazaar was a bit like Woolworth's, with little old men squatting in small cubicles instead of salesgirls standing up behind counters. She could not cope with anything so extravagant as actuality. The streams of British occupation, sometimes in flood, somewhere in ebb, left a silt not only geographical, such as railway lines and offices, clubs and polo grounds, but also and predominantly mental. The stilted language used by Indians today when speaking English is not that of Rambo or James Bond, but Bulldog Drummond or Richard Hannay. Bureaucratic attitudes, the cult of paperwork, and niceties of civilian as well as military hierarchical structures: all these have made upper-crust India in the late 20th century a country not unrecognisable in formal speech from the England of the late 19th century. In Agra you separate the cantonment from the bazaar. In Jaipur one visits the Albert Hall and in Udaipur the Victoria Hall. Billiards tables gather dust in echoing palaces. Cricket is still played on every permissible patch of greenery. Tray tea and bed tea, tiffin and porridge: one reverts almost to the nursery (an ayah for a governess, a tooth for sticky sweets) and to day-dreams of lawns carefully tended under a broiling sun by the over-lavish use of precious water, of tennis courts floodlit at night when parrots and crows have finally dozed off. Game, set and match to nostalgia.

Jaipur's Albert Hall, eccentrically named for Victoria's consort, was devised in the uneasy Indo-Saracenic style by three Indian architects to plans by Colonel Sir Swinton Jacob. Its prototype was London's Victoria and Albert Museum, and the Prince of Wales, Albert's son and later Edward VII, laid its foundation stone in 1876. Jacob spent ten years on the creation of the Albert Hall and other buildings in Jaipur, with others in Delhi, Bikaner, Jodhpur and elsewhere, and his ideology of hybrid architecture which would suit India's present needs by absorbing the best tendencies from the past proved lastingly influential in the sub-continent.

The locked Durbar Hall will be opened on request for you to admire a fine Carpet Museum, its star piece being a great Kirmani carpet of 1632 representing a Persian garden alive with fish, birds, animals and trees. Albert Hall itself was surprisingly packed with Indians gazing in awe at Sanganer prints, tie and dye, gold and silver cloth prints, arms and armour, palm manuscripts, and rock-paintings from the Chambal Valley. I must admit I was equally taken with passing ladies in beautiful saris, doe-eyed, moving fluently like a willow caressed by zephyrs. Sculptures worth study include a tiny turbanned lady of the 2nd century B.C., a stone Shiva head of the 8th century, and 18th-century wooden figures from a chariot in the former Banswara state.

As the capital of Rajasthan, Jaipur feels itself compelled to outline

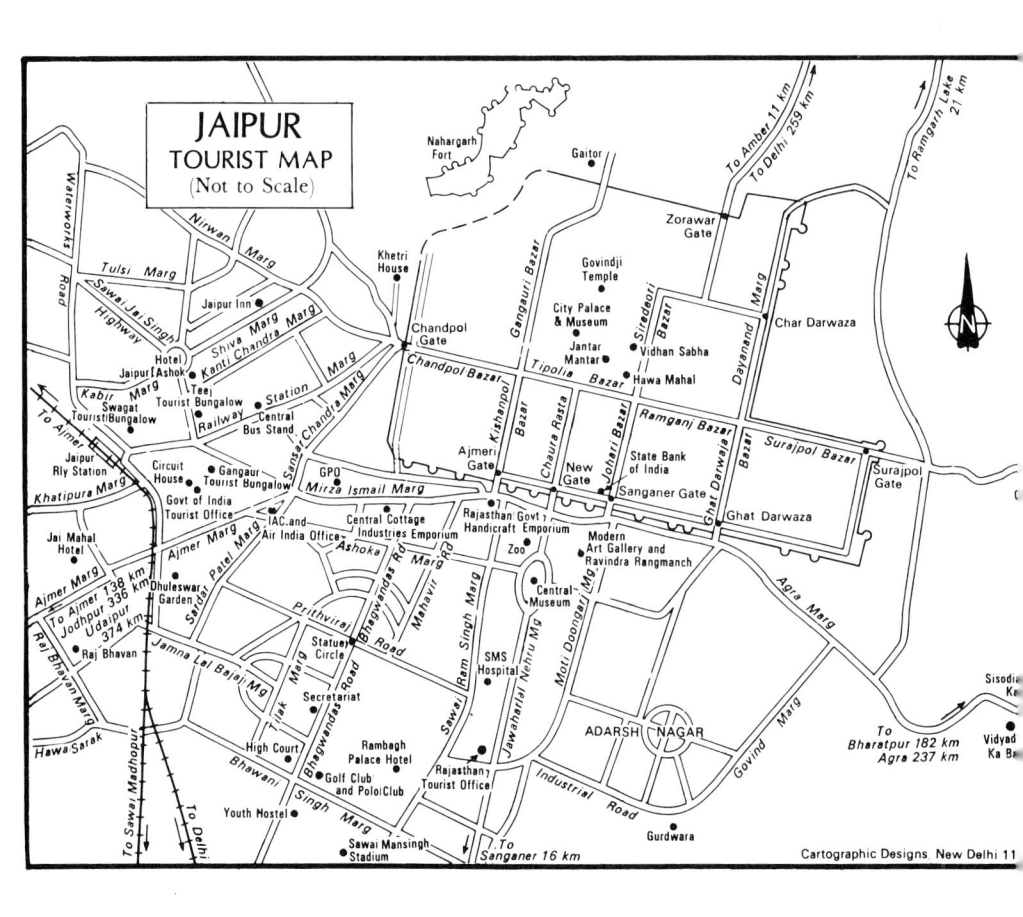

Rajput morality in this museum. 'A Rajput puts his life at risk if he is forced to abjure his faith, if he is deprived of his lands, and if his womenfolk are molested', notes a sign. At first glance Rajput society resembles mediaeval Christian Europe in its code of knightly honour, adventure, and aristocratic vanity, even to the point of repelling Muslim invasions under the Abbasids. But whereas Europe finally overcame the Islamic tide at Poitiers, at Vienna, at Budapest, the Rajputs were heavily defeated by the Turkish conquests of the 12th to 14th centuries, and eventually changed their opposition to the Mughals in the 15th century, to alliances in the 17th. Rajputs may be Hindu by religion, but they lack the sensuousness of the genuine Hindu, they despise the theory of 'life before honour', and they have little feeling for extremes of Hindu asceticism. Rajputs are reckless, disunited in war and politics, and inclined to allow loyalty and romantic love to overrule social conventions. To claim descent from the heroes of the *Mahabharata* and *Ramayana* must be considered in itself to claim the status of a romantic hero, transforming one's life into one's legend. The use of the characteristic turbans (many of which are shown here) dates from at least the 2nd century B.C., when they were portrayed on terra cottas. You will be astonished by virtuoso brass: plaques, vases and bowls which may be engraved with scenes of Indian legend, lacquered or embossed with repoussé. Pottery from protohistory introduces the traditional Jaipuri wares, glazed with floral designs in blue and white. Ornamental stonework has been executed since at least the 2nd century B.C., approximate date of a colossal seven-foot high *Yaksha* figure from the village of Noh: other roughly contemporary examples can be seen in the museums of Mathura (Uttar Pradesh) between Delhi and Agra, and Bharatpur.

Don't miss the incredibly detailed *phad*, a folding screen thirty feet long and five feet high. In stylized orange, black and red cartoon frames, the *phad* is a portable novel or long illustrated ballad, narrating in pictures the life of the Rajput hero Pabuji Ramadeo of the Rabari tribe and his magical mare Kesa Kali, who sensed danger to her master. The folding screens are carried from village to village by minstrels called *bhopas*, accompanying themselves on the *jantar*, an instrument made of two gourds joined by a rod of bamboo. I thought of the wandering chapmen of mediaeval Europe, reciting ballads and selling broadsheets; or the painted churches of Yugoslavia, illustrating scenes from the New Testament for the benefit of illiterate worshippers.

A display introduces Rajasthani marionettes, or *kathputli* dressed nowadays in Rajput costume though presumably their ancestry goes back to much earlier times. The *kathputli* have wooden faces carved usually with Rajput features, with torso and arms usually of wood, but sometimes of padded cloth, but there are no legs, these being replaced by long cloaks or skirts. The puppeteer is always male, and his wife or son will play the *dholak* or drum, and occasionally sing an accompaniment. The puppet-play usually tells events or legends in Rajput history, with fighting heroes and dancing girls, the marionetteer standing above a low stage and manipulating his three-dimensional characters such as charmer and snake with wit and dexterity, farce contrasting with violence, treachery and murder. Edward Braddon noted, in *Thirty Years of Shikar* (1895) that marionetteers in his time slyly dressed some of their dolls in odds and ends of cast-off European clothing and wearing masks designed to represent the European face. 'As far as I can remember', he added, 'the Britannic character thus portrayed was singularly circumscribed. The sahib in mask and scarecrow apparel was a creature of three emotions and no morals. He got drunk, he said d--n frequently, and he thumped his native attendant.'

The first floor of Jaipur's Albert Hall has cases badly lit around three wells, displaying many 18th-century Jaipur School miniatures, and others of the Bikaner School ('Prince with Lotus', 'European and Lady with Dog'); the Kota School (a majestic, glowing 'Seated Heroine', 'Two Seated Ladies', and a view of a prince's lion hunt, the prince at a safe distance in a red boat); and the Jodhpur School ('Bhado Masa with Elephant'). Frustratingly, there are no reproductions of these fine paintings to be bought, so I suggest you acquire Andrew Topsfield's informative *Paintings from Rajasthan* (National Gallery of Victoria, 1980), which is especially strong on the Udaipur School. Topsfield admits that 'the historical development of few (perhaps none) of the many schools and sub-schools of Rajasthani painting is yet fully understood – and many pictures remain difficult to assign to any particular school', yet there is a certain sober refinement in Mughal influence and verve and expressiveness in Rajput influence mingling in different proportions. Artists' names are known, in Udaipur for example, only with the accession of Jagat Singh II (1734-51). Emphasis on festivals in many Rajasthani miniatures reminds one of the local adage 'sat bara, aur nau teohara': seven days but nine festivals, reflecting a resolve to seek joy and serenity in a time of struggle, for instance against the marauding Marathas.

Textiles, ivory, an unexpected Egyptian mummy: the Albert Hall has the bemused air of a 19th-century museum first waving, then drowning, as in the case of the melancholy anatomical displays, a horse skeleton, a human skeleton, and a stuffed cobra. Sparrows hopped about the ground floor as confidently as in a shaded garden. Regrettably, the zoo in Ram Niwas Bagh partakes of the same atmosphere. Badly-nourished birds and animals sadden and droop without adequate sympathy or scientific care.

My cycle rickshaw to the City Palace cost five rupees (25 pence in English money), but the rickshaw-wallah pointed out by a business card printed in English that he could offer a basic citywide tour for only twenty rupees. I stopped Mohan Lal at the Usha Book Agency in Chaura Rasta, to buy Manohar Prabhakar's *Rajasthan Today* (1988) and Hiralal Maheshwari's *History of Rajasthani Literature* (1980), then we continued to the City Palace, where we took a Gold Spot orange drink together and I paid him off. The City Palace takes up two of Jaipur's nine urban districts, which were carefully planned in accordance with the ancient treatise *Silpa Sastra* by a Bengali architect called Vidyadhar Bhattacharya, at the behest of Sawai Jai Singh II, from November 1727. Each of the main tree-lined avenues, in blocks later familiar to rational planners in Manhattan and elsewhere, measures 111 feet wide, with uniform shops on both sides of the wide roads, topped by pleasant mansions.

Beyond 'Iswar's minaret piercing heaven', or Iswari Minar Swarga Sal, to adopt its Hindi name, built by Iswari Singh, successor to Jai Singh who ruled from 1743-51, I came to the triple-arched gate Tripolia, through which maharajahs would pass on gaily-caparisoned elephants, and the extraordinary, romantic but essentially also practical sculpture park known euphoniously as Jantar Mantar (literally 'magic devices') and created as an open-air astronomical observatory, following Jai Singh's own prototype in Delhi (1724-7), where Parliament Street enters Connaught Place. An astronomer-king is not unique to India of course: the Aztec rulers of Mexico and the Pharaohs of Egypt (in particular the sun-worshipping Akhnaten) intuited the link between understanding time, seasons and the calendar on the one hand, and magically controlling their subjects on the other with a show of preternatural knowledge. Jai Singh II, who ascended the throne of Amber in 1699 at the age of 13, knew Mirza Ulugh Beg's 15th-century observatory at Samarkand, but trusted none of his predecessors, repudiating Hipparchos as 'an ignorant clown', Ptolemy as 'a bat', and replacing his original brass astrolabes and armillary spheres with huge stone instruments that relied on observations by the naked eye. Jai Singh's Delhi observatory was once faced with white marble damaged and lost in warfare, that of Mathura has disappeared altogether, that of Benares was restored by the Maharajah of Jaipur in 1912, and that of Ujjain was partly renovated in the 1920s.

Jaipur observatory is the largest of Jai Singh's astronomical parks, and even today the Raj Yantra is used to plot the details of the next Hindu calendar; the Samrat Yantra ('supreme device') is climbed by astrologers on Guru Purnima, an auspicious full moon day, when they consult texts to predict the monsoons. When the circular brass Chakra Yantra is revolved on a diameter parallel to the axis of the earth, you can calculate the angle of an object from the Equator. The Dhruva Yantra shows each of the twelve signs of the zodiac, each taking 30 degrees of the complete heavenly circle, and can be used for finding the Pole Star at night. The bizarre compound of observation and superstition, fact and fallacy, illumination and obscurantism, is deeply entrenched not only in Rajasthan, but throughout the whole of India. Much of the City Palace is still occupied by members of the former ruling family; insights into their private and public lives can be obtained from the memoirs of Gayatri Devi, *A Princess Remembers* (1976), written with Santha Rama Rau. The third wife of Maharajah Sawai Man Singh (known as Jai, she being known as Ayesha), Gayatri Devi is one of the great beauties of the twentieth century, yet she was too intelligent to take a traditionally passive role, and in 1962 won a seat in the Lok Sabha as a member of the second largest Opposition party to the Communists, Swatantra. An index to the popularity of Gayatri, her husband and the ruling family altogether is the fact that her majority over the Congress candidate came to 175,000, still the largest majority won by any candidate in any democratic election anywhere.

The main entrance to the City Palace is Siri Deorhi, off the homonyous bazaar, immediately in front of another monumental *darwaza* or gateway called Nakkar Khana, which leads to the vast Jaleb Chowk.

But the main public entrance these days is via the humbler 'servants' gate' or tradesmen's entrance: Gainda-ki Deorhi (Rhinoceros Gate). In the middle of the courtyard stands the graceful Mubarak Mahal, now a dazzling museum but built originally by Madho Singh II in 1900 as a guesthouse, and subsequently transformed into the royal secretariat. Madho Singh I, who ruled from 1750 to 1768, is alleged to have stood seven feet high and weighed around 500 pounds, or 225 kg: figures supported by the volume of his pink silk winter *atamsukh* ('soul's pleasure'), with dotted designs in gold. Here too are Pratap Singh's wedding robes, a riding outfit made for Ram Singh, and a magnificent Diwali dress in black and gold.

Amid all this lavish pink sandstone, it comes as a shock to learn that the local stone is a muddy grey, and it is this that was used at Amber, though rendered and painted cream. But pink sandstone was fashionable at the time, so Jaipur's mixture of rubble and render was merely *painted* red, and ever since the 1730s, when the city had been completed in less than a decade, the municipal authorities have insisted that all landlords and householders paint their façades pink, failing which the authorities do the work and bill the owners.

The Sileh Khana, or Armoury, possesses a vast range of rifles and curved swords: the treasure trove of a warrior race who now have no further use for brute force. Unlike Jaigarh above Amber, Sileh Khana is regrettably uncaptioned, so we cannot date these shields, swords, muskets, helmets and chain-mail suits of armour, except their Mughal daggers with ivory handles are ascribed to the 17th-18th centuries: vague enough to be useless. I especially liked Jai Singh I's turban-style helmet.

Before entering Singh Pol (Lion Gate), note that its flanking elephants were set there in 1931 to celebrate the birth of a male heir to the Kachchwaha dynasty of Jaipur. So much champagne was drunk at the birth of Bhawani Singh that his British nanny called him 'Bubbles', a name that has stuck with him ever since, and must have annoyed him especially during army years.

Through the bronze doors of the Hindu-style gatehouse we come to the charming Mughal-style Diwan-i-Khas, or private hall of audience, obviously judging from its great dimensions a former Diwan-i-Am, relegated to a more modest function when the later Diwan-i-Am was added by Sawai Pratap Singh (1778-1803).

Jaipur. City Palace. Entrance to Mor Chowk

Mughal influence can be easily explained, for Jaipur is geographically the closest of the Rajput states to the Mughal cities of Agra, Delhi and Fatehpur Sikri, and close ties with the Mughals go back way beyond the foundation of Jaipur itself, to the time of Bihari Mal, whose daughter Mariam Zamani was to become the mother of Shah Jahangir. Man Singh and others of the Kachchwaha house were valued generals and heroes of the Mughal Empire, even against other Rajput states. Diwan-i-Khas is dull and uninteresting for its niches are *drawn* on, making mock of architecture's three-dimensional genius seen so clearly in Rajendra Pol or Chandra Mahal.

The immense Diwan-i-Am, intended for durbars and banquets indoors, has *jali* screens behind which ladies in *purdah* could watch the ceremonies. Since 1959 it has been the Sawai Man Singh II Museum, with eight great carpets, four at each end, from Agra, Lahore and Herat and roughly mid-seventeenth century in age. The twelve-columned audience hall has a staggering display of manuscripts, with a superb 'Jahangir and his Courtiers' (*c.* 1750), a piquant Deccani 'Madonna and Child' (*c.* 1630) evoking recent European influence, and a charming Mughal 'Lovers at Night' (*c.* 1725). My favourite was an exquisite 'Krishna and the Gopis at Holi' (1737) created for Jai Singh, the patron prince, whose collection of astronomical and astrological treatises in Arabic and Persian have artistic as well as scientific and historical value. Wonderful examples of calligraphy from many schools are to be found on paper and palm-leaf: I singled out a Sanskrit text of the *Mahabharata* in old Assamese script.

Next I explored the exquisite Pritam Niwas Chowk, with 'four seasons' gateways and decorated with wondrous peacocks: those birds whose feathers are the symbols of state. As Brahma flies on a gander in Hindu mythology, Indra rides an elephant, and Shiva the bull Nandi, so Shiva's son, the god of war Skanda-Karttikeya, flies on the peacock. Warlike in the manner of all Rajputs, the rulers of Jaipur managed to manipulate the Mughal Emperors by a combination of matrimonial alliance and military co-operation. Jagat Singh, who ruled from 1803 to 1819, was condemned by the British as 'the most dissolute prince of his race (whose) life did not disclose one redeeming virtue amidst a cluster of effeminate vices', according to George Malleson's *Historical Sketch of the Native States of India* (1875). His posthumously-born son Jai Singh III reigned after him until 1835 but during his rule 'corruption and misgovernment' were so rife that an East India Company official was appointed to reside at Jaipur. This precaution proved ineffectual, as the situation deteriorated to the point where Company troops were called in and Maharajah Jai Singh was murdered on the orders of Jotharam, lover of the Maharajah's wife. The Resident attempted to reform the administration and became guardian to the young Ram Singh II and,

Jaipur. City Palace. Peacock Gate

after Jotharam tried to have the Resident assassinated and failed, he was jailed for life. Ram Singh ruled until 1880, when he was succeeded by Madho Singh II (to 1922) and Man Singh II until Partition. While under British 'paramountcy' between 1818 and 1947, Jaipur manipulated with equal intelligence the British administrators who gave the city political, economic and military advantages to the point at which a relatively small state could develop into a virtual absolutist monarchy, as one can appreciate with growing excitement and understanding as one reads Robert Stern's *The Cat and the Lion* (Leiden, 1988).

Chandra Mahal, the Moon Palace of seven auspicious storeys (like Dungarpur's Juna Mahal) is open only on the ground floor, a low peristyle hall with characteristic cusped arches. The other storeys are occupied by members of the former royal family: the second and third comprising a single high room: Sukh Niwas; the fourth and fifth, Rang Mandir and Subha Niwas, imitating Sukh Niwas; and the sixth and seventh, Chavi Niwas (a hall of tiny inlaid mirrors or *shish mahal*) and Mukut Niwas tapering to elegant domes in appropriate homage to Amber's Jas Mandir. In Chandra Mahal, as elsewhere in the City Palace, some floors have been painted to render the illusion that they are carpeted, with rugs and runners in narrower spaces, the whole

Jaipur. City Palace. Chandra Mahal in background

executed in realistic fresco. For in the hot summer months carpets were too hot to walk on and were rolled away, to allow bare feet the luxury of cold floors. Chandra Mahal forms the original nucleus of the City Palace, connected by a watercourse with the Temple of Govind Devji – regarded as the real ruler of Jaipur, being the most sacred of the six forms of Krishna, playing a flute, and with a face typically dark blue. The *darshan* or viewing of the main image is at 11.15 a.m. daily, when each of three successive curtains is drawn back. The idol was saved by Sawai Jai Singh from Aurangzeb's iconoclastic raids on Mathura, and installed here in 1734, when the city was nearing completion. Writing in *The Architectural Review* (September 1982), Michael Carapetian suggests that Govind Devji's temple and Badal Mahal were hunting lodges set within the original hunting ground around which the eighteenth-century city was established; Giles Tillotson takes the view that these two buildings might well stand on the sites of the original hunting lodges, but are in fact later, then remodelled. Badal Mahal is a garden pavilion overlooking the reservoir known as Tal Katora, where crocodiles once lazed in the sun.

Palaces beyond Jaipur city boundaries possess an almost unbearable load of nostalgia, for dust, moss, mist and damp make their natural home in India, as soon as any table, floor or wall is left unattended for even a little while. Entering the city from Agra, you first come to the Sisodia Rani Mahal of the 1750s, 8 km distant from Jaipur. Gardens and galleries, pools and graceful halls recall the Mewari princess who married Sawai Jai Singh II and gave birth to Madho Singh. Enjoy the mural paintings of Krishna's life, polo games and the hunt.

Above Sisodia Rani Mahal runs the gorge of Galta, festooned with monkeys, an oasis of peace and beauty a mere 10 km from the noisy city. A sun temple on the cliff top was erected at the expense of Rao Kirpa Ram during the time of Sawai Jai Singh II, allegedly 'curative waters' gushing from the mouth of a stone cow.

Near the royal cenotaphs or *chhatris* on the road to Amber you can see Jal Mahal of the 1730s, created as a pleasure pavilion for hunting parties shooting duck on the Man Sagar, a lake splendid in winter but dry in summer, before monsoon.

Another enjoyable excursion, by auto-rickshaw or taxi, is the 12-km ascent to the fort named Nahargarh after a local holy man, started by Jai Singh II in 1734. A caretaker will explain how Nahar, incensed at not being consulted by the Mahajarah on the auspices, caused work achieved by day to be destroyed by night, a Hindu Penelope. Only after Jai had propitiated this 'saint' did the work proceed without interruption. If Nahargarh itself is no more interesting intrinsically than Sajjangarh above Udaipur, then the view from it is no less breathtaking. And there is a modest restaurant for the relief of hikers.

Jaipur's city streets and ample bazaars, planned in 1728 on the model of Ahmedabad, are wide enough to allow Indian tumult its megaphonic apotheosis. Elephants of earlier centuries have by and large given way to honking trucks and buses. But buffaloes and sacred cows mooch in their splendid indifference from one side of the road to the other, finding their own laggard way home at dusk to sleep. Goats poke their noses into gutters and piles of rubbish. Bullock-carts pick their slow, deliberate way through five-mile-an-hour traffic, oblivious to whip or shout. Lithe monkeys skip around open shops as if on ships' rigging round wooden cabins. As for the extravagant colours: who can ever forget such vermilions and crimsons, saffron, scarlet, amber, emerald, yellows and purples, deep green, light green, carmine? The women so encased are seldom glimpsed even in these days of relative emancipation. Here is a middle-aged lady speeding on a moped between a bus and fodder-truck. There two young girls gossip and giggle unconcerned with the imminent onset of puberty that will change their lives for good. The ladies of Jaipur are swathed in such saried splendour that one alone looks like a procession: three comprise a carnival.

If you take the southern road from Jaipur after 15 km you will come to a crossroads, leading left to Tonk and right to Malpura: you will be in Sanganer, accessible by bus from the Ajmer Gate. You can see there a commemorative white marble pillar called Kirti Stambha, a Hindu temple devoted to Krishna, and a Jain temple adorned with the usual idols or tirthankaras. But Sanganer is predominantly a village of craftsmen, some specialising in the blue pottery known simply as 'Jaipur', and others in papermaking or calico printing. Virtually all the places where handicrafts may be seen are privately-owned, but that does not inhibit Sanganeris from inviting you in to see designers separating colours, blockmasters cutting wood, printers or embossers of traditional bird, tree, and flower prints for Rajasthani textiles sold in Jaipur bazaars. Chemical dyes have replaced natural vegetable dyes almost universally, but in the nearby village of Bagru there remain a few families of the *chhipa* (printing) caste using natural dyes such as indigo, red from red earth, alum and gum, and black from a mixture of old metal and *jaggery* left for about ten days in a pot of water.

Jaipur blue and white pottery was introduced by Man Singh I (1550-1614) after campaigns in Afghanistan where he led Mughal armies. Falling into disuse, the craft was revived under Ram Singh in 1886, and when the Indian Government foolishly closed his school in 1957 only the vigour of Maharani Gayatri Devi caused it to reopen, and it still produces new master potters at the Sawai Ram Singh Shilpa Kala Mandir. I feel that this determination on the part of a princely ruler is symptomatic of India's ambivalent, on the whole unsatisfactory, relationship with its former royal families. Democratically speaking, it would seem that the princes could play no rôle in a modern India where each citizen enjoyed theoretical equality. But such equality has always been a matter of ideology, not reality. If, for instance, one were to distribute a million rupees equally among a million citizens, none would benefit at all; if the same figure were distributed among a hundred thousand, they would barely notice a change in their circumstances; if among a thousand, their lifestyle could be significantly enhanced; if among a hundred, new factories and enterprises could be started, employing many hitherto unemployed or unproductive. So it seems that equality is a chimaera of little practical value, whereas the affluence of the few leads to the potential affluence of the many. This was recognised by the Government of India's own *White Paper on the Indian States* (1950):

'Moving voluntarily with the times, the Princes, big and small, co-operated in exploding the myth that India's independence would founder on the rock of Princely intransigence. The edifice of democratic India rises on the true foundation of the co-ordinated effort of the Princes and the people. But for the patriotic co-operation of the Princes, the tremendous change that has come over India for the mutual benefit of the People and the Rulers would not have been possible. Traditionally habituated to an order of personal rule, the new order has involved a radical shift for them. They have given evidence of imagination, foresight and patriotism by accepting the change with a good grace'.

Generalising about the maharajahs is unwise, because they varied from state to state and generation to generation in character, imagination, foresight, patriotism and every other quality. Some were dissolute and worthless; others showed a passionate concern for the wellbeing of their subjects. A monarchy is only as good as the reigning monarch: thus it is with the princely states. Once they seemed immutable, invincible. In 1971 they were 'derecognized', their privileges, privy purses and titles all abolished at a stroke. But, as always in India, matters have not turned out to be so simple. In some states the former wealth and property of the rulers has not diminished, so that they remain significant policy-makers and formers of opinion, as well as influential employers. As hereditary owners of great palaces and forts of national and international importance, their possessions and traditions play a part altogether out of all proportion to their numbers: in Jaipur as in Udaipur, Jodhpur, Mandawa and Bikaner, much of what you visit was constructed and maintained by the rulers, even to the hotels where you stay. 'The first duty of a political officer is to cultivate direct, friendly, personal relations with the ruling princes and chiefs with whom he works', observed the *Manual of Instructions to Officers of the Foreign and Political Department* (1924), and the British Empire's tactical interest in the all-powerful rulers paid off in terms of co-operation and long-term understanding, but naturally led to suspicion from Indian democrats, not necessarily socialists or communists, that after Independence the rulers would remain as detached from the everyday cares of the rural poor as they were before Independence. An egalitarian society was doctrinally committed to the elimination of princely privilege, no matter what the cost. Brigadier Sukhjit Singh, Maharajah of Kapurthala, who retired from the Indian Army to farm, after receiving the gallantry award of Maha Vir Chakra, ruefully reflected on the news that privy purses of four crores of rupees were to be withdrawn from the princes. He pointed out that ten times that amount was being lost in bad management, embezzlement, bad procurement, and various other losses to the Exchequer. 'But this four crores a year that was paid out to the Princes helped maintain vast establishments, kept people going who had no other form of sustenance, people who had given their lives in the execution of what we call 'the honouring of their salt'.

The first royal palace to be converted into a hotel (in 1958) was Jaipur's Ram Bagh Palace on Bhawani Singh Road. Of course, as elsewhere in India, you do not have to spend the night there to take tea, or a buffet meal, and I suggest a drink in the Polo Bar, celebrating Sawai Man Singh's almost obsessive polo exploits. He died in 1970 following a fall in a polo match at Cirencester. Ram Bagh goes back to 1835, when Sawai Ram Singh II created a pavilion which later developed into a hunting lodge as a base to bag the abundant game in the area. Over the next century it became a large palace, with its wilderness transformed into formal gardens, Sawai Man Singh's private home and polo ground. After adapting it into a hotel, the Maharajah known as Jai moved with his family to the 18th-century Raj Mahal, the former British Residency on Jumna Lal Road which was originally the *zenana's* summer quarters, but that too has become a hotel. I stayed in the opulent Jai Mahal Palace on the Jacob Road, in the top price range, like the Mansingh Hotel in the city centre, the Jaipur Ashok in Bani Park, and Clark's Amer near the airport. But I confidently recommend cheaper accommodation with quite as much character, if not more, as family houses run for guests, such as the adjacent Bissav Palace Hotel and Khetri House in the west of the walled city area.

These last will enable you to walk out into the bazaars without need of a rickshaw. Don't be surprised at seeing jewellery fanciers from all over the world in Durlabhji's emerald store at 139 Jauhari Bazaar, or at Gem Palace, Mirza Ismail Road. You can acquire rubies, diamonds and sapphires for a fraction of the price you would pay in London, Amsterdam, and New York, but gold is not such a bargain. Copies of original Mughal designs are the speciality of Sajjid Khan at B41-2 Bais

Godam. Over thirty thousand stone-cutters are stated to find employment in Jaipur, a tradition begun by princely patronage and never permitted to die out: look for some of them in the alleys leading off Jauhari Bazaar, where you will be welcome to watch. Enamelled jewellery known as *meenakari* is a craft centred on Jaipur: superb examples from the 17th century are illustrated in the standard *Arts and Crafts of Rajasthan* (1987) by Aman Nath and Francis Wacziarg.

Painters of miniatures, carpet-weavers, makers of batik and scroll-painters, embroiderers, brass-beaters: it seems no skill of the human hand is alien to the artisans of Jaipur, and you can find handsome cotton quilts at Anokhi, 2 Tilak Road, who also sell a range of dazzling cotton clothes, including the fine quilted dressing-gowns called *atamsukh*.

And then you find the quarter of stonemasons, sculptors, call them what you will for the hazy line dividing artist from artisan never bothers a Rajasthani. Alleys are strewn with great blocks of stone, ready to be carved, or part-hewn with Ganesha, Shiva, or Vishnu. You could have flown on a magic carpet to Vedic India, for masters with white beards are supervising younger men and apprentices of eight or twelve, each elaborately intent on the form below the chisel, not yet incarnate. Listen to the noise of chisel on stone, of creative thought, but no human voice interrupts the hammering and contemplation, the whole enveloped in a gauze of the finest dust filming over not only the alleyways and the ground, but the sinewy brown bodies and the very still air, stiflingly hot and incorrigibly timeless. The Old Testament tried to persuade us that God made the world in six days; the sculptors of Jaipur make so many gods in six days that I doubt if they have ever been counted. For this, too, you must come to Rajasthan.

After such unceasing activity, making one vicariously thirsty and exhausted, it is good to return to one's hotel, along pink-tinged avenues that gleam and glow a different hue at every succeeding hour of the day, from grey-pink flamingo dawn to brightest noon, and shadowy, watery pastel-pink twilight. I sank, tired out, on a gilt chair in my hotel garden, sipping iced orange juice and awaiting trouble. A well-dressed western-educated Indian in a pinstripe suit with a handkerchief in his top pocket and a carnation in his button-hole joined me with a beatific smile.

'Excuse me, sir, I am fortune-teller.'

I smiled non-committally. 'Won't you join me?' (He already had).

'From your face I can tell you are cheerful, very happy, open disposition, you like travelling, you will live long about 96 or 98 and you will die suddenly of heart attack, no grief.'

'Really?'

'From your face you are tiger or snake.'

He scrutinised my hand, ringless in complicity with my wife, who assents to my opinion that finger-rings are unmanly. 'You are not married, but you will marry very soon, and have many sons, no daughters.' I forbore to reveal that I have two grown-up daughters, but am never likely to have sons.

'Here, sir, will you think of flower, one flower.' I thought. 'Now, sir, watch, I write down the flower name you thought of. Will you tell me any number below six?' I thought. 'Now I write down number you thought of and you hold paper on your left hand. You show right hand. How interesting. Most fine hand, you like fun, plenty fun, morning, afternoon, during dinner, all night, you like too much loving.' I gingerly removed my hand from his and backed away. 'What flower and number you thought of?' 'Antirrhinum and one'. He backed away and melted into the dusk. I opened the crumpled bit of paper. 'Rose', was written on it. Above the number 'three'.

Ranthambore

From Jaipur you can reach Sawai Madhopur, and the nearby Ranthambore National Park with its celebrated tiger reserve, on a metre-gauge railway which connects with the main line between Bombay and Delhi at Sawai Madhopur. The ancient fort has walls extending some seven km, and was self-sufficient in water. In 1303 twenty thousand women committed suicide in a *jauhar* after a siege by Sultan Ala-ud-Din Khilji of Delhi. Akbar laid siege to it for a year and the fort eventually gave way in 1569, due to its isolation and the superior power of the imperial army. Once an alliance had been forged with the Maharajahs of Jaipur, they were again allowed suzerainty over the area, and royal protection offered wildlife a chance of survival, apart from organized hunting. Between them, the British and the Maharajahs slaughtered nearly 39,000 tigers in India between the turn of the century and 1971, when killing tigers was outlawed. Project Tiger was set under way here in 1973, when only 14 tigers roamed free. Now the total has risen to forty, and the confidence of the great cat has grown to the point that since 1981 it has been seen diurnally as well as nocturnally. A tiger called Genghis, well known to Valmik Thapar of the Ranthambore Foundation who spends a couple of weeks here every month, now pursues sambhar deer from the lakeshores into the water, dragging out his victim on to dry land for gradual mastication. Tigers kill only what they need, and there are enough sambhar, chital and minor groups of nilgai to feed the tiger population, though a hungry tiger will even take pheasant or peafowl if need be. Forests near the lakes consist of banyan, pipal and mango, though the hills and valleys are populated by dhok, whose scientific name is *Anogeissus pendula*. Since 1981, Ranthambore has been a national park, and in 1984 a further hundred square km were annexed to the south as the Sawai Man Singh Sanctuary. Fateh Singh Rathore, the former Field Director, can distinguish a tiger's age, sex and size from its pawmarks in the dust: they like to prowl on the dusty roads that run through the reserve for the convenience of game wardens and tourist jeeps. There are wonderful views from the fort, soaring 215 metres above the park, and you will encounter warriors' tombs, guard-towers, and the great fort-gate studded with nails to prevent elephant-charges. To clear the area for wildlife, sixteen villages had to be evacuated, and the villagers resettled outside the park boundary. Valmik showed me the overgrown royal garden, Raj Bagh, where one tigress prowls. On all sides, in the valley and in the forest, you can hear the bellowing of a tigress summoning her wandering cubs. Bears in Ranthambore try to avoid the tigers by seeking their prey on higher ground, where they can see the animal Jim Corbett called 'the jungle gentleman', though 'lady' is a term I could scarcely apply to the tigress. Other big cats you may glimpse on your peregrinations include the caracal and the leopard, and I recall my shock on finding a statuesque monitor lizard in a glade, and two marsh crocodiles still as Hindu bronzes beside one of the artificial lakes. For an hour I sat and listened to a panoply of bird calls below the huge banyan tree near the fort, though I missed seeing the crested serpent eagle for which this reserve has also become celebrated. The only accommodation within the Reserve is at Jogi Mahal, controlled by the Field Director's office, but you can stay outside at the Castle Jhumer Baori Forest Lodge on Ranthambore Road, Sawai Madhopur, and the Maharajah Lodge in Sawai Madhopur: both lodges can arrange for you to visit the national park by jeep.

Ajmer

Between Jaipur and Jodhpur (to the southwest) or Udaipur (to the south) your way will bring you to Ajmer, founded in the 7th century by Ajaipal Chauhan, whose Taragarh is considered to be one of the earliest of India's hill fortresses. In 1150, the Chauhan Ana (1135-50) created the artificial lake still called Ana Sagar. Known as Ajaimeru ('Unconquerable Hill') on account of Taragarh, the city remained a Chauhan possession until the Muslim invasion of about 1193, when the Chauhan Prithviraj III lost both Ajmer and Delhi to Muhammad Ghuri. Ghuri's representative was Qutb-ud-Din Aibak, ruling Ajmer from Delhi until 1326, after which it was a prize to be won and lost by the Sultans of Gujarat and Delhi, and the rulers of Marwar and Mewar. Shah Akbar created Ajmer a full province in the 16th century, and walled the town.

Akbar's idea in creating this red sandstone fortress with a perimeter of thick double walls was clearly to provide himself with an invincible stronghold at Ajmer against rebels while on tour. The fort of 1570 does not belong to the series of forts at Agra (which we have seen), at Lahore (now in Pakistan) or in Allahabad. Akbar never intended to live there for any length of time, for the spacious two-storeyed pillared hall in the centre of the fort's courtyard could not have provided the quarters for a stay of any length, and served primarily as an audience hall. A Government Museum now occupies this audience hall, and can be visited daily from 10 to 5. It has sculptures dating from the Gupta period (4th-5th centuries) to the 18th century. From Kaman, west of Mathura, come two figures of the marriage of Shiva and Parvati, and two tetramorphic lingams, with Brahma, four-armed Vishnu with Garuda, and the sun-god Surya, and four-armed Shiva with Nandi. Tenth-century works from Sikar district show Brahma and Vishnu measuring the lingam of Shiva, and the gently-smiling Surya. A Lakshmi on Garuda in black stone (12th century) comes from the Ajmer region, while a fine Kali, goddess of destruction, in black marble (early 18th century) comes from Awa, south-east of Pali. Coins, weapons and inscriptions will interest the specialist, but everyone will be enchanted by miniatures showing the struggle of Rama against the evil Ravana, and the youth of Krishna.

Away from the museum, the pulsating life of Ajmer can be found in the bazaar which assails every sense as you walk from Station Road to the mausoleum of Khawajah Muin-ud-Din Chishti (1142-1236) and the nearby mosque called the 'Hut of $2\frac{1}{2}$ Days' not because of the extraordinary speed with which an earlier theological college of 1155 was transformed into a mosque by the orders of Ghuri in the last years of the 12th century (with arches and screen dating from 1266), but because of a religious festival, established later, which lasted each year for that length of time. The great Adhai-din-ka Jhonpra is thus one of the earliest monuments of Indo-Muslim art, as well as one of the finest. Domes and pointed arches characterised Islamic architecture, but Hindu masons at that period could not adapt to true radiating arches and domes and improvised by creating the effect without the substance, by horizontal corbelling. We saw this at the Qutb Mosque in Delhi and here at Ajmer a screen of seven arches shows quite dramatically the Hindu construction techniques of the time, and the conical dome inside that is much lower than if Muslim masons had been responsible. The Islamic calligraphic decoration, itself honey-brown just like the arches, makes a quite different impact from the tiled calligraphy on most early mosques in Western and Central Asia, towering above visitors suitably overawed by these remarkable arches. But there are many more visitors at the shrine of Muin-ud-Din Chishti, the Persian Sufi saint who at Makkah – the story runs – was inspired by a vision to settle in Ajmer, which he achieved with Ghuri's army. His order follows Chishti's example in devotion to the poor, and remains as widespread as ever. Akbar paid frequent, if not annual, visits to the shrine of Muin-ud-Din, and built a mosque. Two large cauldrons for gifts of food are not the originals given by Akbar and Jahangir, but recent replacements. Another mosque in white marble was founded by Shah Jahan, and nearby there is a charming portico given by his daughter Jahanara. Muin-ud-Din's simple brick tomb has been enriched by gifts such as a silver railing and arch; doors are totally plastered with votive horse-shoes. Non-Muslims are forbidden to enter the tomb of the saint's daughter, Bibi Hafiz Jamal. By no means all the pilgrims to Muin-ud-Din's tomb are Muslims: I saw bent crones and old men buckled under the weight of their age fingering the silver rail, and kissing the white marble walls, as though the sanctity of the Sufi could transmit itself not only through time but also through the space between crumbling bones and outer air. Parables of Lazarus and others skimmed into my mind, overstressed by heat, dust and polybabble: Sindhi, Rajasthani, Urdu. What can the atmosphere be like when the dargah is *really* crowded, on the first six days of Rajab every year, when the anniversary of Muin-ud-Din's death about 1236 is celebrated by huge crowds, crushing and pressing in from all parts of India?

And just when you thought that Islam had carved itself an exclusive niche in Hindu Rajasthan, you come to the 19th-century Jain temple called Nasiyan, with charming wooden gilt figures in a two-storeyed hall resonant to all appearance with great age and extraordinary mythic strength yet no older in fact than St Pancras Station in London. From Nasiyan Temple you can take a tonga or auto-rickshaw on the Circular Road around Ana Sagar. Arid, jagged hills encircle the lake, which is adorned by majestic embankments and marble pavilions endowed by Shah Jahan. Then from the centre of Ajmer an auto-rickshaw or taxi will convey you the 5 km up to Taragarh Fort, situated on a road above the dargah. Taragarh, once a British health resort, possesses a mosque and a shrine to Sayyid Husain, a governor of the fortress who died in 1202 and achieved renown when Akbar came to pray at his grave; the final approach has to be made on foot.

You can stay in Ajmer at the Khadim Tourist Bungalow on Savitri Girls' College Road or at the Circuit House south of Ana Sagar. If you have read about the education of Rajput royal families, you will frequently have come across the name of Mayo College, founded in Ajmer in 1872, barely two years after the first college for princes (Rajkumar College) was established at Rajkot in Kathiawar. As early as 1835, Lord Macaulay had observed: 'We must at present do our best to form a class who may be interpreters between us and the millions whom we govern – a class of persons Indian in blood and colour, but English in tastes, in opinions, in morals and in intellect'. If one can forgive for a moment, in the context of those embarrassingly white supremacist days, Macaulay's tacit assumption that British taste and intellect were unarguably superior to those of Indians, there is in at least one way something to be said for his opinion. This education for a new middle class was essentially outgoing, in the sense that Indians were to be allowed to break out from their restrictive, traditionalist society which may have been tolerant to a point (except as regards women's potential) and in some places pluralist, but was certainly never secular or sensibly sceptical. Despite this, a new professional middle class *did* emerge, based however slightly on the meritocratic principle that the English had borrowed ultimately from the successes of the Chinese examination system for graded posts in the civil service.

As in England, a class raised on a classical literary education placed conservatism at a premium, undervaluing innovation, experimentation, and cross-fertilization from, for instance, Russian, German or French literary styles and modes of perception. B.B. Misra, in *The Indian Middle Classes* (1961), has indicated that this professionalism and sense of citizenship was based 'not on religion or caste but on the discharge of certain common civil obligations to the State', a view closer to Confucius and Lord Curzon than to Aurangzeb, but acceptable to Indians as a continuation in some useful sense of the life and work of Akbar, undermined by the proletarian sentimentality of Gandhi. As in England, vocational, scientific and technical experience and competence were seen in India to be irrelevant to a 'proper education' and only after World War II have the better-educated classes migrated, still reluctantly, into management, business, industry and technology. Even so, the civil service and literary professions continue to be dominated by Brahmans and higher castes.

Mayo College had a succession of British headmasters and followed the code of discipline of public schools such as Eton, but 'boarding-school life' was very different. For one thing, each state had its own 'house', so that boys from Kota would stay in Kota House and boys from Bikaner in Bikaner House. Boys had to join in every activity of the college from sport to history, but then at night they ate and slept in their own house. Karni Singh of Bikaner, a former Mayo pupil, has noted: 'When I was a boy we had English officers who were in charge of the police, English principals in charge of schools, the railways were manned by British people, and Indians and British played tennis together. States like Jaipur, Jodhpur and Bikaner were all trying to bring British technology into their states. The English language itself was a very binding force and for three hundred years these two countries had lived together. So to my generation England isn't another country'. Maharajah Karni was born in 1924.

Pushkar
You can take a bus or auto-rickshaw 10 km from Ajmer over Snake Mountain to the three sacred lakes of Pushkar, which sees its greatest pilgrimage season at the full moon of November, or Kartik Purnima, in 1989 the days from 10 to 13 November. By booking in advance you might be able to stay at a charming palace once owned by the Maharajah of Jaipur and now called the Sarowar Tourist Bungalow in Pushkar, but when the pressure for accommodation is at its height the Rajasthan Tourist Development Corporation sets up a tented village with good bathrooms and communal dining areas. Fifty thousand camels, horses and bullocks are traded amid the most exhilarating scenes of colour, chaos and hubbub. Pilgrims use the lakes as a kind of second-class Ganges. Take the chance to visit the red-spired temple of Brahma, for there are extraordinarily few such throughout the length and breadth of India, considering that Brahma is one of the four leading aspects of the divine in Hinduism. But most of all, just allow your senses to revel in scenes which nobody outside India could ever experience, not even in Bangkok or Bali, one Buddhist and the other Hindu. You might be alarmed by snake-charmers, dazzled by huge bulls with jewelled collars and silver anklets, enthralled by magnetic minstrels and bards, with their folk-tales and Rajput legends. You can buy bangles of ivory, sherbets and cold drinks, tea and curry, textiles and brass. On the marble steps down to the lake, genealogists record the names of pilgrims at this, one of the five sacred places of Hinduism, and feverishly try to discover how many of their ancestors had visited the lakes.

Pushkar has been sacred since the time of Rigveda and perhaps even before, if the fire rite is considered pre-Vedic. Brahma, while preparing for the fire rite in the heavens above Rajasthan, saw a demon devouring Brahma's children at Pushkar. Brahma killed the demon with one touch of the lotus he held, and three lotus petals fell to earth as the three lakes of Pushkar. Brahma's temple is not the only one to celebrate this legend: there is another to his consort Saraswati, goddess of wealth and learning, and a third to a milkmaid called Gayatri who took Saraswati's place at the fire rite when the goddess was delayed. Such tales, reinvented and refurbished for every generation with elaborations and ever-entwining anecdotes, endure in one's memory long after the facts and figures of Pushkar's more prosaic life have disappeared.

Kishangarh
From Ajmer, you can reach Kishangarh 31 km away on the road to Jaipur. Modern Kishangarh has its own attractions, but you will want to explore first and foremost the old town founded in 1611 from Jodhpur, by Udai Singh's son Kishan Singh. By the 18th century, alliance with the Mughal Shahs had brought elegant luxury to the court of Kishangarh,

Kishangarh. Fort Palace

and great painters such as Nihal Chand and Bhawani Das fled from Aurangzeb when his fanatical Islamic zeal threatened their lives and livelihood. Raj Singh (1706-48) and his son Sawant Singh (who abdicated in 1757 with his great love, the singer Bani Thani) fostered the arts, and under their patronage Kishangarh reached possibly new heights in sensuous Mughal miniatures, or alternatively a cul-de-sac from which these painters of Krishna and Radha could not logically develop, exemplified by a refined yet decadent mannerism in posture, costume, and smothering trees in such works as the *Krishna and Radha* (1800) of the National Gallery of Victoria, a work far inferior to the *Tambula Seva* (c. 1760) in Delhi National Museum. Before visiting the forgotten city, read *Kishengarh Painting* (Lalit Kala Academy, Delhi, 1959) by Eric Dickinson and Karl Khandalavala, and apply to see the former ruling family's collection by writing to the private secretary of His Highness the Maharajah, Kishangarh. You could stay in the royal Manjhela Palace. The palaces and fort (in which red chilis are spread out to dry during the season) overlook a splendid lake where ducks and herons swim and squabble almost undisturbed, and the lake palace (accessible by boat), reminds you inevitably of wondrous Udaipur.

4: SHEKHAVATI

Nawalgarh — Mandawa — Fatehpur Shekhavati

Shekhavati comprises a region of desert plain in the triangle whose points are Delhi to the northeast, Bikaner to the west, and Jaipur to the south. The name 'Garden of Shekha' derives from a Kachchwaha prince, Rao Shekhaji who, as the ruler of Barwada in Amber region of Jaipur, proclaimed his sovereignty in 1471. Since then Shekhavati has constituted a disparate sequence of small fiefdoms known locally as *thikanas*, the most notable of which are Sikar, Nawalgarh, Dundlod, Mandawa, Fatehpur, Chirawa, Churu and Khetri. Private car is the best way to see these towns, but if you have more time, buses can be used. The daily Shekhavati Express train from Delhi to Jaipur calls at Jhunjhunu and Sikar, and the metre-gauge railway from Jaipur to Bikaner stops at Sikar, Fatehpur and Churu.

Since Shekhavati was omitted both by Eustace Reynolds-Ball from his *The Tourist's India* (1907), and by Nagel's more ambitious *India: Encyclopedia-Guide* published seventy years later, it may reasonably be asked why the locality deserves close attention. The answer is that in 1982 the Frenchman Francis Wacziarg and the Indian Aman Nath produced the first full-scale documentary illustrated study, *The Painted Walls of Shekhavati*, which has revolutionised our understanding and appreciation of the wall paintings carried out since the mid-18th century on forts, temples, cenotaphs, and since the early 19th century on opulent private houses called *havelis*. The worldwide taste for naive art, from Henri Rousseau and Grandma Moses to L.S. Lowry and the many Yugoslav *virtuosi*, has awakened a great deal of interest in the skills and imagination of the Shekhavati craftsmen, who applied fresco to wet plaster in a technique quite possibly derived ultimately from mediaeval Italian practice. The Mughals knew of true fresco from the Persians, and Fatehpur Sikri, Akbar's capital, was close enough to Shekhavati for artists to learn the technique and pass it on to their families and apprentices. The name *haveli* too is Persian, defining at least in the Mughal period an aristocratic self-contained town house of fortress-like dimensions, virtually closed from the outside except for a stout wooden door. Life within revolved around an open courtyard, with its own well and laundry space nearby, and a communal 'playground' for children in the open air but not risking their vanishing or being hit by passing vehicles or animals. Several small families or one or two large families would live in one *haveli*, which might be four or five storeys high. An inner courtyard usually protects the women's quarters from prying eyes.

We first come across frescoes in Rajput art when rulers commissioned a mason, or *chhitera*, to decorate a room or *chhatri* with wall-paintings, the same artisan fulfilling both functions. Later, the Marwari merchant families (Goenka, Birla, Kanoria, Singhania and others) emulated the noblemen by decorating their vast mansions with splendid, inventive frescoes which make up in colour, wit and originality what they may lack in aesthetic qualities. Shekhavati is by and large flat and sandy: a monochrome lionesque brown. In the absence of great Mughal gardens, the merchants of Fatehpur and Khetri brought joy and sparkle into their lives with a ravishing sequence of designs based on natural pigments: indigo for blue, lamp-black, lime for white, and saffron for orange, with all the intermediate shades, fiery reds, cobalt, aquamarine, and refreshing green. Religious themes recur throughout the history of Shekhavati fresco, but family pride and prowess form another vital thread, from Shardul Singh's *chhatri* at Parasrampura (1750) to fierce hunting scenes in the Chokhani *haveli* at Lachhmangarh (1860), the town with a fine fort overlooking the town, a regular plan based on that of Jaipur, and the *havelis* of Kedi (1880) and Rathi (1910).

As you leave Jaipur northwestward towards Sikar, mango orchards shimmer green under a clear blue sky. During my visit the monsoons had failed for seven years, and cattle fodder was being trucked to Western Rajasthan on grotesquely overloaded trucks which had to drive only a foot off the left or right edge of the uneven tarmac roads to overturn: on the way to Jaisalmer I saw several such disasters, massive beached mechanical whales stranded and waiting for police or army assistance. The driving is not so much noisy or reckless (though it is both) as *central*. These are no longer motorways or trunk roads, but ribbons of asphalt, patched and holed like a tramp's shirt, and as ragged at the edges. So all vehicles, to avoid snagging their tyres, try to drive in the middle of the road, and the greater the truckload, the more vociferously and arrogantly you assume the crown. It only takes two such juggernauts to refuse to give way, and both are inevitably sanded in, their wheels buried up to the hubs. Accidents are frequent, and foreigners are not permitted to drive cars, so if you want to hire a car you must also hire a driver, who may be reliable and may even know some of the places where you want to go, but he may have a different idea of road safety from yours, so it is in order to encourage him to slow down.

Wheat and mustard fields spread around us, as if denying the scarcity of water farther west. Artesian water lies closer to the surface in this area than in Bikaner, so wells are shallower here. A government afforestation plan began by offering free eucalyptus trees to farmers, but eucalyptus was subsequently found to be absorbing water at an alarming rate, and *prosopis cineraria* were planted instead. Plum orchards delight the eye in Chomu, and you can tell the abundance of the grain crops here because the old fort has been converted to a granary. If you have time, take a right turning from the Sikar road to Samod, where you will find a strange, quiet palace a mere century old, with a durbar hall glowing with *meenakari*, an enamelling technique introduced by Man Singh I (1590-1614) when he brought master *meenakars* from Lahore. You can stay at Samod Palace.

At Ringas village we were held up by a goods train at a level crossing, then a passenger train, while a wrinkled old tribesman in a turban gazed unblinkingly at me – a European specimen to be labelled in the storehouse of his memory or forgotten the next minute as a fragment of inlaid mirror will reflect an eye and then empty again.

Now motor vehicles seem to be decreasing in number, as camel carts proliferate. Vultures congregate hopefully, patiently, untidily on upper branches of spreading trees, sprawling as ungainly as their own nests. This is a land of quarries, where soft stone can be hewn out with few tools and little effort. Local people can quickly put up a stone house against summer heat, but their animal byres still consist of old-fashioned

Ringas. Waiting at the level crossing

vegetation: straw, branches, packed foliage. Food is plentiful and children dart around with enormous zest: nobody goes hungry, and a Urea Distribution Centre helps the crops and the ground to remain fertile for some time to come. At Sikar, I stopped off at the squat toilet near the bedrooms, then asked for a cup of tea, but none was to be had in the middle of the morning. I explored this rest-house for Public Works officials, with its holed mosquito nets on the windows, its flat roof with a whiff of a breeze. In the 1970s, old tin hoardings for Craven A cigarettes, Gold Flake, Brasso, and Mansion House polish still reminded us of the 'Forties, but now most of these have disappeared, and in any case there are relatively few customers for Western imports in desert Rajasthan. A grid at the entrance to the garden deterred cattle from coming in, but plenty of pigs snuffled hopefully for kitchen scraps. Crows carked aggressively below the shady trees.

Nawalgarh

We turned right, along the road for Nawalgarh, heart of Shekhavati. The bazaar there is hectic with excitement, not only because all markets are occasions for argument, meetings, and watching strangers, but because tomorrow is Holi, the festival of colour, and stalls and carts are piled high with pyramids of coloured powders, sold by weight in little polythene bags. Crows flutter and stab with their beaks at offal covered

Nawalgarh. Well

in sand. Scooter rickshaws laden with brilliantly saried women zigzag past the Sethi Anand Ram Eye Hospital. A garden with a children's playground stands deserted, wrecked swings flapping uselessly in a sudden gust. Painted walls urge me to patronise 'Texla – the right choice. Colour-Black & White TV' and others 'Sony Orson'. Nawalgarh takes its name from Nawal Singh, who established its fort in 1737, and encouraged the founding of the surrounding town with a large number of Marwari merchant *havelis* and mansions built by nobles or *thakurs* ('thakur' being a transliteration of the Hindi word which gives 'Tagore' in Rabindranath Tagore, Bengal's classical poet). You can stay in the Roop Niwas *haveli* overnight in Nawalgarh, where a *bhopa* or local minstrel with his *bhopi* wife will sing to their own accompaniment on the *ravanhatta*. The fort, normally locked, may be opened to reveal a fresco of Jaipur on the dome. Visit the temples of Ramdeoji and Gopinathji. But the telephone exchange with its colourful murals causes the greatest sensation, bright and glittering in the midday sun. Forty thousand inhabitants mill in the streets, where bakers offer delicious pastries, and drapers can so easily persuade you into buying the fine 'tie-and-dye' fabrics. The influence of 'the Company' can be seen everywhere. Indians took a natural interest in the curious behaviour of the formalised, ritualised English who lived among them, with their trains, bicycles, cars and strange clothes. Rajputs made excellent soldiers, and

Nawalgarh. Street scene with performing bhopa

Nawalgarh. Frescoed haveli

their recruitment into the Army proved as much of an asset as the recruitment of Sikhs, say, or Gurkhas. The Chokhani *haveli* of 1820 has a charming procession of soldiers bearing a flower in one hand and a rifle in the other. The Chhawchhariya *haveli* (1875) has intricate decoration, with portraits of Britons riding bicycles, and an elephant fresco unusual in its three trunks, which may be a reference to Indra's mount Airavata, though its goad or *ankush*, howdah, bells and caparison are all realistic enough. Fireworks and rockets were being set off beside a statue erected to a favourite local politician: Kesar Deo.

If you have your own car, take a road east to Parasrampura which will bring you in 9 km to the *chhatri* erected in 1750 for Shardul Singh, eighth descendant of Rao Shekhaji, founder of Shekhavati. Battle-scenes and processions vie with scenes from the *Ramayana* and *Mahabharata*. Shardul Singh (1681-1742) was responsible for ending three hundred years of Muslim rule in the region by capturing first Jhunjhunu (1730) and then Fatehpur Shekhavati (1731). These paintings might reasonably be considered the remote ancestors of the frescoes we are to see at Mandawa and Fatehpur.

Mandawa
From Nawalgarh you could visit westward in Dundlod two important *havelis* of the Goenka family and their more distant *chhatri*, and you

could spend the night in the frescoed fort, built in 1750 by Keshri Singh, a son of Shardul Singh. Much larger and more interesting is the town of Mandawa, with Nawal Singh's fort of 1755, and an impressive sequence of *havelis*, now tenanted without charge on behalf of the absentee owners, who have multi-million rupee businesses in Calcutta, Delhi, and Bombay, in fact all over northern and central India. These merchants originally grew rich on trade between the Near East and the Far East and between Delhi and the coast of Gujarat. Building great mansions for themselves and their extended families, they could afford to enrich their native villages with wells and reservoirs, for there is only one river in Shekhavati and the Katli, roughly bisecting the district north-south from Pilani to Sri Madhopur, fills only during irregular monsoon rains. Their homes were decorated with scenes from daily life, Indian myth and legend, and with birds, animals and foliage compensating in brilliance for the monochrome sand around them. The wealthy families left for newly-rich cities, allowing poorer families to look after their houses rent-free. The most frequently recurring motif is Lord Krishna with the *gopis* in his incarnation as Gopinathji. But these naive mason-craftsmen see no incongruity in depicting early aeroplanes, sailing ships or cars. The British are figures of fun and perplexity, painted in their period costume, both civil and military.

Hotel Castle Mandawa has been run since 1980 by members of the former royal family of Mandawa, who greet visitors personally and make them feel most welcome. Yet bed and breakfast in 1988 came to only £19 (US$35) for two. All rooms are different, of course, for you are living in a former palace-cum-barracks, but I greatly enjoyed my tiny look-out cell with a low ceiling and windows facing the sandy courtyard and (from a new bathroom annexe) over the oasis. The former Maharajah Keshri Singh took me into several unoccupied bedrooms, all spotlessly clean, each with a unique touch such as a fine carpet, a raised concrete bed, or a round tower. You take an evening drink on the terrace at sundown. Mosquito nets protect you from night invasions.

I drew various estimates of the population of Mandawa: the 1981 census put it below 13,000, but Kanwar Devi Singh, Keshri Singh's father, indicated a figure of 17,000, of whom 12,000 are Hindus and 5,000 Muslims. A distinguished nobleman, married in 1941, Devi Singh is a scholar and historian, whose *History of the Rajputs* (Jaipur, 1985) recently appeared in Hindi. Among his anecdotes were memories of Mayo College, Ajmer, that prestigious school for the sons of noble families. Both he and Keshri Singh are on the school's management committee to this day. Devi Singh's grandfather, when asked whether he wanted the railway to run through Mandawa, refused indignantly, much to the rueful amusement of his descendants. Mandawa basks in a trainless serenity, without the racket of India's floating railway population and the rather arrogant bureaucracy that comes with the state railways system: even if you benefit from the trains, you may be repelled by the levelling, tiring, interminable transience of strangers who pass you with scorn or indifference in their crowded carriages. The Coca-Cola culture, with its transistors and colour television, emerges incongruously into much of India that still for the most part thinks at walking-pace, and worships the Hindu gods as it has always done. Youngsters emigrate for education and for jobs, and few come back into the countryside which they consider backward, in some senses quite rightly. Devi Singhji showed me around his private museum, displayed in the former Audience Hall or Diwan-i-Am. In the three rooms seven generations of royal costume take your breath away, and coins from

Mandawa. Maharajah Keshri Singh in his palace

every period of Indian history include fine examples of Indo-Scythian, Kushan and Gupta minting, as well as state coins of Jaipur and Jodhpur, reminding us that in the 19th century Mandawa had its own currency. The last battle of Mandawa was fought in 1828: relics of it include rusty matchlocks and kukri daggers. Games played locally include *shatranj* (our chess), the variant *atranj* with four extra pieces, *chirbhir*, and *chaupar*, a kind of Chinese ludo normally (except at Fatehpur Sikri) played with dice.

Keshri Singh pointed out an early ceiling painting in the fort, showing a courtesan with a bottle of wine gazing passionately into the eyes of Rajput who clasps her in his arms. We strolled out to the gateway of the castle, two painted elephants being ridden by mahouts. The wooden main gate, immensely strong and thick, is planted high up with long nails fixed with the point outward against charging elephants. Then we hopped into a Japanese four-wheel-drive vehicle and Keshri Singh parped on his horn to scatter fowl, goats and cows from the sandy trail leading behind the castle just about one km to a delightful desert camp complex opened in 1986 and described in *Architecture and Design* (Bombay), November-December 1987. Twelve indigenous-style cottages have private showers and very comfortable rooms with running hot and cold water, each individually designed on a hill to catch the breeze; you can arrange to get there by camel from the Castle. The camp, ideal for barbecues and private parties, is regularly booked at weekends by embassy and business groups anxious to get away from Delhi, 250 km distant.

At three next morning I was woken up by chanting in Rajasthani, and at five by loud laughter outside my room. By six the screeching of foraging peafowl had been challenged by the call of myna birds, and within fifteen minutes radio music had begun to blast out not only within the castle, but from the town far below: there it must have been literally deafening. I will not draw attention to my diarrhoea beyond warning that western stomachs are not immune from attack by strange bacteria, germs, and microbes in any African, Latin American or Asian country, and eating curries if you do not eat them at home is a foolish indulgence. Within a few days in India I was reduced to a limited culinary repertory of bread, plain boiled rice, sweet tea, and salt tablets, plus the occasional potato for dinner and porridge for breakfast, and bottled soft drinks against creeping dehydration. It distresses anybody to lose valuable days in India through stomach disorders, but I was determined not to miss hours in Mandawa, where every *haveli* has its own extraordinary paintings.

Sagarmal Gulab Rai Ladia's *haveli* (1859) is illustrated in plan and cross-section by Wacziarg and Nath in *The Painted Walls of Shekhavati*, from which we can see the fascinating scheme of access ramp, courts,

Mandawa. Ladhuram Tarkeshwar Goenka haveli, *from the gateway*

terraces, and balconies, combining roofed and roofless chambers to ensure comfort at all seasons.

I asked a passing resident for directions to the *haveli* of Ladhuram Goenka (1870), originally constructed for two brothers, and subsequently bisected through the external courtyard by their descendants. A twelve-year-old Hindu boy called Anil and his Muslim friend Salim took me inside, where I found a most intricate range of balconies, all painted with engaging realism and humour, elephants and horses, all with riders, filling arched spaces which are surmounted by delicate friezes, dominant colours being red and blue. Frequent windows fail to interrupt the artist's inspiration, for they are taken into

Mandawa. Ladhuram Tarkeshwar Goenka haveli, *showing frescoes*

account, much as a Venetian would take into account the windows of a *palazzo*. The Chowkhani and Madan Lal *havelis* both date from around 1890; the former again shows the interest in horses and elephants, twin signs of wealth and prestige, whereas in the latter we see a European riding a newfangled bicycle and wearing a helmet: the handlebar is roughly accurate, but in the absence of pedals, the unfortunate cyclist is reduced to pushing along the front wheel by its spokes. The Company School influence appears in the scene of a train passing through a tunnel through a mountain, but the simultaneous rendering of sun and moon returns us to traditional miniature-painting.

The bluish-green Mormoria *haveli* nearby glittered in the morning sun. I sat in the shade to admire the overhanging balconies of another Goenka *haveli*, and Anil took me to see a temple, well and *chhatris* built by the wealthy Goenkas, one of whom is Editor of the influential English-language daily *The Indian Express*. A pimp in the middle of a sandy track offered me for five rupees the services of a simpering, quite pretty girl of about seventeen with a baby at her breast, then in his excitement at the prospect of a client found himself nearly cut down by a pacy camel-cart. Fireworks announced the proximity of the Holi festival. In the pimp's wrathful confusion, as he remained shaking his fist and calling insults on the head of the camel-driver, I disappeared discreetly in the direction of one of the Saraf *havelis*. The Saraf family has become one of the most successful jewellers in Calcutta: a trade always likely to prosper where money is invested for show, to exalt feminine beauty, is subject to fluctuation in value, and to low interest-rates. I was discouraged from proceeding beyond the outside courtyard into the interior, where as usual ladies prefer to confine themselves against the wandering eyes of men outside their extended family. An old man hinted broadly that, as the tap in the courtyard gushed water only for one hour in the morning and another in the evening, I should make every effort to do something about it, but I shrugged in the hopeless fashion of any stranger caught up in circumstances beyond his control. I greeted a man I had met earlier in the bazaar, beside a pipal or wild fig tree outside a second Saraf *haveli*. 'Namasteh!' he bowed. It was the head cook from the castle, who lived in this mansion with his family and was delighted to show me around in his spare time. Rajput beards and moustaches characteristically curled up (Muslim moustaches curl downward) entrance the eye, as do fleeting horses and cumbersome elephants painted *al fresco* with a fantasy of decorative line and colour. A hundred and twenty-odd *havelis* make of Mandawa almost an abode of patricians, though contemporary inhabitants have as it were 'come down in the world' to relate as uneasily to their majestic surroundings as a jeep in the Grand Canyon. Take for example the superb *haveli* of Sneh Ram Harmukh (1905), with huge elephants flanking the doorway, galloping horses portrayed lifesize in the next arches, and above them a frieze of diminutive human figures, scarcely visible. Or the Newatia *haveli* (1937), in which one of the aviator brothers Wright is shown precariously balanced on a plywood platform, while the other stands in mid-air, a lyrical poem to the 'flying ship' known possibly to the artist from a magazine photo.

That evening, after an excellent meal in the Hotel Castle Mandawa. I attended a marionette performance in the floodlit gardens, on a human scale altogether more reassuring than the vastnesses of Bikaner's Lallgarh Palace or Jodhpur's Umaid Bhawan. Mughal arches about two feet high were surmounted a red horizontal strip, then a blue, then finally another red, behind which the marionetteer plied his art. The first item was a sword dance, accompanied by a male drummer, a woman singing low and high squeaks from the marionetteer as if his creatures were denizens of another aural land accessible only to dogs. Then came a crazy camel and rider from Bikaner, followed by a horse with a fiery rider somersaulting like fury, a snake-charmer with cobra, a juggler, Jonah and the Whale's counterparts in Hindu myth, and fighting Rajputs, concluding with a voluptuous dancing girl. The turbanned Rajput kathputli-wallah emerged at the curtain, holding the strings of the dancing girl aloft, to polite applause from the Western audience.

Fatehpur Shekhavati
Out of Mandawa, a road northeast will bring you out to the important town of Jhunjhunu, Bagar and Chirawa, all with more intriguing *havelis*. My road westward to Bikaner brought me to Fatehpur Shekhavati, below a cloudless blue sky, the landscape pricked with *prosopis cineraria* trees, thorny against voracious goats. Fatehpur's ruinous fort of 1521 has decaying, paling Company-style portraits, but you have come here too for the fine *havelis*. A slim Hindu was ironing trousers on the pavement, amid humped bullocks, and the darting, cheeky flight of parakeets. A little local hotel in the centre was opening its doors, and a smiling turbanned Rajput outside twirled his moustache in a style mingling hauteur with contemplation. A sacred cow pissed thoughtfully over his feet. Above the open arcades in the bazaar, faded awnings propped on poles drooped in expectation of a long day's sunshine. A donkey moped by an open gutter, flicking its bitten ears against attacking flies. The *havelis* of Ram Gopal Goenka and Motilal Bhotika both date from around 1850: in the latter a colossal painted elephant is framed by a decorated arch, flanked by a girl playing with a yo-yo and another playing the *vina* above a camel-rider and horse-rider respectively. Symbolic slender women's hands painted in red commemorate women who have committed *sati*, illegal *de jure* but by no means unheard of *de facto* as in the case of a widow at Lohargal in 1972. In the Goenka, a *navakunjara* painting forms an elephant for Krishna of eight *gopis*, an example of the so-called 'Arcimboldo' effect. Ask to visit the Nand Lal Devra *haveli* (1890), with its portrait medallions on the upper walls and ceilings ranging from Shah Jahangir to an Englishman with a little dog. A courtyard of the Singhania mansion of 1870 is painted with a fine composition of four elephants worshipping Lakshmi, goddess of wealth; within, lithographs evoke the taste of the time for voluptuous, Rubens-style beauties. These same lithographs have been copied in fresco outside the Rameshwar Lal Chaudhuri mansion, also of 1870.

Prosopis cineraria *in sand dunes*

Krishna appears cloned many times on the entrance ceiling of the Nand Lal Devra *haveli* (enabling each milkmaid to dance with him simultaneously) and three times around the window-screens of the Poddar mansion of about 1888, adoring cows making a charmingly asymmetrical frieze.

From Fatehpur you can head north to Churu's 18th-century fort, or south to Lachhmangarh. I took the western road for Bikaner which passes through Ratangarh, a stop for a 'Break. Enjoy your Jourany Here' in the words of a sign at the Chinkara Midway rest-house run by Rajasthan Tourism Development Corporation. I had by now become accustomed to the notices offering 'Child Beer'. Culture shock (or was it dysentery?) had taken its toll of a middle-aged bearded Italian, lolling glassy-eyed at a table being dive-bombed by a confident squadron of carefree flies. His hot sweet cup of tea stood unsipped, a rock cake and sugar-bowl the object of keen attention by a train of ants. India cannot be said to steal up on your senses gradually, like a morning mist, but to assault you suddenly and frequently, like monsoon rains interjected by lightning. I needed to sleep long and undisturbed to cope with the flooding sensations from morning till evening, and those who choose to remain unaware of creeping emotional exhaustion may find themselves inexplicably wrecked, gaping with open mouth and attention confused. For one thing, hundreds of people will come up to you to sell you something, show you something, engage you in interesting conversation, or beg. The heat of midday can be dehydrating and ten hours of heat can be enervating: exposure can become unexpectedly serious within a matter of a few hours when the dry atmosphere is cloudless and you are walking for hours. When you feel that India is whirling around you like a hot tornado, just take a seat, like the Italian at Ratangarh, and wait until tranquillity returns.

5: BIKANER

Bikaner — Gajner — Holi at Bikaner — Deshnok

Now the road to Bikaner and the Thar Desert becomes steadily less busy, camels graze acacia and other scrub plants. Villagers live in huts here, and not stone houses. Far away to the left I glimpse the cenotaphs of the former royal family of Bikaner, then on the right the Bikaner Boys' School and Sophia Girls' School. The general air of desolation is due partly to drought and the experience of famine alleviated by Central Government's determination to provide canal irrigation and animal fodder. But it is due also to a population scarcity hardly credible in one of the world's most populous countries. At a time when seventy thousand people can live in Calcutta's 'city of joy', barely twice the area of two football pitches, throughout Rajasthan the average density is as low as a hundred persons per sq km, and in Bikaner district the figure declines to thirty, reducing in Jaisalmer to merely six.

It follows that you can breathe as easily here as in the Sahara, or Kazakhstan. Bikaner itself seems as widespread as Algerian oases in the Kabylie that never really peter out because a watercourse is always close by. On the right the Border Security Force is headquartered. On the left a Temple to Durga, then the Town Hall. Bikaner has the longest 'dry' golf course in Asia, which is to say it has no grass. A large painted advertisement on a wall proclaims 'Pyramid No Doubt About It', leaving me in a quandary: of what is there no doubt? I believe that Pyramids in India are colour television sets, but the ad gave no hint of this. I gratefully sank into an easy chair in the open foyer of Lallgarh Palace Hotel, with a cool Limca, and meditated on the exhortation in large capitals behind the reception desk, 'The highest point of perfection is to do small things in a perfect manner'. I gazed around me in astonishment, for there is not the slightest sign of anything small (if one excludes scurrying chipmunks) either in the former royal palace now a luxury hotel, or apparently in the whole of Bikaner.

Junagarh Fort, with its dizzying array of great palaces, exemplifies the urge to grandeur displayed by Rai Singh, who demolished the original fort and in 1588-93 commissioned a lavish monument worthy of the house of Jodhpur. Rao Bikaji, younger son of Rao Jodhaji and hence without any real hope of inheriting Jodhpur, in the 1480s conquered this

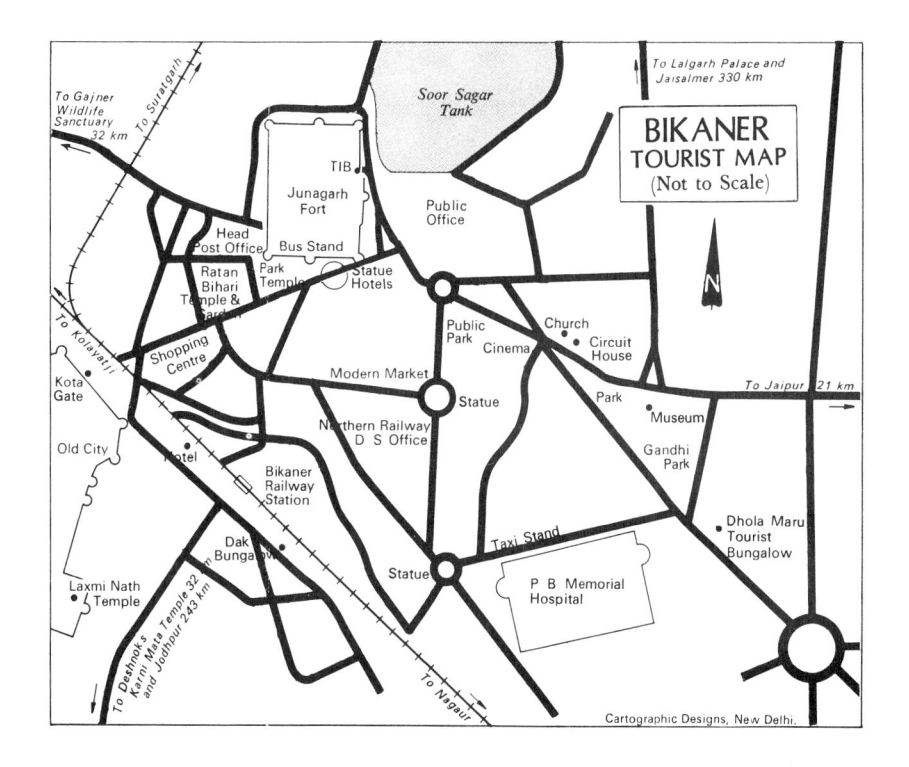

small desert oasis on the trade route between Central Asia and the Gujarat coast, but it was only with Rai Singh's rapid rise to military glory under Shah Akbar at the end of the sixteenth century that Bikaner's star came into the ascendancy. Rai Singh's brother Prithviraj, a scholar and poet, became one of the celebrated 'Nine Gems' of Akbar's court. Interestingly, despite its vulnerable position on a plain, in contrast to Jodhpur Fort's rearing hilltop stronghold, Junagarh Fort has never succumbed in war. Its great ramparts, protected by numerous thick bastions, guard numerous palaces in a palimpsest created almost continuously up to the early years of the present century. The first gateway is Karan Prol ('prol' being a local variant of the usual 'pol' or gate), followed at right angles, to deter mounted invaders, by Daulat Prol and Fateh Prol, but the first true gate is the sunrise-facing Sun Gate or Suraj Prol, considered auspicious. From the gallery, musicians would hail the maharajah's exit or entrance. Royal ladies (I counted forty-one) are celebrated by symbolic *sati* handprints on a left-hand wall by the Karan Prol. The custom of *sati* may theoretically have been proscribed, but how can one finally exterminate among Hindus a practice based on the spontaneous incineration of Shiva's wife (Sati) in her distress at the quarrel between Shiva and her father Daksha? Karan Prol is fitted with horrifying spikes and studs to deter elephant attacks.

Suraj Prol, its name reminding us that the Rathore dynasty belongs to the 'sun' clans as opposed to the 'moon' clans of Rajasthan, is built of yellow sandstone, though most of the rest of the fort buildings are of red sandstone. Two huge red sandstone elephant statues, with mahouts (and disrespectful pigeons aloft) flank the gateway, which opens on to a gigantic courtyard, to the left of which rises the Tripolia, or triple gateway. In *The Tourist's India* (1907), Eustace Reynolds-Ball could write that Junagarh 'is little more than a straggling group of bungalow-like buildings, containing an enormous number of rooms. This is due to the Rajput custom, which makes it undignified for a ruling chief to live in his predecessor's apartments'. You could equally confess that Petrodvorets and Versailles contain 'an enormous number of rooms' and leave it at that, because the range, beauty, and exquisite detail of many of the Junagarh palaces might in a sense be considered on a par with those of Louis's France or of Imperial Russia.

Between the first and second courts rises the huge durbar hall called Ganga Niwas, in which its builder, Ganga Singh, celebrated his golden jubilee in 1937: altogether he ruled for 56 years, being succeeded in 1943 by Sadul Singh, who acceded to the Union in 1949 (thus terminating the State's autonomy) and died the following year. The second courtyard is flanked by Har Mandir, the private temple where the former royal family celebrates births and marriages, where arms and horses are worshipped on the holy festival of Dussehra, and where Gangaur is commemorated. The main deities served by the hereditary priests are Lakshmi Narayan, Vishnu and his consort. The third courtyard has a charming pavilion in a white marble basin, with the Karan Mahal to the south (that is, the left). Named for its builder, Karan Singh (1631-69), Karan Mahal is a public audience hall, or Diwan-i-Am, with fluted columns reminiscent of Shah Jahan's times, but the dado and ceiling decorations are later, by Anup Singh's command, in the last third of the 17th century. Anup Mahal (1690) is his private audience hall, or Diwan-i-Khas, though the elaborate decoration such as inlaid polychrome glass, intricate mirror-patterns, and red and gold paint are the contributions of Surat Singh I (1787-1828). A coronation chamber, it possesses a bolster seat recess, which can be used as a throne. This must be one of the most fantastically ornate rooms in Asia.

Anup Singh was also responsible for the other ranges at the west end, and the Anup Mahal courtyard itself. You can tell by the little projecting balconies or *jarokhas*, and by the pierced screens or *jalis*, that the higher ranges at the west were inhabited by the palace ladies in their *zenana*, for they could see without being seen. The ground floor of the

Bikaner. Junagarh

northern range, or Badal Mahal ('Weather Palace') has a lovely painting of a Dundlod chief from Shekhavati visiting the Maharajah of Bikaner, each with his very different turban. The room derives its name from painted rain near the floor beneath painted clouds, wishful thinking in a land stubbornly arid for so many months every year. Photographs show men standing on nails, wood, swords, and saws, enduring a great deal by the force of faith – or could it be the opium which Rajput soldiers took (and gave their horses too) before engaging in combat?

I leapt up the stairs to the famous eighteenth-century Gaj Mandir, a suite of five rooms named for Gaj Singh (1745-87). A view down into the gardens, once carefully cultivated, is now depressing because so much has been left to run riot: look for the ruined Shiva temple, stables for horses, enclosures for elephants, barracks, and a room where a printing press was operated during the British period. Above Karan Mahal, Gaj Mandir has one central chamber with a raised floor and four external rooms connected with each other by doors but with the central chamber only by windows, except that one (and one only) of the external rooms has steps up to the centre. That Gaj Mahal's courtyard might be covered (for privacy, or during sudden rainstorms) is proved by the existence of round hooks from which to hang a canopy. The bench, tables and box are original, but Krishna's swing is later. The most southerly room is a *shish mahal*, or mirror palace, with gold leaf on the ceiling and a wonderful painted gallery. Each doorway is painted with scenes of Krishna and the milkmaids.

Late 18th-century additions include the west range of Karan Mahal courtyard and Vikram Vilas courtyard, but the Chhattar Niwas was added atop Gaj Mandir, by Dungar Singh (1827-87), to benefit from the breezes, and with a fan operated from without by the punkah-wallah. The short, low Rajput bed is traditional: as a warrior, a Rajput must be able to reach his sword and stand upright within a moment. If you examine the angles, from the bed-head the warrior could recognise whomever was coming up the stairs before they reached the top, a valuable advantage gaining seconds when treachery and jealousy caused fratricide, parricide, and all other conceivable familial strife. The Ras Lila ceiling paintings were added between 1872 and 1887. If the blue and white plates sunk into the wall look familiar, you may well be right: they derive from Samuel Howitt's *Oriental Field Sports*, prints published in London early in the 19th century.

On the way downstairs, note two more painted rooms: Dungar Niwas and (past a former lift) Lal Niwas with a painted ceiling depicting clouds, rain, the god Indra, and angels.

Ganga Niwas has become a museum, with wings from planes shot down in World War I in one room and bodies of planes in another. A staggering range of weapons confirms the predilection in Rajasthan, the abode of kings, for accoutrements of the military life: swords, daggers, kukris, shields, helmets, chain mail and maces. Complex arms include knives which expand on entering the body assailed, and a combined pistol-dagger. The great hall of Ganga Niwas displays the imperial sandalwood throne, sweet-scented and majestic. The architect, Colonel Samuel Swinton Jacob, you will remember from his Albert Hall in Jaipur, but Ganga Niwas is more successful in its eclecticism, cunningly concealing European technology, and absorbing classical columns and arches (in the courtyard without) into harmony with pierced screens that alleviate any sense of heaviness or gigantism. Ganga Singh became maharajah at seven, but did not assume sovereignty until he was sixteen. In 1911 he was made Knight Grand Commander of the Star of India by George V, and represented India at the Treaty of Versailles. Stuffed animals around the wall provide clues to the passion for hunting that joined British and Indians in mystical amity when they could agree about little else. Here is Ganga Singh's ceremonial elephant howdah, but my eye was taken by dazzling examples of the Bikaner school of miniature painting. I tried to reconcile the urge to power and destruction exemplified by the massive double-edged sword of Rajkumar Padam Singh (which an average man cannot lift) with the elegance and almost feminine beauty that such a Rajput would commission as a patron. Contrast for example the miniature of about 1715-20, depicting Kesari Singh on horseback overcoming a lioness, now in Lallgarh Palace and reproduced in Stella Kramrisch's *The Art of*

India (1955) with the slightly later 'Hot Month' attributed to the last years of Ustad Murad and reproduced in Naveen Patnaik's *A Second Paradise* (1985). In the first, a disciplined horse stands its ground at the fulcrum of the composition while the Maharajah spears a leaping lioness through the neck, the formal triangle they make echoed in the landscape behind them. In the second a palette of palpitating reds and oranges evokes parching days of the driest month of the year: *Jyestha*, languishing women in the open pavilion available for unspoken pleasures.

From Junagarh I stumbled into brilliant golden sunshine towards the hurly-burly of Bikaner bazaar. Around a rusty green tin table sat two middle-aged men in stained vests and shirts devoutly shlurping their sweet tea in little glasses and scooping little balls of rice into their open mouths like quick urgent postmen eager to finish off their round by shoving the rest of their mail into the nearest letter-box. Thirty-twenty-four; thirty-one, twenty-five; thirty-two, twenty-six; shlurp, twenty-seven.

'Listen, sir', whispered a youth in a yellow vest and grimy off-white shorts, waggling his body in an obscene parody of a nautch girl, 'I am having very fine package one hundred rupees, best quality, you coming to my room, o.k. we talk.'

'No, thank you'.

'Fine, you are sniffing, you take up nose, good feelings. Only ninety rupees, maybe you are having friends?'

'No, I have no friends'.

'I am finding you many friends, girls, boys, who is counting them all?'

'Not I'. (Do I *really* look so desperate for company?)

'Are you not refreshing by yourself?'

I pondered the answer to this conundrum while the two shovellers stabbed up the last grains of rice from the tin plates, their long nails predatory as curlews' beaks. One burped in appreciation of the wholesome fare, to show his host's ample hospitality. The other attempted by facial and bodily contortion to burp louder as an extra compliment but managed only a deep sigh. His companion straightened his back in supercilious gratification, and they hastened away in the direction of the clock tower I had christened Bik Ben.

Exhausted and overwhelmed – as usual after every few hours in India – I took a passing tonga to the Lallgarh Palace Hotel. Another masterpiece by Swinton Jacob, the palace was completed in its first phase in 1902, and in three further phases in 1926. An example of Indo-Saracenic eclecticism, the great palace is created entirely from local red sandstone, which has aged very gracefully. A slogan in the hallway that could have been extracted from Norman Vincent Peale's *The Power of Positive Thinking*: 'Work Commenced With Perseverance

Bikaner. Lallgarh

and Resolute Determination Ends In Success' is separated by an Air France route map from 'Do Not Guess When You Can Make Sure: Guess In A Careful and Reasoned Manner Only When You Cannot Make Sure'.

The name does not mean 'Red Fort' as in the case of Lal Qila at Delhi and Agra, but 'The Fort of Lall', built in honour of Lall Singh's memory by his son Ganga Singh. The main part of the hotel is Sadul Niwas, where Sadul Singh lived until he moved as Maharajah to Lakshmi Niwas from 1943, and each room is spacious, elegant, even regal, with furniture of the 1910s and 1920s that carry you back to 'art nouveau', Edwardian days, those uncomprehending years when Europe was plunged into chaos and bloodshed. Former Maharajah Karni Singh, the present owner of Lallgarh, lives in one wing and, as a former Olympic clay-pigeon shooting champion, trains a new generation of shooting experts on his own range. The Anup Library of Sanskrit Manuscripts accommodated in Lallgarh Palace consists principally of treasures taken by Anup Singh from Golconda and Bijapur as Shah Aurangzeb's general in those campaigns of 1687, but this collection is open only to scholars of Sanskrit, and the western visitor will roam instead the many atmospheric rooms of the Shri Sadul Museum, opened in 1976. Paintings and portraits of all the maharajahs of Bikaner line the walls near a map of Bikaner State divided into three main physiographic regions: 'Nali' in the north, watered by the river Ghagga; 'Thali', meaning 'pebbles'; and 'Magara' meaning 'dunes'. A substantial library in locked glass cases runs the gamut from local administration reports and statistical analyses to classics like *Kim* and forgotten 'period' writers like Edgar Jepson and Vernon Loder. The English-speaking curator, Raghuvir Modi, showed me leatherbound photograph albums of Sadul Singh's trophies on hunting safaris in 'Tanganyika 1932-3', 'H.R.H. the Prince of Wales' Tour of India, 1912', and 'Royal Visit of Gwalior, 1905', fading sepia records of an age recalled with nostalgia by all those intimately connected with it. Ganga Singh's personal switchboard, once in the vanguard of intercommunications, now sits silent and glum as a Brownie camera. Another melancholy sight: old toys such as wooden ships, wheelbarrow, and rocking-horses. An American lady nudged me in admiration of a gallery of Indian princes. 'Handsome devils!' she sighed in envy of an autocracy not even a billion dollars can buy you in Denver. One room is devoted to the life and times of Maharajah Sadul Singhji and another to Mountbatten, who visited Bikaner in 1948.

Even if you don't choose to stay at Lallgarh, you can visit not only the museum, but the grounds alive with chipmunks and peafowl, blue jays and pigeons, bee-eaters, humming-birds. Lakshmi Vilas has suites for guests, a billiards-room, card room, and drawing-room. Shiv Vilas includes a very large dining-hall, its walls littered with stuffed heads of animals shot on *shikar*. Wide, endless corridors are also pocked with trophies of leopard and tiger, deer and antelope, interspersing old prints and photographs recollecting past glories. Democracy comes very hard in Bikaner: the prevailing wind appears to murmur, 'What has it ever done for us?' and frankly it is hard to find an answer. How has the transfer of princely power to the Government benefitted the average Bikaneri? If you are thinking of land reforms, something has been achieved on paper but not much in reality. The greatest achievement has been in the Rajasthan Canal Project, later renamed Indira Gandhi Canal Project, which reached Jaisalmer on 1 January 1987. Colonisation has taken place, resettling young families and the landless as farming communities in the canal zone running through what was previously arid desert. But very little light or heavy industry has been promoted by the Government throughout Rajasthan, and tourism remains underdeveloped to a level where the independent traveller can truly and enjoyably feel that he is faring forth in terra nova.

I took a tonga, asking the wizened old cabby in grey cotton vest and dark blue shorts to drive me round the bazaar and railway station. *Holi* fever had struck Bikaner already, and tomorrow I should experience the festival of colours for myself, but for today the pandemonium of tambourines, drums, songs and fireworks prepared me for the joyous day. The wheat crop will be harvested, and the age-old fertility festival grips the soul and spirit in Rajasthan just as the pagan Nowruz or New Year festival encompasses Iran. In the noisy, brilliant market-place tides of people ebbed and flowed like the sea, a panoply of colour intensified by the deepening of the afternoon sun. Exotic vegetables and fruit are piled high on carts with chipped paint or none at all, while countrywomen in ankle-length skirts and blouses bare at the midriff haggled with all the sharpness of poverty. Frustrated by the small size of my suitcase, I had to shake my head when offered fine hand-woven cotton rugs, silk carpets, and lacquered lanpshades. I drank a Gold Spot soft drink at a stall while admiring a lacquered camel-hide wall panel, and women tinkling and jangling past in their bangles and anklets. A turbanned merchant sat cross-legged, deep in the study of a thick accounts ledger. A shop with video cassette recorders and Indian-made colour television sets was crowded with the curious, none of whom was actually buying anything. A barber shaped his chin with thumb and index-finger at me meaningfully and I guiltily remembered that in my excitement I had not shaved since yesterday. In the old quarter I passed the exquisite Kothari *haveli*, which may be visited by appointment.

The oldest fort of Bikaner is now in ruins: it is dated to 1488 by Goetz and is thus of Rao Bika's original foundation, but it is difficult to believe that he should have taken so long to fortify his new town after seizing it, and it may be earlier, or replace an earlier mud-brick site. Nearby are two temples dating from roughly the same period: the Jain Bhandasar Mandir, and the Vaishnavite Lakshmi Narayan. The former was established in honour of the tirthankara Parshvanatha and completed about 1514 in yellow Jaisalmeri sandstone. The *mandapa*, galleries and porches in red sandstone are 17th-century additions by Karan Singh. The interior has been charmlessly wrecked by appalling modern paintings. The next Jain temple was Chintamani, finished in the last year of Bikaji's life using yellow sandstone, and enlarged in 1535 in red sandstone. Unfortunately its spire is too short and heavy for the ensemble. In 1583 the Adinatha temple in the Natha quarter was started, as an almost exact replica of Chintamani, with delightful later ceiling paintings of devatas like those we have seen in Chandra Mahal, Gaj Mandir and Sardar Niwas in Junagarh. But the finest Jain temple in Bikaner is that dedicated to Neminatha in 1535, near the original fort. The cella is again surmounted by a high *shikhara*, the closed *mandapa* has lateral doors, and the open *ardhamandapa* is accessible from three sides. There is an inventive use of diamond lozenges, and an exuberance of ornament such as the leafwork scrolls that had been fashionable since Gupta times.

Wandering around Bikaner, I found that private houses by and large followed the model of the royal palaces in style, though they tended to the vertical rather than the horizontal: see the house of Shri Krishnan Das and other homes of the late 16th and early 17th century in Nath Chowk and Banthiya Chowk.

I waved to a near standstill a one-horse tonga under the ruminating control of a thin, wrinkled sage named Nand Lal, with an emaciated nag reminiscent of Quijote's Rocinante. Together, they heaved into motion with me aboard, swaying on the splintered wooden deck towards the railway station, where the Palace on Wheels was standing beside the platform, its tourists away for the afternoon before continuing to Jaisalmer overnight and thus deliberately (some might say wilfully or absurdly) missing the extraordinary desert landscapes of the Thar. Nobody moved on the station platform. Why should they? There would be no movement for several hours: no tickets to sell, no left luggage to receive or produce against a coupon.

I resumed my hard seat at the back of the tonga and asked Nand Lal to trot to the Town Hall, where the Ganga Golden Jubilee Museum (founded in 1937) has been lodged since 1954. You may like the weapons and historic photographs, but the main treasures are the miniatures of the Bikaner School of the 17th and 18th centuries, illustrating the *ragas* and the months of the year; and the sculptures, especially Kushan- and Gupta-era terra cottas from Rang Mahal, Badopal and Munda, and a superb 11th-century Jain white marble sculpture of Saraswati, the beautiful goddess of learning, lithe, full-breasted, holding her book, rosary, water-pot and lotus, each in one of her four slender hands. The carving of her encircling *torana* (rounded arch) is in the exuberant Jain style of abundant narrative detail.

The Golden Age of Bikaner art and architecture comprises the 15th-17th centuries, when Muslim art forms from Delhi's Lodi dynasty and from Gujarat were adopted for secular buildings, and traditional Hindu forms freely assimilated for religious purposes as the Rajput style found its hybrid self-confidence in Bikaner, Bundi and Amber. After Rajah Rai Singh's time however (1573-1612), Bikaner relapsed into temporary provincialism, repeating Fatehpur Sikri motifs and outmoded Rajput painting styles, regaining its artistic creativity only when it resumed political influence under Anup Singh (1669-98) and with Amber taking full responsibility for the introduction of the apparently alien Mughal art into Rajputana. But then a detailed chronological study of Rajput arts will reveal the successive influences of Sassanid Iranian, mediaeval Hindu, Jain-Gujarati, and Central-Indian Muslim manners, so the acquisition of a Mughal aesthetic could be understood as a link in the chain of acquisitions rather than as a colonisation. Intermediate between Hindu and Iranian art, the Rajput mode might be characterised, with reservations in time and place, as lacking in sensuality but compensating in the romantic exaltation of life, love and adventure, with a strong rhythmic feeling, flowing outlines, and simplified colour and plastic surface.

Gajner. Palace

Gajner

On this side of town you can spend the night at the comfortable Dhola Maru Tourist Bungalow, on Major Puran Singh Circle, but an alternative place to stay (which may be arranged in advance at Lallgarh Palace Hotel reception) is Gajner Palace Hotel, though meals may be more difficult, depending on the time of year and the number of people booking. The summer palace of the Maharajahs of Bikaner, it is still used by the family quite often on Sundays, but during the rest of the week it can be seen, and its wildlife sanctuary enjoyed, by visitors in small numbers. Some 30 km from Bikaner on the road to Jaisalmer, Gajner was once the scene of indescribable carnage as the royal shoot 'bagged' thousands of sand grouse in a single day, leading a joker to refer to Ganga Singh as Maharajah of Bikaner 'by the grouse of God'. Nowadays an inevitable sense of decay touches the sandstone palace, increased by the drought that shrivels the area of Gajner Lake. No picnics by order, no parties by order: Gajner seems still a fastness of exclusive royalty. Yet a honeymoon couple may (by arrangement with Lallgarh Palace Hotel) stay in the isolated Shabnam Cottage erected by order of Sadul Singh to overlook the lake. Dr Karni Singh's deerpark and sanctuary for wildlife harbours gazelle, sambhar, blackbuck and nilgai. Wild boars are still found, and a bearer estimated that thirty thousand Imperial sand grouse from Siberia wintered here last year.

I looked up at a brushing in the trees and found peacocks preening. On another pipal vultures brooded, emissaries of carnage. Near the esplanade I was presented with a garland of holed biscuits by a palace retainer under a mango tree, then another brought pale sweet tea and betel nut. Oleander trees dotted gleaming pink around me, and chipmunks, nostrils quivering, stood up on their sturdy little haunches to survey the situation. A myna bird flapped by the water's edge, above a covered rowing boat. Hoopoes and wagtails, blue jays and kingfishers rejoiced in the relief of Gajner Lake, set in such a vast desert. The elegant pavilion with dining-room and sitting-room has overlooked the lake since 1944. For some reason I was touched to find bathroom fittings by Shanks of Barrhead. Sardar Niwas is the original palace, but I explored, under the discreet but beady brown eyes of attendants, Ghalub Niwas, where overflow visitors who cannot be accommodated in Lallgarh Palace can be accommodated in splendid art deco surroundings, with horse prints and hunting scenes by Cecil Aldin. 'Forrard away! Forrard away!' one is captioned, encapsulating effortlessly the ethos of this 'twenties fantasy palace, where ghosts from Noël Coward's bitter-sweet comedies may charleston the nights away to the tinkle of champagne glasses, and the giggles of sweet young things. Then at dusk, the animals come down to the lake to feed, and with a pair of binoculars I could distinguish chinkara and a lone padding jackal.

Gajner. Vultures in a pipal

Around Gajner, look for settlements of the Brahmin landowners from Pali near Jodhpur whose homes have red sandstone carvings influenced by the *bangaldar* niches and late Mughal-style ornamentation of Gaj Singh's time.

Gajner lake, like those of Devi Kund and Kolayat, depends on dams to hold the monsoon rains in the *sar* or depression. The gardens in Bikaner depend on wells. Sur Singhji's great Sur Sagar, or lake of Sur, was surrounded by trees in the 17th century but had no formal garden, so a *char-bagh*, or quadripartite garden, was designed in 1808 by Anup Singh on the southeastern side of the fort: this Anup Sagar, larger than Sur Sagar, and in Mughal style, also depended on an important well.

After a visit to Bikaner Public Park, with its small zoo and equestrian figure of Ganga Singh, one day I chartered an auto-rickshaw for the white marble and red sandstone cenotaphs or *chhatris* of the Bikaner princes at Devi Kund Sagar, 8 km back on the Jaipur road to the east of the city. The princes' final resting-places are shown by their solar symbol; their princesses' by a lotus. The earliest *chhatri* is to Rao Kalyan Mal (1542-71) and the latest to Sadul Singh (1943-9) erected in 1950. In the afternoon I had been invited with my friend Birendra Singh Tanwar to the Camel Breeding Station, where the 'National Research Centre on Camel', as the board outside proclaims, is headquartered. The camel's term of pregnancy is thirteen months and its average life span, at least in Rajasthan, some twenty-six years. The first young are born when a she-camel is five, and an active mother will continue to breed until she attains twenty or twenty-one. Their attendants, Raikas, form a special caste skilled in camel-breeding. The camel farm began in 1960 and has succeeded in improving the strength and health of these finely-adapted creatures. Of the five Indian breeds, the slim Jaisalmeri is considered the best camel for long-distance riding, whereas the Bikaneri, sinewy and strongly-built, is believed the finest beast of burden. With the use of aircraft tyres on wheels, carts drawn by camels can now carry 1,000 kg instead of the previous average of 200 kg. I heard a Raika call 'Je! Je!' to persuade a camel to sit down, and 'Kho! Kho!' to make it get up again. Without the familiar call, a camel will stubbornly refuse to move. A typical camel at the time of my visit cost around five thousand rupees (£250), and a superlative specimen upwards of ten thousand.

Holi at Bikaner

The following day was the long-awaited Holi, when foreigners were kindly requested to cower in their rooms for fear of coming into contact with an authentic Hindu festival, and even modest Indian women kept indoors for fear of being touched by immodest, drugged or drunken men. For Holi is the fertility festival when licence and concupiscence are allowed, Carnival (if you like) after Lent, and streets are empty of traffic, except for those who enjoy spraying others with coloured water, or smearing each other with coloured powders. Young men brandish phallic emblems and sing songs devoted to love and sex. The morning was quite hot after breakfast at eight thirty, so I thought I should prefer to take the $2\frac{1}{2}$ km ride to Bikaner town by rickshaw. 'Impossible', nodded the only receptionist in sight. 'They are too frightened to come outside for japes'. So I headed out for the road to town. A friendly gang of singers and drummers surrounded me and coloured my forehead chastely with red powder. The tonga I had ridden on the day before clip-clopped round a corner and I hopped aboard, with a greeting of

'Holi Mubarak' to the driver, Nand Lal. We trotted past a crowd of boys lathering coloured dyes over a prone drunkard, and then a motor-bike roared up, its pillion passenger with a perfume spray squirting red liquid on to my face and chest.

We were then totally surrounded by a crowd of drummers and youths with plastic bags of purple, yellow and scarlet powders. Each in turn insisted on spreading colours into my receding hair, offering me his head and neck for me to reciprocate. We then embraced and chanted 'Holi Mubarak', 'Blessed Holi'. Forewarned, I was wearing my oldest shirt, disreputable jeans, and an old pair of sandals. So none of the high spirits caused me any distress at all: on the contrary, I felt closer to the Krishna-worshippers than ever, being hugged and kissed on both

Bikaner. Selling powders during Holi

cheeks. Tugging out my handkerchief to clean my daubed glasses, I also pulled out bits of popcorn and diarrhoea pills. Sparrows in the gutter pecked voraciously at the popcorn, but to this day I cannot imagine what they made of the diarrhoea pills. A baker's van had been commandeered by a man plastered in scarlet and green, and was bursting at the seams with revellers falling in and out as they took part, when they remembered, in the hilarious hurling of exploding plastic coloured bags.

During Holi you may be able to see village women dance the *jhumar*; it is also performed at Diwali and to celebrate the monsoon rains during Tij celebrations. The *jhumar* is a pirouetting circular dance, and looks to me as though it too originated as a fertility rite, connected with the turning of the year; it has permeated all levels of society now, and can be seen even in towns, and in palaces.

At the railway station I saw the station-master, poker-faced but grimly determined to act the sportsman, accept from an underling the reverent purples as they trickled gingerly down his neck. My abiding recollection of that magical morning when India fireworked into my subconscious is of a cyclist demented with hashish who pedalled slowly and remorselessly *across* the road from left to right and, hitting his front wheel on the far wall, accepted his fate like a man, picked himself and his bike up again with resigned fortitude, and zigzagged back again. I hope he finally worked out how to escape that particular *karma*.

Deshnok
One of my reasons for wanting to see Bikaner during Holi morning was that the afternoon was to be my last in the city, and I wanted to visit Deshnok, which is to the south but too far east to be visited en route for Jaisalmer next day. The hotel could not fix up a taxe because it was Holi and they assured me that none could be found. Yet with a kind of sublime optimism derived from long experience, I didn't believe that my hopes of seeing the temple dedicated to Karni Mata, with sacred rats scurrying over my bare feet, could be quite so easily dashed, and in fact I just stood at the entrance to Kota Gate and stopped the first person who came along. This gentleman was Jagdish Singh Chaudhury who, yes, did happen to own a taxi and, yes, would meet me at the hotel at 1.30 this afternoon, take me to Deshnok and bring me back for 150 rupees. Yes, he would gladly risk having his taxi assaulted by roughs with syphons. But it turned out not to be like that at all, for in the heat of the afternoon the youngsters had retired to sleep off their high spirits, the girls were out (in shielding numbers) wearing their new spring raiment, and Mr. Chaudhury avoided the odd *bhang*-crazed lunatic with an ease born of amiability and shrewdness. Once away from the town, Jagdish relaxed in his Bombay-made jeep and told me about himself. A B.Sc. at Bikaner's

Nomads on the road to Deshnok after seven years of drought

English-medium Agricultural College, he is 32 and his Hindu wife is also a graduate, though in a Hindi-medium college, which in India is considered less prestigious. He has a small home 'with three cows' in Bikaner itself, and also three sons, plus a new farm in the Rajasthan Canal Project Colony in the desert. 'Please come and stay with my family tonight', he urged, but I apologetically explained that I was due to leave the next morning by bus to Jaisalmer so early that I should inconvenience his family much too much.

Gazelles fled the approach of our jeep on both sides of our road; family-plagued families with their bony cattle tramped sluggishly beside the road to the possibility of better grazing near Jodhpur. Jagdish seemed philosophical: they will return home when the next monsoon rains arrive, and meantime the government makes sure they will have enough fodder to keep their animals alive. The scale of hardship here is minimal compared with Ethiopia, Sudan and the nations on the rim of the expanding Sahara. Furthermore, communications for transporting food and drinking water long distances are adequate, plenty of money for relief is being made available, and there are no conditions of war such as bedevil Ethiopia.

Central to the little town of Deshnok, 32 km from Bikaner, is the temple of Karni Mata, a Charan mystic locally considered a reincarnation of Durga, who was worshipped as a goddess during her own lifetime. It is said that she blessed Rao Bikaji, founder of Bikaner, on his way to found the new city, and prophesied his victory, since the temple has come under the special protection of the Maharajahs of Bikaner; indeed the great silver gates through which I passed were the gift of Ganga Singh.

Rao Bikaji may have founded a simple shrine to Karni Mata during his reign from 1472 to 1504 but Hermann Goetz's *The Art and Architecture of Bikaner State* 1950) proposes that the original shrine was provided by Rao Jetsi, who ruled from 1526-42, and that it is this which was destroyed or overlain by successive enlargements to cater for Karni Mata's growing popularity. As usual, the sacredness of the rats is explained in more than one way, but one explanation is that a women relative once brought Karni the body of her newly-dead son and begged her to restore the boy to life. Giving in to the woman's entreaties, Karni Devi fell into a deep trance and encountered Yama, Lord of the Kingdom of Death. He said that the boy's soul had already been reincarnated and returned to the world of the living in another form, so could not be recalled. Karni refused to accept Yama's explanation, and defiantly said that none of her tribe of Charans, a caste of minstrels, would be governed by Yama, but at death they would enter the bodies of rats, and when the rats died they would reincarnate as Charans. So it is that Deshnok's rats are fed off silver plate with grain and sweets, and protected from swooping hawks and crows by wire mesh fixed across the courtyard. Ramkishan Dhan, the head priest, allowed me to take out a silver dish with fresh water for the scampering rodents, and I saw the kitchen where their next banquet boiled in a cauldron. Of course you have to take off your shoes and socks, as you would to enter any Hindu temple, removing leather objects such as belts or handbags, purses or wallets. But these *kabas*, or sacred rats, are unlike any others you will have seen, for they are neither terrified nor famished, and hence pose no problem to the nervy. Since a human soul may inhabit one or more of these rats, and there is no knowing which, it is religiously prohibited to injure or kill a rat, and anyone so doing must make retribution by

Deshnok. The silver gates of Karni Mata Temple

presenting the goddess with a silver or gold replica of the animal. I found the constant stream of scuttling animals so valified in our society (like harmless spiders and snakes) an unforgettable experience, and I shall never feel able to wince at a rat again. Instead, I shall remember the sanctuary image carved from Jaisalmeri golden sandstone, and the silver low relief of the full-face goddess on a door panel, holding in her right hand her *trishul* (or trident) and in her left, like Judith with the head of Holofernes, the bloodied head of Mahishasura, the buffalo demon, well-fed rats scampering around her feet in joyful freedom.

The fortunes of Bikaner contrast notably with those of Jaisalmer. Under Sardar Singh (1851-72) and his successor, Bikaner flourished.

Ganga Singh (1887-1943) founded the Chamber of Princes, co-sponsored the first parliamentary reforms in British India, and represented India at the League of Nations. Jaisalmer, on the other, lost half its population between 1890 and 1930, and by the 1971 census had lost 86 of its 518 villages, abandoned and deserted. It was not until 1968 that Jaisalmer was linked to Jodhpur by rail.

6: JAISALMER

Pokaran — Jaisalmer — Lodruva

By now, I had read enough, thought enough, and observed enough Indians in their everyday lives to match, however fuzzily and anxiously, the practice of living to Hindu theories. *Dharma*, or the code of social behaviour, instructs a man to carry out his duties as a member of a particular varna, class or caste, in exercising virtue, justice and morality. *Artha*, or the striving for material gain, teaches a man to work for financial rewards, temporal power, the creation of a prosperous household and a well-regulated family. Just as the Vedic scriptures provide the textbook for Brahmins, the priestly caste, so Kautilya's *Artha Shastra* lays down precepts for worldly success in politics of the second caste, warriors and princes, in a way that the Italian Renaissance will later recognise in Machiavelli's *Il Principe*. The third goal of life is *kama*, or the pleasures of the senses, a central text being the *Kama Sutra* of Vatsyayana, though there are many more. As the life of the senses is built into Hindu orthodoxy, the average Hindu seems, and actually is, far less guilt-ridden about sex and fertility than the majority of Christians in the mainstream tradition, though he is punctilious about not showing too much affection in public. The fourth goal of a Hindu's life is *moksha*, or liberation from the cycle of rebirth, a pursuit familiar in Jainism and Buddhism as *nirvana*. Once a man (for Hinduism is dominantly masculine, like Judaism, Christianity and Islam) has fulfilled his *dharma*, or social duties, provided for his family's wellbeing or *artha*, and sated himself with earthly pleasures or kama, he reaches the stage of trying to attain *moksha*, the isolation of the unique inner reality from all past and present influences.

He might, when fifty or sixty, cast aside quite literally his previous garments, his former life, and start to wander as a mendicant, seeking wisdom from travel and from meeting teachers and fellow-aspirants toward *moksha*.

There is something intrinsically valuable about such a willingness to slough off one's inheritance, humbly to go back to nakedness and poverty. I tried, at exactly fifty years of age, to transform myself into such a seeker as I prepared to leave Bikaner for the westernmost city in Rajasthan: the last halting-place before the closed frontier with Islamic

Pakistan. I breakfasted at 5.45 on weak tea with coarse sugar, an omelette, and toast with Bhutanese orange marmalade. Stuffed heads of stag, rhino, tiger and antelope silently reproached me (an accessory after the fact of their murder) from the four walls of Lallgarh Dining Hall.

As my bus sped in the light of dawn towards Jaisalmer, the first procession of girls walked with empty pots to their nearest community well. Later the unmarried girls would worship Gangaur, also called Durga, the consort of Shiva, for the fifteen days after Holi during the period of the waning moon 'till there is no moon in the sky' as Birendra put it. Pink oleanders brightened the road. We overtook trucks bringing

Bap. Women at the salt-pans

sugar cane and hay for cattle from Punjab; they would return laden with salt, wool, goat and sheep from western Rajasthan. Four gazelle crossed the road as confidently as reindeer in Lapland or cattle in Agra. Beyond Gajner, a mining enterprise was in full swing, producing gypsum for cement and plaster of Paris. Water coots scampered into a lake near Kolayat, where the soil is excellent for brickmaking, and a kiln was being lit. A road to the right led to the Rajasthan Canal Project and its irrigated area, a lifeline for western Rajasthan. Around a wayside shrine peacocks screamed and preened, aloof from sheep grazing among tussocks. An eagle, volative Simeon Stylites, stared arrogantly at us from the top of a telegraph pole.

The salt lakes of Bap were too good to miss, and I walked around the rough crust beside the rectangular pans. Water is pumped into the pans, then channels are dammed for fifteen days until the salt leaches out. The local salt enterprise is run by Muslims who lease the pans from the Government. Four hours after leaving Bikaner, our bus pulled into Phalodi, where a great milling crowd of cows had arrived at a fodder station. Some local women had of course arrived immediately afterwards, and started to make dung-cakes for fuel, yet another use for cattle. The Aryans arriving from Iran and Central Asia probably brought cows and cattle-worship with them as a trait of life and lore that would never vanish while Hindus continued to practise the tenets of their distant ancestors. The prohibition on killing cows is of course a well-known economic catastrophe that India bears with resignation, because all common sense must bow down before religious zealots, as in Khomeini's Iran, or Mao's Cultural Revolution in China. An Indian cow, ill fed because of lack of resources, yields less than a tenth of the milk yielded by a Swiss or Danish cow; so that if seventy per cent of Indian cows were gradually to be killed off as useless the other thirty per cent might receive adequate feed and India could afford the techniques to rear a new generation of fit, milk-giving cows. But despite Pandit Nehru's fervent support of such a plan, and despite the rational plans of foreign agencies anxious to finance projects to improve stocks and benefit children suffering from malnutrition, nothing is done.

Pokaran
From Phalodi to Pokaran, poor scrub and flat sand give little encouragement to settlement, and the whole area is so sparsely populated that one might only speculate what could be done if date-palm plantations were founded along water-courses, not far from the roadside. Similar desert conditions in Morocco or Oman do not inhibit the multi-purpose date-palm from flourishing if properly looked after. Past the Hindu cenotaphs on the left and a Muslim cemetery on the right we eventually drew up at the front of Pokaran for lunch. The

bazaar's populace had by now thinned out, with the heat of midday; amid gunny-sacks of spices, shining pans and bright clay pots, crouching figures glanced up without much expectation of a sale. A hoarding advocated 'Adhunik Suitings, Shirtings and Dresses'. At lunch the talk was about Holi in Punjab, where yesterday Sikh terrorists had massacred at least forty people while they were watching a religious play in the village of Kari Sari, Hoshiarpur. Responsibility for the massacre was claimed by the Khalistani Commando Force, a terrorist group alleged to have murdered more than two hundred innocent victims within the previous few months, urging its claim for an independent Sikh state, to be called Khalistan. The massacre coincided with the release

Pokaran. Fort

from jail of five Sikh head priests and forty extremists arrested during the storming of Amritsar's Golden Temple in 1984. The head priests returned to the Golden Temple, where they were welcomed by a gun salute from armed terrorists controlling the shrine as a kind of mini-state where Hindu police and soldiers did not *de facto* enter. Subsequently the State has reoccupied the Golden Temple, but extremists remain at large.

Strategically located midway in the triangle between Jaisalmer (112 km west), Jodhpur (172 km southeast) and Bikaner (224 km northeast), Pokaran also has a modest Dak Bungalow where you can spend the night and obtain a soft drink or cup of tea. My host at Pokaran Fort was young Dilip Singh Rathore, informally dressed like me in jeans and sneakers, though his forebears are very much more eminent, going back to Rao Maldeo of Jodhpur, the city where Dilip Singh's family still resides. The fort itself is four centuries old, self-sufficient with grain-stores and wells, though its charming, cool dining-hall dates from the late 19th century. We visited after lunch the temple in the second courtyard and the former *zenana* upstairs. Architecturally, I preferred this Flower Palace (Phul Niwas) with its delicate, suitably feminine arches and *jali* screens inviting fantasies of slender maidens gazing out in yearning. From the roof of the fort we could see the town, which Dilip Singh estimated perhaps with exaggeration at twenty thousand souls, thirty five per cent or so being Muslims. The early wooden doors still contain lethal spikes against elephant charges, though one cannot easily imagine elephants enduring with any patience the long, hot stages from Jodhpur.

Jaisalmer

And now I began the final road to Jaisalmer, below a pitiless sun, past thinning acacia and listless goats. A cassette of Rajasthani folk music blurted out a man's longing for his beloved, and I experienced that familiar welling-up of uncontrollable excitement that once overwhelmed me on reaching Roman Djemila high in the Algerian mountains, or the faded Oriental exoticism of Portuguese Macão. When I climbed the summit of Ollantaytambo in the Peruvian jumgle, and when I first encountered Leonardo's anguished *S. Jerome* in the Vatican Galleries and realised how inner agitation could be expressed by sunken eyes and straining tendons.

The bus was still twelve km away from Jaisalmer when I made out in the mid-afternoon haze a table mountain ahead, turreted and walled like Ávila, Carcassonne, or the Levantine Krak des Chevaliers. 'No trees interpose their verdant foliage to relieve the eye, or shelter the exhausted frame of the traveller', complained James Tod, though with respect nobody comes to the Thar desert in the expectation of foliage. The city's golden bastions rise like a crown on the head of the limestone outcrop, amid gently undulating but hard pebbly desert folds. No perennial rivers can survive this climate, but monsoon rains occasionally and fitfully fill local reservoirs such as Amar Sagar and Gharsisar, and allow trickles in such watercourses as the Chandan and Sukadi, Kak and Lathi. The walled city is supplied by the wells called Ranisar and Jaislu, in the fort, but other brackish wells in the vicinity have to tap water at a depth of nearly three hundred feet. As well as cattle-breeding, a surprising activity in a land so hot and dry, and camel-breeding, the villagers grow millet, barley and sesame.

Jaisal, ruler of Lodruva (16 km westward from Jaisalmer), conscious that his fortress on the plan lay susceptible to invasion, wandered in the neighbourhood to find a securer vantage point. Local legend relates that he came upon a Brahmin hermit living by the spring Kak, overlooked by the triple-peaked hill known as Trikuta. The recluse told Jaisal that many years earlier the hermit Kak, after whom the spring had been named, had been visited by Arjuna and Lord Krishna, who foretold that a descendant would build a town beside the spring, and a fort on top of Trikuta. Jaisal consequently founded Jaisalmer in 1156, and the inhabitants of Lodruva, now unprotected, moved their residences too, beginning the turbulent history of 'the hill of Jaisal', or Jaisalmer. At the end of the 13th century, the Muslim sovereign of Delhi, Ala-ud-Din Muhammad, seized Jaisalmer from Jait Singh, but Gharsi (1316-61) ultimately persuaded Ala-ud-Din that Jaisalmer lay too far away from Delhi to benefit from the ruler's direct control, and a local Rawal (the traditional name for a rajah in this region) should be appointed as a deputy. Shah Jahangir appointed Kalyan Das in the first quarter of the 17th century, and Shah Jahan commanded Jaswant Singh of Jodhpur to place Sabal Singh on the throne of Jaisalmer, which he enjoyed from 1651 to 1661. Sabal was succeeded by his son Amar Singh (1661-1702), who fought back invaders from Bikaner. A fine garden and reservoir were created in his honour by Akhai Singh (1722-62) are still known as Amar Sagar. Other notable rulers of Jaisalmer include Gaj Singh (1820-46), Ranjit Singh (1846-64) and Bairisal (1865-91), but the strategic importance of the city disappeared with the evolution of Bombay and Surat. We know about Jaisalmer's intrigues during the reign of Rawal Gaj Singh because the British Political Agent at that time was the observant scholar Colonel Tod, who describes how the 15th-century ruler Rawal Chachakdeo managed to seize the heads of hundreds of prosperous Jain families, and agreed to their release only after their families had been brought to settle in Jaisalmer. This early example of a 'brain drain' had the expected result of increasing the city's long-term prosperity, but the less easily foreseen consequence that the Mehta family rose to prominence over the ruling dynasty itself, to the point where the sovereigns' indebtedness led to virtual servility. An

JAISALMER TOURIST MAP
(Not to scale)

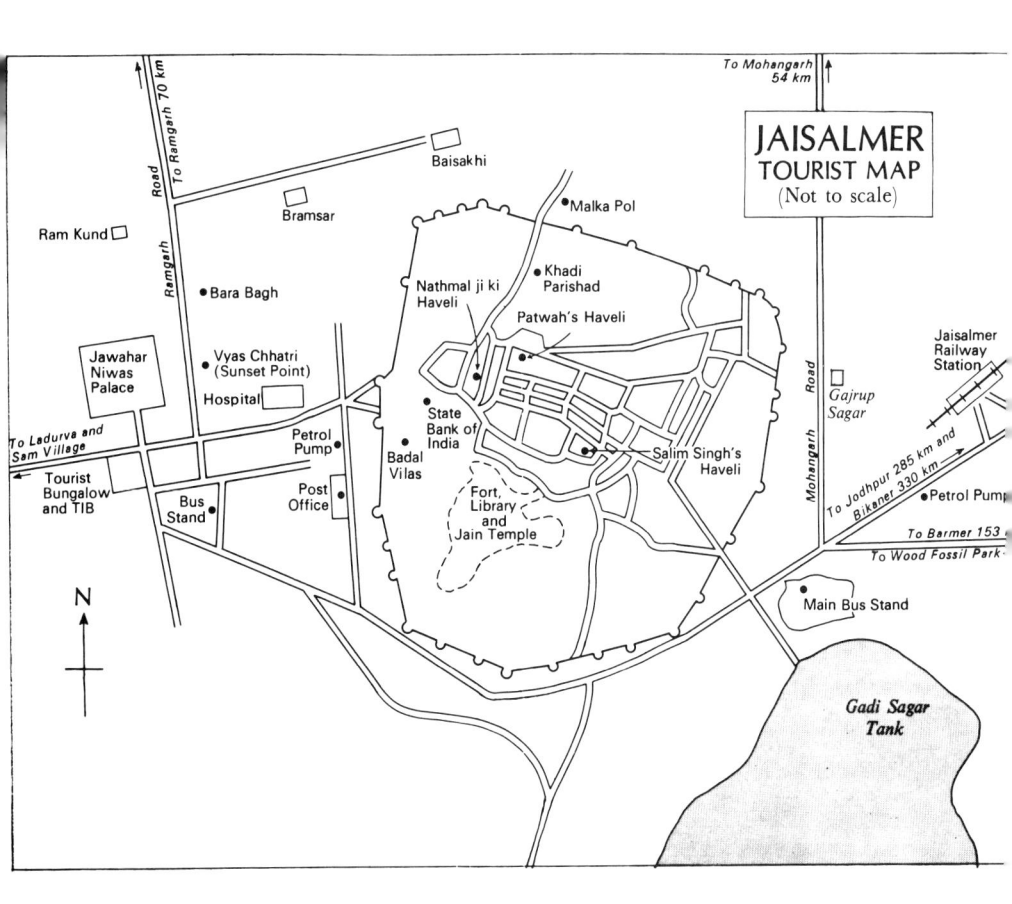

18th-century Prime Minister, Swarup Singh Mehta, challenged a Rajput prince to repay a loan in public, and was murdered for this insult. His eleven-year-old son Salim Singh Mehta took up his hereditary position as Prime Minister with a burning if concealed desire for vengeance. Thus it was that Salim gradually increased his usurous demands on the royal family, imposing higher taxes too on the merchants to increase his own wealth and influence. Thus it was that in the 19th century Jaisalmer lost its power and wealth, as Jain families moved out to escape the impositions of the Mehta, and the impoverished royal family succumbed to humiliation, lacking any money for projects to modernise or industrialise. In 1824, a Rajput stabbed the detested Salim Singh but, lest the wound might heal, his wife made sure by administering Salim poison. The trade route fell into almost total decay, and Jaisalmer sits and dreams today in its golden crown, abandoned by the rest of the world, yet oblivious to its isolation for it has happened not suddenly, by conquest and sacking, but as gradually as the wearing of Jurassic sandstone by the elements. The population of the city was 115,000 in 1891, 88,000 in 1911, 73,000 in 1921, 67,000 in 1931, and today it has fallen to 22,000. Yet all that has happened is that the previous overcrowding has vanished; there is now room for all to breathe. It is not a sad place, like the Cracovian suburb of Cegielnania in February evenings, when everyone has fled upstairs to their crowded high-rise apartments to escape dank smog. Or a Tournai square in late autumn, when shamefaced sallow leaves batten themselves close to an ancient, peeling brick wall. In the depths of a velvet Jaisalmeri night beats the palpitating heart of Marco Polo, having entered the city with his caravan to general amazement before the wooden gates had clanged shut at dusk. I dreamed of the Peacock Emperor with his train of glory, the world and its pendulum bowing before his iridescent majesty.

The place to stay is the Hotel Jaisal Castle, its laconic address being 168 Fort. Phone 62. Cable Jaisal. As simple as that. It has only twelve double rooms, but they are laid out in traditional rabbit-warren levels (each with unobtrusive bath and shower), whitewashed and with superb views down over the the higgledy-piggledy town. I come from northern Europe, where grey skies stain grey stone grey with rain, and like most of my compatriots I see a great deal of sunshine only when I travel. Every desert will dazzle you (it is a property of deserts), but the Western Thar will dazzle you more than most, for sandstone changes to a more golden tinge in these parts, and Jaisalmer radiates gold like the treasury of Midas.

The 12th-century Fort was constructed on Trikuta over a period of seven years, and its bastions rear thirty feet above the rock, itself about 250 feet above the plain. A second stage of construction took place between 1577 and 1623, when Bhim and Manuhar Das added three fine gateways: Suraj Prol, Ganesh Prol, and Hawa Prol, and seven bastions. At this time a second wall was erected parallel to the first but only fifteen feet high, and both Hindu and Jain temples were built within. Between 1633 and 1647 a further ninety-two bastions were added, each with a sentry's window and a platform from which cannon could be fired at approaching enemies.

Akhai Singh's period of strong rule (1722-62) encouraged residents to leave the fort and build their own houses on the lower slopes. He opened the new Akhai Prol near Gopi Chowk and started to lay out streets by trade or profession.

Mulraj II (1762-1820) was responsible for the long city wall protecting the enlarged town with six new gateways: Mal-ka Prol, Gharsisar Prol, Amar Sagar Prol, Biron-ki Prol, and two on the south side now sealed. The great *havelis* we so admire today date from the early years of the reign of Gaj Singh (1820-46), after whom the palace Gaj Vilas is known. Maharawal Bairisal (1865-91) moved the royal residence down the slope to Badal Vilas, where his descendants still live today. The multi-storey Tazia tower was created by Shi'a Muslim *silavats* to imitate the bamboo and paper towers modelled by the Shi'a community to commemorate the martyrdom of Hasan and Husain.

If we stand by Jaisal's legendary well in the old fort palace, the earliest building (dated by Tillotson about 1500) is the Juna Mahal behind the *zenana*, its relatively heavy *jali* screens similar to Hindu craftsmanship for Muslim rulers in Gujarat such as the Begada Tomb at Sarkhej (about 1511).

On each side of Hawa Prol you can see the original *mardana*, with Gaj Vilas (*c*. 1844) on your left. Left again is Moti Mahal, and as you swing on your heel you see a royal temple in front of two ranges of mansions. This is a Temple of Kali or Durga, goddess of destruction, where the traditional horse sacrifice or *arsha puja* was once carried out, and in this square or Chauhata, mass suicide or sacrifice of Rajput women took place: the infamous *jauhar*, which decreed that Rajput women must not risk being captured and ravished, and children not be seized and taken into slavery. They must die or be killed by their own menfolk, who would then don the saffron robe, take opium, and rush out of the city walls to a ballad-singer's death.

Much of the old royal palace is opened only by prior appointment or invitation, but if you have a chance to explore the *mardana*, or men's quarters, look at the fine painted murals of Rang Mahal, showing Jaisalmer, Jaipur and Udaipur, dated probably to the latter part of the 18th century, though the buildings may be older, probably of the 17th century. Giles Tillotson has drawn attention to a peculiarity of so much of Jaisalmeri architecture: a contrast between heavy form and fine detail characteristic not only of the *mardana* here, but also of Suraj Prol and the Amar Sagar Pleasure Palace.

Moti Mahal, like Rang Mahal a construction commanded by Mulraj II, dates from 1813, but has been converted from its original function to a school.

Jains seeking refuge from Brahmanical persecution in the Middle Ages found it in the desert states of Bikaner and Jaisalmer, nowhere more than in this golden city. The austere Jain merchants, so keen to avoid giving pain that priests will wear muslin or gauze over their mouths to avoid inadvertently swallowing or wounding a flying insect that might enter their mouth, created beautiful temples all over northwest India wherever they were allowed to do so, as at Mount Abu, Ranakpur, and here in the 'Sonar Qila', as Satyajit Ray entitled his film set in Jaisalmer.

Jaisalmer. A haveli *in the fort*

Seven of the Jain temples are linked in a kind of protective chain: the eighth, Mahavira Swami, is located near Moti Mahal in the fort. Before entering any Jain temple, remove your socks and shoes and any leather items (it is a good idea for men to wear plastic belts and for ladies to carry plastic handbags in India). In Jaisalmer the Jain temples may not be visited after midday, as a rule. The first of the linked temples is that of Rishabhadevaji, commissioned by the family of the Marwari merchant Seth Sachcha and consecrated in 1479. The Jain *Kalpa Sutra* relates of Rishabha that he was 'clever, of great beauty, lucky, modest and in control of his senses. He lived two million years as a prince, and six million three hundred thousand years as a king'. After neglecting his body for a thousand years, he fasted three and a half days without drinking water, being engaged in deep meditation, and reached the infinite, to adapt the translation by Hermann Jacobi in *Jaina Sutras* (1895). Unusually for a Jain temple, Rishabhadevaji has a ceiling without sculpture but retaining traces of paintings, including a procession of *tirthankaras*. Through a carved archway or *torana* you enter the main hall, where splendid heavenly maidens or *apsaras* may induce feelings not altogether chaste. The central image of the first *tirthankara*, or 'fordmaker', the bridge between humanity and eternity, Rishabhadevaji, inevitably draws one's attention, but a circle of meditating *tirthankaras* on the right presents a physical representation of that chain of tradition enunciated by Mahavira, founder of Jainism, who was a contemporary of Buddha, being born in the mid-6th century B.C., and considered himself the 24th and last ford-maker.

Taking the next flight of stairs up from the same square you come to Chandraprabhuji (1448), similar in style to the Chaturmukha temple at Ranakpur. Beautiful amorous couples, slender and lithe, transform this temple into a brilliant sculpture gallery, but when you ascend to the roof you are overcome by the shimmering grace of the *sikharas*, or temple towers, so different from English church spires. For one thing, the curving line of the graceful main *sikharas* is formed by miniature *sikharas*, and the parapet is itself formed by a number of tiny *sikharas* in a kind of decorative frenzy below a radiant sky.

The next temples to visit are Kunthunathaji (the 17th *tirthankara*) on the ground floor, below Shantinathaji (the 16th *tirthankara*) on the upper floor with its wonderful pyramidal roof decorations spilling over with little affectionate lions not so much roaring as mewing.

Opposite this dual temple complex stands a triple temple complex. The least significant, crowded temple is Shitalnathji dedicated to the 10th *tirthankara*, in 1451. Much more impressive is Parshvanathaji, named for the 23rd *tirthankara*, who is believed to be the first historical figure in the protohistory of Jainism, having lived in the early 9th century B.C. It is said that, having been born into a royal Kshatriya house, he renounced the world at thirty, then for another seventy years or so wandered over India as a preacher, attracting many disciples. His temple in Jaisalmer, consecrated in 1416, dances and sings with slim girls in high relief, every column swirling in an ecstasy of line and form, with *yaksha* sentries and girls at play in every conceivable posture familiar from Indian classical dance. *Vraddhiratnamala* calculates that the temple has 1253 images. A priest in a saffron robe briefly bowed to me as we passed. I was on my way to sit cross-legged for a while before the central image, which was brought from Lodruva to the new Bhatti capital here. A sign reminds you 'Please don't give any gift or presents to any workers here', an injunction which you may ignore. Sambhavnathji (named for the 3rd *tirthankara*) was consecrated in 1420; its superb images were carved by, or under the control of, the master Shiv Deva and total, according to *Vraddhiratnamala*, 604, the best figures being the radiant female dancers and a single male musician showing us the joys of Jain heaven, figures on the ceiling appearing to sway and chant as one's eye flits from one to the next. Below Sambhavnathji is guarded the Jinabhadra Suri Gyan Granth Bhandar, a locked library of unique manuscripts and miniatures. Some are exhibited in display cases outside the locked library, and one may of course ask to see more by prior appointment. This is an opportunity not to be missed, though photography is not allowed here any more than in the rest of the Jain temple complex. You could ask to see some of the five hundred palm-leaf manuscripts, especially the earliest known surviving palm-leaf manuscript from India, Dronacharya's *Oghaniryaktivritti* (1060). Two string-holes, one a third of the way along the centre of the strips and another two-thirds along, are the means by which the manuscript is bound, heavier boards at front and back keeping the strips flat. Paintings fill framed panels between two passages of text on leaf 105, for example, one showing a rampaging elephant, and another Kamadeva shooting an arrow. A series of 13th-century wooden boards also bear Jain iconography, and there are a few miniatures too, notably a charming Jaisalmeri Jain painting of Parshvanathaji cross-legged above the Goddess Padmavati on a lotus flower. The antiquity of the library goes back to 1443, when Shri Jinabhadra Suri rescued Jain manuscripts, secular as well as sacred, from Muslim iconoclasts in Gujarat threatening Patan, Anhalapur and Khambat. In 1951 conservation measures carried out including the preservation of each MS in its own aluminium box in an iron safe.

Even in this lost oasis of the Thar Desert, the Indian devotion to a good story cannot be denied. The Indian equivalent of the *Thousand and One Nights* is the lost *Brhatkatha* or 'Great Narrative' compiled in Prakrit by one Gunadhya before the sixth century. There is an 11th-century Sanskrit recension by Somadeva Bhatta called

Kathasaritsagara or 'Ocean of the Streams of Story' edited by N.M. Penzer (10 vols., C.J. Sawyer, 1924-8) which can be recommended to anyone trying to anticipate or recreate their experiences in India through the complexities of fiction. What could a Mormon or Christian Scientist or Seventh Day Adventist, with their quirky single-strand theologies, make of the untidy conglomeration of Indian ideas and emotions tangled in the briars of approximate history? I, believing in no political or religious dogmas, marvelled at Hindu myths in miniature, Jain cosmology in temple carvings, Rajput chronicles in manuscript, Sikh notions enshrined in white marble *gurdwaras* and Guru Adi Granth Sahib, pseudo-historical fantasies in popular guidebooks, yogic practice beside Pushkar Lake, Muslim traditions in Delhi's Pearl Mosque, pagan rites among the Bhils of Mewar, tribal genealogies concocted to please *kshatriya* rulers, allegories of Shiva dancing and men transmogrified into animals, reincarnation and the rats of Deshnok, explanations more fanciful than the events they profess to explain. You are told the truth that you want to hear and that is what makes it your truth. Opium is available, so are hashish, hopes of reincarnation, rice-wine and illicit sex: any medicine that will cure you of despair is tacitly permitted, any prospect of salvation or of comfort. You do not

Jaisalmer. Salim Singh haveli

educate your wife or daughters because they must not become your equal; because they are uneducated they are not worth talking to, so you spend your time carousing with male friends of the same caste, same background, same age-group, shoring yourselves up against the tide of desolation by regular doses of oblivion.

I asked for a lunch of *thali* at the Treat Restaurant opposite the Salim Singh *haveli*, just for the joy of concentrating on every shift of sunlight touching the golden mansion. Daulat Singh, in his homely guide *Jaisalmer* (1987), suggests that you ascend to the roof of the facing house: 'The house lady is very helpful; of course demanding little money, but a good bargain for this extra ordinary photo'. Salim Singh Mehta was Chief Minister to Mulraj II, and created this remarkable mansion, its intricate balconies flowering high above street level, in 1815. The highest surviving level is known as Moti Mahal (pearl palace) or Jahaz Numa (hanging apartment), with twelve delicate arches on the front and seven on each side, peacocks dancing between the balcony arches. The decoration of this Moti Mahal resembles that of its near contemporary, the fort's own Moti Mahal.

Thematically, it seems sensible to concentrate on other major mansions before losing one's way in Jaisalmer's riot of colour, alleyways like those in a Cairene *suq*, and carts piled with fruit and vegetables. But what can you do? I wandered through the vegetable market near the Famous Tailor, past cows still bearing red smears from the recent Holi festival, admiring all the private house façades and overhanging balconies. A little girl at a niche stone window waved to me as I passed a post office with its letter-box hanging from a hook. A woman crouched over her pans in an outer courtyard, boiling up water on an open fire, one of her sons laughing, his bronzed arms crossed over his bare chest. A chubby-faced little girl with plaits trustingly took my hand as I sauntered past a new portico being carved with all the ancient craftsmanship by white-robed masons. One of them hailed me, and said he was the only member of his family still working in Rajasthan. Many masons and woodcarvers too from Nagaur and Shekhavati have been recruited to work on palaces in the Middle East, in Saudi Arabia, Kuwait, Oman and the United Arab Emirates, and their remittances were benefitting the extended families they had left behind. Steps up to the mansion were powdered purple and red from Holi and gold from the worked stone. In a narrow lane otherwise reminiscent of mediaeval Orvieto, a sacred cow nudged past me, and a family celebrating a wedding tried to pull me inside to take part with carefree hospitality in their celebrations. They had painted on the facing wall an invitation in Hindi to all their friends to participate by a representation of Ganesha the elephant-headed god. Silver and coloured tinsel had been stretched across the street in a mesh above cow-height to attract party-goers. In

Jaisalmer. Vegetable market near Famous Tailor

the absence of pipal leaves, the party had hung propitious mango leaves over the door, and the sound of women singing in jubilation echoed along the alley. I kept glancing down to avoid cowpats while enjoying stone-carving on both sides of the road.

I finally arrived at the remarkable Nathmalji mansion almost by chance, but once there you can have no doubt because its five storeys are, unlike the lower storeys of Salim Singh's, equally finely carved, with intricacy and yet oddly asymmetrical patterns due to the fact that the left-hand and right-hand sides were carved by Hathu and Lalu, two brothers working independently. The mansion was completed in 1885 by Nathmal, prime minister to Bairisal. Nathmalji diplomatically presented the house to his Maharawal, who bestowed the *haveli* on his

Diwan as a royal favour. Scrutinise the motifs and you will find that this apparently traditional edifice is carved not only with elephants and birds, which you might expect, but also with a European horse-and-carriage, a bicycle, and a steam-engine. Lovely balconies seem to swarm up the façade like monkeys up a banyan: all is brilliance and motion as the sun's rays play like floodlights on walls partly shrouded in deep shadow. You remember how caravans from the Central Asian steppes would have brought thoroughbred horses, wine from Iran, silks and pottery from China to barter for Indian spices, rare birds, brocades and jewels. Rich merchants would take their ease on shady balconies overlooking crowded streets in the cool of the evening, as the anonymous poet says:

Galiyo sir gaddal bichhe, amal bate apraman,
Mahal changi drav mansa samajhtiya Jaisan.

(Bedrolls are spread on projecting balconies,
and opium is shared out.
The wealthy reside in beautiful mansions
in Jaisalmer the delicate and radiant)

The Nathmal family rents out their ground floor to shops these days, and I suppose I am not the only visitor to be amused at the oddity of 'Mehta Engineering Company' renting out a shop opposite. A lovely woman in a new rose-pink sari hinted a smile at me as we passed outside 'Famous Haircut Ladies and Jents'. Nearby the Golden Restaurant offered 'golden musht potatoe and porrage' for three rupees. Signs for 'Hotel Fort View' and 'New Jaisal Restaurant' competed with 'Laxmi TV and Radio: Only One Palace of Repairing Philip TV, VCR, Tap and Transister' facing masterly walling (remember Mycenae?) sloping up to the fort.

Exhausted by the incessant pounding of sensations that even the smallest cities in India provide, I returned to the quiet of my room at the top of the fort but, resting my eyes on the bed, I kept wanting to go and switch off the light in the early afternoon because it was too bright. It was of course already off. My front and back shutters were drawn: the light entered only by tiny cracks and underneath the door, yet its concentration yielded so much illumination that I could see to read and write without any electricity.

My stomach still churning, that evening I took only soup and poppadums, plain boiled rice with cauliflower and omelette, halwa and coffee to keep up my liquid level and restore enough energy for a chat with Nihal Singh of Bikaner, owner of the new Himmatgarh Hotel, who commissioned the well-known architect Pillu Modi to design this new de luxe hotel, with 40 circular cottages, in November 1987. In 1988 a swimming-pool was added. Other places to stay include the comfortable Narayan Niwas, just inside Mal-ka Prol in the northern sector of the walled city; the new Moomal Tourist Bungalow in the chain of Rajasthan Tourism Development Corporation, emulating the old style of building; the royal Jawahar Niwas; and the modest but clean Neeraj near the Post Office. New enterprises of one sort or another are springing up for the nascent tourist industry, and it may be possible to obtain rooms from time to time in the Badal Vilas royal palace or in the traditional Shri Nath mansion near the Jain temples. Near Jawahar Niwas are the economical Dak Bungalow and Tourist Bungalow.

I felt ready for the surprise of the Mansions of the Brocade Merchants, or *Patwon-ki-Havelis*, created between about 1805 and 1855 for the five sons of the brocade merchant or Patwa called Guman Chand. It is in fact one vast mansion divided into five more or less equal self-contained homes, so that each family could enjoy a measure of privacy and the extended family could together counter any threat to their security. The house opposite, obscuring the extraordinary view of this patrician palace, was demolished and its owner compensated by order of Indira Gandhi after she visited Jaisalmer. The view from the Patwon Gate down the cul-de-sac to the six-storey *haveli* is unforgettable, like a delirious Oriental Venetian palace in Marco Polo's

Jaisalmer. Women cooking inside a haveli

wildest dream. Each is entered by steps with slabs for resting at intervals, the main halls being at a level much higher than the road outside to protect the floors from desert dust. The *mol* or drawing-room has a ceiling which protects the vestibule from summer heat, but the main feature of these beautiful homes is their fleet of sixty-six *jarokhas* or balconies, a maritime term used to convey the sense of curved sails in motion with fine *jali* screenwork, and oriel windows placed at different heights and depths, an effect totally different from the idea of a façade in western terms, which would be flat and even. The ground floor of each mansion served as a warehouse for merchandise such as embroidery, brocades, ribbons and other rich textiles. The family later dealt in opium, and with wealth derived from this turned its many hands to tax-collecting and banking. The first son of Guman Chand, Bahadur Mal, took up high position in Kota state; the second, Sawai Ram, in Jhalarpatan state; the third, Magani Ram, in Ratlam state; the fourth, Jorawar Mal, saved the exchequer of Udaipur from ruin and settled at Indore; the fifth, Pratap Chand, remained in Jaisalmer where his son Himmat Ram sponsored the lovely temple of Adishvara at Amar Sagar. The first floor has fragments of the original paintings, and two *havelis* are adapted as souvenir shops, while part of the remainder has been converted into a museum and may be visited.

Dawn in the desert exerts a distinctive spell, whether at Kufra in Libya, or Petra in Jordan, Nefta in Tunisia or Palmyra in Syria. In Jaisalmer, thousands of birds filling invisible trees produce a chorus worthy of Fez. Dogs whine and howl in apprehension of another day, for they are more badly treated in India than cows are pampered. Each cur with its tail between its legs looks as though it fears for its life and limbs. Cockerels try to make themselves heard above the bedlam. Pigeons, cooing privately, make only a local impact.

I had negotiated with a jeepdriver called Soman to make his four-wheel-drive vehicle available for me during the whole day, since the environs of Jaisalmer are packed with interest in several directions. We started at the artificial lake of Gharsisar, where rainwater is carefully conserved during the monsoon. Begun by Maharawal Gharsi and completed, after his death, in 1367, the reservoir is skirted by four Hindu temples and numerous cenotaphs. The ceremonial gateway was offered by a 19th-century royal courtesan called Tila to the people of Jaisalmer as a goodwill token. The royal princesses were so incensed at her brazen gesture that they threatened to pull the gateway down, but Tila promptly added an image of Krishna as Satya Narayan above the gateway and so rendered it sacrosanct!

From here we visited Amar Sagar, another reservoir 7 km away from the town dating from 1740, when Maharawal Amar Singh established the Shivaite temple. A bony cow and desperately thin goats grazed what they could. Three Jain temples are also well worth visiting, especially the Adishvara of 1928. Nearby buffaloes were tied to a water-wheel, a leather bag emptying the precious liquid into fields trying to grow a vegetable that looked like spinach. Amar Sagar had completely dried up during my visit in March, before the monsoons were due, so I was able to stroll across the bed of the lake to a new Jain temple dedicated to Parshvanathaji. Masons from southern Rajasthan and Gujarat greeted me respectfully as I praised their delicate craftsmanship.

Lodruva

We sped on to the previous capital of Lodruva, 10 km farther, having stopped to give a lift to a leatherbound ancient of about seventy, wrapped in loose rags like votive wishes on holy trees in Armenia. In justification for gesticulating at us, he explained that only one bus connects Jaisalmer with Lodruva daily, and he had missed it by about five hours. We crossed the once-rushing watercourse Kak, making out the ruins of the palace of Moomal on the bank, then drew up at the Jain temple of Rishabhadevaji, the first *tirthankara*, whose symbol is a bull, the meaning of his name. This bull is (not by coincidence) also the animal sacred in Shivaism, which derives from the pre-Aryan Indus Valley civilisations known at Harappa, Mohenjodaro in present-day Pakistan, and Kalibangan north of Bikaner.

The Jain temples of Lodruva antedate those of Jaisalmer, just as the city itself antedates Jaisalmer, but its ruins are all the more touching for the silence caused by the suffocating centuries of drifting sand. I wandered over mounds yet to be excavated: the paradox is that lack of funds and insufficient trained personnel to carry out a wide-ranging and scientifically successful archaeological project here as elsewhere in India will guarantee the best possible results, in that practical techniques and theoretical knowledge advance so quickly that sites excavated only a few decades ago are considered almost 'spoiled' by ignorance. The longer we wait, the better the results are likely to be.

Lodruva's major Jain temple, to Parshvanathaji, was destroyed in 1152. We see today a reconstruction commissioned in 1615 by Seth Tharu Shah, with additions of 1675 and 1687. Its *torana dwar*, or main archway, must be the most ornate in Rajasthan. Interestingly, the temple guardian is not a Jain at all, but a Rajput. I removed my shoes, left my camera with the attendant, respected the stricture 'Use of eggs, meat and vine is strictly prohibited here', and began to explore the temple in the approved direction, that is to say clockwise, like the Hindu swastika (and contrary to the Nazi swastika). We have already seen the original idol, or *mulanayaka*, of Parshvanatha in Jaisalmer fort; its place has been filled by a later Gujarati image of Parshvanatha in black stone, with a multi-hooded serpent canopy.

The Rangamandapa is surmounted by an octagonal pyramidal roof. A fortification wall reveals anxieties felt by Jain communities throughout the ages in a potentially or actually hostile Hindu or Muslim environment. A temple in each corner of the compound is dedicated to a different *tirthankara*: Rishabhadevaji in the south-west, Sambhavanatha (of the horse symbol) in the north-west, Parshvanatha in the north-east, and Ajitanatha (of the elephant-symbol) in the south-east, all dating from 1618. A tree once believed sacred grew in these grounds, and when it died it was replaced by a lifelike sculpture in an alloy of eight different metals, making an 'eternal tree' or *Kalpavriksha*, which would symbolise the tree of enlightenment. The 'leaves' of the tree are protected from vandals by a mesh.

Near the tree you can see on the main temple's outer wall a low-relief carving on a stone. Every summer a black cobra 'which has lived there for four hundred years' comes out ten to fifteen times, and lucky the man who catches sight of it!

A few km further on you arrive at the typical desert village of Rupsi. You can distinguish the wealthier of the women at the well because they use expensive, infrangible brass pots (some two up), whereas their less affluent neighbours continue to use time-honoured terra cotta waterbowls which, all will doubtless agree, keep the water much cooler in these hot dry wastes.

As Soman took me back to Jaisalmer, he pointed out the minor Hindu

A village near Jaisalmer

temples. The most significant is situated in the fort area: Maharawal Vairisi's Lakshmi Temple of 1437. But I should mislead the unwary if I were to suggest that Tikam Rai near Hawa Prol, or Ratneshvar, or Surya or Rajeshwari were worthy of close examination. Instead we made for the 'Great Garden' or Bara Bagh, eight km to the north, where rulers of Jaisalmer have been cremated, with cenotaphs raised in their honour, since the times of Maharawal Jait Singh, in 1554. An equestrian statue of Maharawal Bairisal in marble shows his date of death as 1898; another equestrian figure depicts Akhai Singh (1722-62). Three wives who committed *sati* are commemorated on the right under a dome of golden sandstone. On the bare hill, earlier *chhatris* lie partly derelict, for the tradition is that the royal family never visit these cenotaphs except for ceremonial occasions. A dam here fills with rain during the monsoon; during the rest of the year pilgrims and visitors can refresh themselves with water pots kept full by an attendant. The mango trees round about belong to the royal family, but are leased to local families.

Returning to the city from the north we stopped at the *chhatris* of Vyas Brahmin, many of whom live in Bikaner and Jaisalmer, a familiar sunset view towards the fort, where camels transport visitors every evening from Narayan Niwas Hotel. There little boys wrestled with each other to hold my hand, sell me fossil shells, and beg for rupees: it was all very goodhumoured. A jeep screeched up to disgorge several ladies in unnecessary hats and a great deal of gaudy jewellery that should have been confiscated by the Imam of Good Taste. After restlessly taking each other's snaps in a spate of high-pitched English-language noise, one of them picked up something from the outcrop on which I was sitting crosslegged. 'What kind of rock is this?' she demanded of her swarthy dragoman, a patient Jaipuri in a khaki suit. He examined it politely for a few moments and after only a moment's hesitation returned it to her: 'We call it dried camel-dung', he replied.

The Fossil Park is reached 17 km on the road south-east to Devikot and Barmer. Since 1961 the site of a forest of great deciduous trees has been protected by the state. The forest, over 175 million years old, can be found near the village of Jodha Akal, 3 km off the main road.

About 44 km to the southwest of Jaisalmer, a jeep (or bus) will bring you to a very different ecosystem: that of the sand dunes of Sam. You will be offered a camelride, and if you decide to accept, stay *very close* to your guide or *raika*, for only he can guide you through these treacherous loose sands which has sucked unwary goats and cattle to their gruesome death by suffocation within a few minutes. Since there is no communication with Pakistan through Rajasthan (all borders have been closed since the last war), the Desert National Park of three thousand square km suffers no through traffic. It is political and military cul-de-sac which (with appropriate legislation) has resulted in the

Jaisalmer. The hill city seen from chhatris *at dusk*

protection of rare species such as the chinkara, the smallest Indian antelope, blackbuck, and the nilgai. You may not glimpse desert cat, desert hare or desert fox, and the crested porcupine is nocturnal. But you may well see the pintail sand grouse in winter and other seasonal migrants, such as Imperial sand grouse, demoiselle cranes, bee-eaters, eagles, falcons and harriers. The Houbara bustard is outshone by the spectacular Great Indian Bustard, once on the verge of distinction but now reviving to a level of a thousand. Those of us who believe that every living thing has the same right to live as humankind will be grateful to the Bishnoi people who live in many parts of western Rajasthan in villages where they identify closely with every aspect of creation, including trees and shrubs. A 15th-century saint called Jambhoji laid down twenty-nine (in Hindi, *bishnau*) commandments, including vegetarianism, and his followers today practise his tenets with great, praiseworthy devotion. If you have never seen a great desert, Jaisalmer's Desert National Park will be a revelation, its sand dunes whirling and whistling in times of high wind.

A word of advice: if you come to Jaisalmer by train, you will wake up in the morning already there, for it travels from Bikaner, very slowly, by night. Instead, try to arrive by car or bus, so that the shock of Jaisalmer catches you fully awake, and longing. I am ecstatic that my destiny has allowed me to walk around the dusty lanes of Jaisalmer instead of sending letters there to strangers asking: 'What is it like?'. 'How does it feel to gaze out on the fossil forest of Jodha Akal when you have felt no rain on your cheeks for seven years?' 'As you stand, lips flaking with heat and drought, before the Patwon fivefold mansion, what is it that you hear, and see, and feel?' Now I know.

7: JODHPUR

Osiyan — Jodhpur — Mandore

Leaving Jaisalmer by a seven o'clock bus one morning I arrived at Pokaran at nine, and there, stretching my legs in the pin-prick brightness of the maturing desert day, I was invited to join a group of three Indian Army officers as they sat round a table with a pot of tea. They had come from Delhi for artillery training in the desert, and were keen to find out my impressions of their country. What can one say, that will not seem naïf or gushing, not even a quarter-truth? I spoke of the gifts that have transformed such a vast nation from a multitude of warring tribes into a democratic fabric. There are appalling wounds inflicted by Tamil separatists, by Sikh separatists, by sectarian extremists in many places and at many times, but I quoted lines by G.M. Carstairs engraved on my memory from twenty years back. 'A Hindu pictures a quarrel as typically a drama with three actors: two contestants and a peacemaker. And it is not the protagonists but the peacemaker who is seen as the victor in the dispute'. This explains the key function of a figure like Gandhi in India, as opposed to a de Gaulle in France or a Franco in Spain or a Wellington in England. We take martial figures as our icons; Hindus take as their leading cult figure of our time its leading pacifist. The Indian Army can be seen in a similar light: its rôle is not that of a NATO Alliance war machine; nor that of a Warsaw Pact force. It is one of the instruments used by an All-Indian Government to ensure that the inevitable riots due to racial or religious or political conflict will not terminally injure the nation-state.

Osiyan

The desert spreads far east of Pokaran. At Dechhu you have the choice of proceeding directly to Jodhpur on the main highway through the strange *kraal*-type villages of Agolai, their round huts surrounded by stone slabs and protecting their animals from wandering by hedges of matted acacia branches; or heading off for the marvellous temples of Osiyan.

Osiyan (on the railway linking Jaisalmer with Jodhpur) is renowned for its Jain temples, but apparently no Jain family lives there today, and indeed the once great city is now demographically little more than a

Walled village near Agolai

phantom of the desert. It owed its importance in the period between the 8th century and the 12th to its position on trade routes, where Jain merchants were given free rein not only to carry on their commercial activities, but also to build temples of stunning architectural and sculptural quality. D.R. Bhandarkar's study 'The Temples of Osia' appeared in the *Annual Report, 1908-9* of the Archaeological Survey of India (Calcutta, 1912) and is well worth consulting even today.

The temples can be visited in two clusters. Eleven temples, some Hindu, can be found at the limits of the modern village, while the remainder, all later, stand on a hill to the east of the village. Among the earliest of all mediaeval Rajasthani temples, they are remarkable for both variety and vitality, both elegance and originality. Three early temples, exquisitely small, are dedicated to Harihara, that is to say the union of Vishnu with Shiva. In these fresh and exuberant temples, raised on plinths, with their sculptures profusely covering almost every surface, one can sense the dawn of a new architectural and sculptural age, which will pass its lessons on to future masters, for instance in the complexity of the porch pillar sculptures.

At Ranakpur we shall enjoy the Temple of the Sun, or Surya, and here at Osiyan a 10th-century counterpart may be equally neglected but is considered by Percy Brown (who illustrates it, in his *Indian Architecture (Buddhist and Hindu Periods)*, Bombay, 1942) 'in some respects the most graceful of the entire group'. Most spectacular of all is the Jain temple to the last *tirthankara* Mahavira, dating to the late 8th century, with repairs and additions of the 10th. The *mandapa's* pillars are original, and the second porch or *nal mandapa* (*nal* means staircase) are later, so you can see the stylistic development. The *torana* or entrance archway (with lovely nymphs sculptured in a manner not considered conducive to religious meditation in a more puritanical religion) and the superb *sikhara* roof both date from the 11th century. The Pipla Devi has a large *sabhamandapa* (assembly hall) with thirty pillars and dates from the late 10th century.

The other group of temples is dominated by the temple to Sachi Mata or Indrani, wife of the god Indra who chose her from a selection of other goddesses because of her voluptuous attractions. Originally of the 8th century, Sachi Mata was amplified in its extant form in the mid-12th century, a period given away by the complex spire with added turrets called *urusringas*. We are aware of the different Greek 'orders' which have made such a decisive impact on western architecture, so it might be appropriate to see the 'vase-and-foliage' motif of Osiyan pillars as a kind of Indo-Aryan 'order'. A good example of this style can be seen in the Mahavira temple's porch pillars, where the artist introduces it in both pillar and base. You might also compare the lavish decoration of Osiyan doorways with the spirited, imaginative use of decoration in French Gothic cathedral porches.

Jodhpur

On the road to Jodhpur, and before we experience the majesty of its rock stronghold, the bustle of its bazaar, and the extraordinary elephantine bulk of Umaid Bhawan Palace, let us dip into the legend ascribing the origins of Jodhpur's Rathore clan of Rajputs to Rama, seventh incarnation of Vishnu. The Kachchwaha clan of Amber and later Jaipur claim descent from Rama's son Kusa, whose family is alleged to have founded Gwalior.

The Rathores narrate how their dynasty reigned from 470 to 1193 at Kanauj, near modern Kanpur in Uttar Pradesh, but fell to Muhammad Ghuri's Muslim army on the rampage from Afghanistan. After a period of wandering, described in Tod's *Annals*, the Rathore dynasty split from fertile Mewar and seized Marwar and its capital Mandore in 1453. The usual hermit, encountered by the young Rao Jodha (born in 1444), suggested that Rathore fortunes might more effectively be protected from the great outcrop called the Birds' Nest than from the leafy, watered but essentially vulnerable Mandore. Thus in 1459 did Rao Jodha start the Chintamani Fort, the stronghold later to be known as Meherangarh.

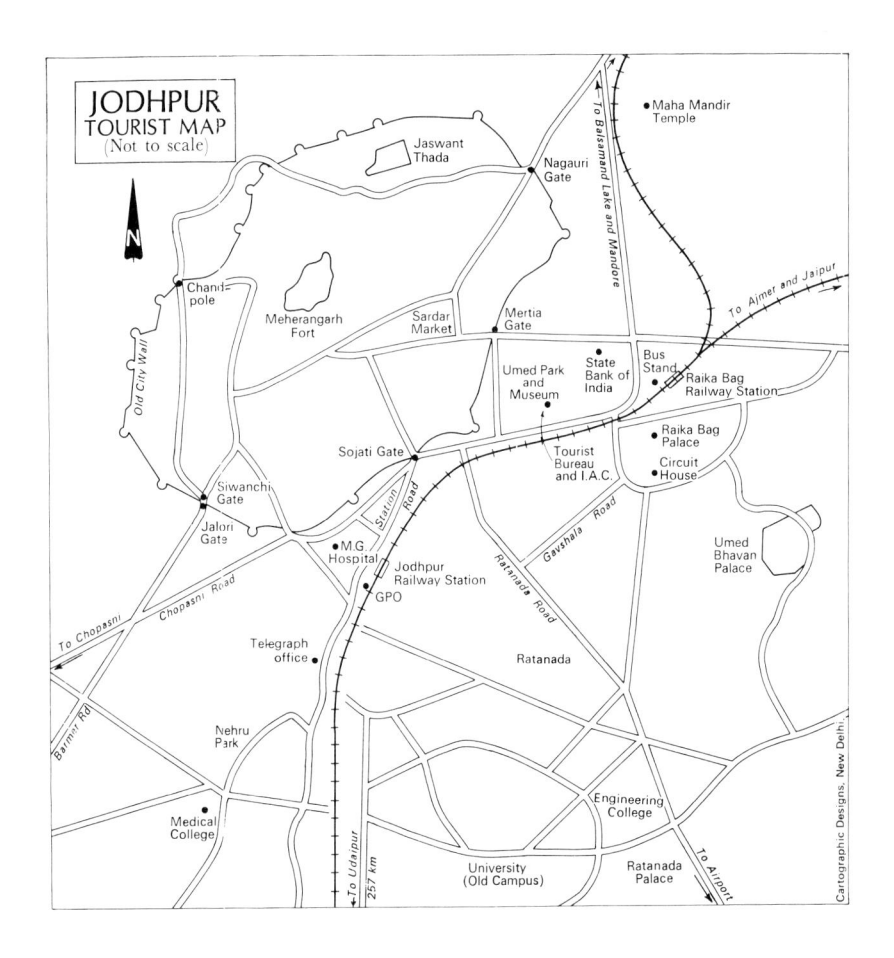

Since the visit to Meherangarh takes so long, it is a good idea to take an auto-rickshaw for the climb up the rock, though on the return journey you can walk down a flight of steps which will bring you out near Sardar Bazaar. By taxi or auto-rickshaw the road swings round from Sardar Bazaar to Nagauri Gate, then past Jaswant Thada to Jai Pol, in Hindi 'Victory Gate', dating from the triumph in 1808 of Man Singh (1803-43) over Jagat Singh of Jaipur, so the name was assumed in punning mockery. Now the fort's main entrance gateway, Jai Pol is a magnificent vantage point from which to survey the city wall, snaking

Jodhpur. Meherangarh from below

brown across the hills amid which the fort sails like a great brown battleship in stormy billows. At one time only Brahmins were allowed to paint their houses blue, and all others were white, but now blue has been adopted as the native domestic pet of Jodhpuri households, though flecks of white roofs like foam remain visible everywhere you look. Five hundred metres above the plain, Meherangarh rises sheer on bare rock. Its protective walls range in thickness from seven to twenty-four metres, and in height from seven to forty metres. Defensive towers at frequent intervals combine to puzzle the most ingenious besieging general. The western gate is called Fateh Pol ('Fateh' being 'victory' in Urdu) and was constructed by Ajit Singh in 1707 to commemorate his recapture of the fort from the Mughals.

Jodhpur. A city view from Meherangarh

Jai Pol's doors are war booty won by Abhai Singh (1724-49) from Ahmedabad. Note the pump which was built to bring up supplies of fresh water from Gulab Sagar, a crucial factor during sieges. The *chhatri* of Kirat Singh commemorates the courageous death of a Rajput in the struggle against Jaipur. Lakhna Pol (otherwise known as Dod-Kangra Pol) is a 16th-century gate made by order of Rao Maldeo (1532-62), bearing dents from cannonballs fired by the invaders from Jaipur: the wall extending between Jai Pol and Lakhna Pol is a 19th-century addition. Rao Maldeo was also responsible for the next gate: Amrit Pol, beyond which (on the left) you can make out the original entrance to the fort of 1459. Two holes on a stone slab took wooden logs which formed a provisional barrier.

The gatekeeper, smiling tolerantly at another awestruck Englishman, waggled his curved sword to prove his entitlement to my wonder, and with his other hand held up a hookah. He blew some smoke lazily into the warm, clear air and it vanished into the centuries-old red sandstone. Loha Pol ('Iron Gate') dates from the 15th century, though in the 16th Rao Maldeo added the façade we see today. Maldeo was a great leader who extended Marwari territorial power to Sind in present-day Pakistan and Gujarat the fertile. Carved hand-prints symbolise the royal *satis* who gave themselves to death on their husbands' funeral pyres, impressing their hand-prints in red paint on a wall or door. Ajit Singh was accompanied in death by no fewer than six queens and fifty-eight concubines in 1731, and tradition dies so hard that a royal *sati* occurred in Jodhpur as recently as 1953, a hundred and twenty four years after British law had forbidden the practice.

Instead of entering the palace complex on your right, glance at the temples: the Rathore family temple dedicated to Nagnechiji, an idol brought to Marwar by Rao Dhuhad in the early 14th century. Chamunda Devi's temple has an idol of Durga brought by Rao Jodha from Mandore in 1459, but the building itself, accidentally destroyed in a gunpowder explosion in 1857, was reconstructed by Takhat Singh (1843-73). The building between the two temples, Salimkot, served formerly as a prison for rebel nobles.

'What happens nowadays to noblemen who offend?' I enquired, for in a society still effectively dominated by caste and privilege it is inconceivable that a single prison system could encompass all wrongdoers. Mr. Sagat Singh of Jodhpur explained that nobles are held in first-class prisons with all comforts; in second-class prisons graduates are confined with no work to do; in third-class jails non-graduates are forced to work to earn their meals and lodging. 'We have many tragic cases of graduates who cannot find work and to avoid starving commit some petty offence in order to be fed and lodged at the state's expense. All this could be avoided with a welfare state like you have in Europe, but the size of our population and our gross national product makes a welfare state just pie in the air, dear friend.'

You will be serenaded by one or more musicians of the Mirashi caste, whose pipes and drums traditionally kept soldiers alert at times when their concentration might have been alloyed with pleasure. From the ramparts (vainglorious with famous cannon such as Gajnikhan won by Gaj Singh from the Pathan rajah of Jalor in the early 17th century) a view extends far across the city of Jodhpur to the serpentine walls and far beyond to Umaid Bhawan Palace and the airport.

More than two thirds of the royal palace complex was taken up with the *zenana*, for the rulers demanded large numbers of wives and concubines, all of whom had servants and retainers. Retainers even now in royal livery keep watch over the palaces, which have become a superb museum requiring a whole day for study and contemplation.

Entering Suraj Pol ('Sun Gate'), you ascend the stairs to the Moti Mahal, or Pearl Palace. Moti Mahal courtyard forms part of the *zenana* and its light feminine *jali* screens in the superb balconies or *jarokhas* is a continuous refreshment of the senses, in a way comparable to Bikaner's Anup Mahal courtyard, both dating to the 1670s. After the death of Jaswant Singh in 1678, the Emperor Aurangzeb seized Jodhpur in vexation at the repeated turning of Jaswant's coat, and the Rathore clan did not recover Jodhpur until Ajit Singh's accession in 1707, when a new building phase began.

The first object before you is the red sandstone coronation seat or Sangar Choki, where every ruler after Jodha has been crowned; its white marble facing was added in the 1750s by Bakhat Singh. You then come to ranks of royal palanquins, and silver howdahs, one of which was a gift by Shah Jahan to Jaswant Singh I in 1657. Other howdahs are draped with traditional flags of the nine saluting Rathore states of earlier times, eight of them offshoots of Jodhpur itself, founded by sons of Rao Jodha. These eight are Bikaner, Kishangarh, Idar, Ratlam, Sitamau, Sailana, Jhabua, and Alirajpur.

Climbing steps to the next level we emerge into a third courtyard with two rooms forming the Khabka Mahal (literally 'sleeping' palace) with pseudo-Ionic capitals and sandalwood roof, raised by Ajit Singh in the first quarter of the 18th century. The first room, Dipak Mahal, was used by the Prime Minister of the former State; the second, Chandan Mahal, was used by the ruler for consultations with visiting nobles and his own ministers.

A European mural of 1893 (by the wandering painter A.H. Muller) portrays the hero Durga Das, who in 1688 conveyed from Delhi the posthumously-born son of Jaswant Singh during Aurangzeb's reign and protected the young Ajit Singh until he could be set on the throne of Jodhpur in 1707, doggedly maintaining the Rathore dynasty's hold on Marwar.

A long gallery, Jhanki Mahal, is called 'glimpse palace' because it was a viewing area through whose screens ladies of the *zenana* could enjoy processions and other functions. The space is devoted to a series of royal cradles, one (powered by an electric motor) having been presented to the Maharajah in 1948. Elaborate gilding and painting characterise these splendid cradles.

Moti Mahal is dated by Sagat Singh, former Director of the Meherangarh Museum, to the reign of Sawai Rajah Sur Singh (1595-1620), but Giles Tillotson is convinced on stylistic grounds that it cannot date before the time of Ajit Singh (1707-24). The Mughal throne from the time of Shah Jahan was presented by Aurangzeb. Here

Jodhpur. Meherangarh. Khabka Mahal

is the Diwan-i-Am, or general audience hall, glittering with coloured glass and with a mirror ceiling; from five unobtrusive openings royal ladies could observe the splendour of ceremonial. The triple band of niches sadly no longer flicker with flames from oil lamps: at very little cost what a charming vision they could again conjure up!

Reverting to the third courtyard, we can explore Sardar Vilas, with its examples of wooden carving, particularly lacquer and ivory inlay on doors, and a marble table given by the ruler of Kabul. Next door the Umaid Vilas houses an enthralling gallery of miniatures, mostly of the Jodhpur School. Amar Das created a fine portrait of Maharajah Pratap Singhji, and here too you can find a resplendent equestrian portrait of Maharawal Jaswant Singhji of Jaisalmer. Mughal and Deccani delicacy is allied with a strong line, bold colour and simplified design. Above Sardar Vilas, Takhat Vilas (added by Takhat Singh, 1843-73) was frescoed with stories from the Krishna-Lila and the legend of Dhola and Maru. Its ceiling is supported by great wooden beams on corbels. A punkah fan was used to ventilate the room, which has a patchwork carpet.

Between Umaid Vilas and a long picture balcony comes the Shish Mahal, or Mirror Palace, possibly a slight disappointment after the exhilaration of similar effects at Amber and Bikaner, but still of great interest, with murals of Krishna, Shiva and Parvati, Brahma, Durga, Rama with Sita and Hanuman, Ganesha and Vishnu.

Amkash Mahal is a museum of regional folk instruments, with an effective tape presentation that allows you to hear them in concert as you look at them. A side flute (*banshi*) and a front flute or *algoja* can both be seen in the countryside today, though I never saw a conch shell or *shankh* being played. A good range of drums represents one of the most enduring of Rajasthani instruments, like the trumpet or *karna* and a sophisticated string instrument called *deshi sarangi*. Sparrows attracted by the music cocked their inquisitive heads at us, hoping for crumbs. Ajit Vilas is a costume museum especially rich in Jodhpuri turbans, possibly the longest in all Rajasthan. Shepherds keep their mirror, comb and tobacco in their turban, and it can be a lifesaving device for in the countryside around Ranakpur it is long enough if tied to a bucket to drop into a well and haul up for a precious drink of water. Here is a figure of Gangaur in silver, and pearl shoes that belonged to a concubine of Gaj Singh I (1619-33).

As I descended steps I saw a tennis court netted to prevent stray balls from flying over the castle walls. The royal cenotaph of Jaswant Thada (1899) is best seen from this vantage point. We have come to the Flower Palace or Phul Mahal, added by Abhai Singh (1724-49) with a clear European influence as a private audience hall, or Diwan-i-Khas. This room alone is worth at least an hour's close study, for the murals added by Jaswant Singh II (1873-95), and the rich painted and gilded ceilings. Thirty-six paintings on the frieze delineate emotions of the Raga-Ragini, the thirty-six musical modes which allowed artists their freest expression. A pictorial royal genealogy and portrait gallery stresses the importance of lineage and tradition in a state, like Udaipur and Jaipur, fiercely jealous of its privileges and autonomy. Even after the important Rajput Hindu states had apparently united to rid themselves of feared Muslim hegemony, internecine stuggles weakened them collectively and individually, so that a strong East India Company could force Jodhpur to sign a treaty in 1818 for Jodhpur's 'defensive alliance, perpetual friendship, protection and subordinate co-operation'.

Below Phul Mahal, Daulat Khana is distinguished by a magnificent red silk and gold brocade Mughal tent made for Shah Jahan in the 17th century, and captured from Aurangzeb by Jaswant Singh I. Daulat Khana's time machine whirls us back to periods of heavy locks and ornate hookahs, maharanis' vanity boxes and carpet weights, coin boxes (before paper money became acceptable worldwide) and wine bottles that on military campaigns would be wrapped in wet cloths to keep safe and cool.

An armoury reminds one of Jaipur's Sileh Khana in its variety and

Jodhpur. Meherangarh. Phul Mahal

selection of the choicest items, such as the sword Khanda made for Rao Jodha and weighing over seven pounds. Here are swords made for Tamerlane, ancestor of the Indian Mughals, and for Shah Akbar, curved daggers and battle axes, shields covered with precious gems, and sword hilts made of jade. Other sword-hilts conceal a tiny pistol...

I took lunch in the cool, informal museum restaurant, choosing 'poch egg on toste' with 'patato fingus chip' and 'tamoto egg (soup)', the whole costing the equivalent of about a dollar and a half in U.S. currency, still allowing me change for a postcard and a chilled drink. Scholars should know that the fort also accommodates a very fine library: the Maharajah Man Singh Pustak Prakash, with about three thousand manuscripts in Sanskrit, and two thousand in Hindi and

Rajasthani. Account books and other archives devoted to the royal household offer a detailed picture of the exotic and almost incredible ritual of life in Jodhpur Fort before Independence.

By prior arrangement, parties of visitors can arrange a live recital of folk music in the 17th-century Rang Mahal, a hall with frescoes and an elaborate wooden ceiling.

Jodhpur struck me as harsh, recalcitrant, enduring for all the wrong reasons, with the tenacity of vengeance, keeping its secrets by a law like the Sicilian *omertà*, a mafioso euphemism for 'silence'. Though Rajasthan is the land of bloodshed and violence, unreasoning fealty to an ethic going back to tribal Europe (like the warring Gegs and Tosks of Albania), Jodhpur has exceeded the other states in obsessive victory of the strong over the weak. The very name of Jodhpur state, Marwar, is a corruption of the former Marusthan: the 'district of death'. It haunts one to remember the reign of Udai Singh (1581-95), who possessed twenty-seven wives and concubines, but chose to add to their number a virgin daughter of a Brahmin. James Tod recounts, 'As there was no other course by which the father could save her from pollution but by her death, he resolved to make it one of vengeance and horror. He dug a sacrificial pit, and having slain his daughter, cut her into fragments and, mingling therewith pieces of flesh from his own person, made the *homa*, or burnt sacrifice to Aya Mata and, as the smoke and flames ascended, he pronounced an imprecation on the raja: "Let peace be a stranger to him! And in three hours, three days, and three years, let me have revenge!" ' The Brahmin then leapt into the flaming pit, and the ghoulish events were narrated to Udai Singh, who fell prey to endless remorse, expiring as expected at the appointed time.

As everywhere else in Rajasthan, in Jodhpur I wandered as far as possible from the great forts and palaces. Down lanes where carpenters sawed and hammered I found children watching wide-eyed as their mothers and aunts picked over mounds of spices while wary shopkeepers glanced hither and thither like parrots in a cage. Effortlessly I floated back to adolescence, when nobody counted those hours in school holidays I passed in daydreams, allowing my imagination the liberties of Dante's paradise and Bosch's hell. That woman in a blood-red sari wearing silver bangles and a yellow head-shawl: she must be another of my great mothers, like Sita or the South Indian Maryamman, goddess of epidemics, who would give me rice if she found me starving, or bandage my arm if I grazed it while falling under a bullock-cart near her side. I penetrated her soul, with its deep anxieties, its brief satisfactions, while a cross-legged Rajput beating brass in the next alleyway deadened his emotions in a fiery clashing like the cymbals reverberating above the battling Pandavas. A cow excreted in the middle of the road, dropping her turds between cyclists ringing their

Jodhpur. Bazaar. Women and girls in procession

bells and auto rickshaw-wallahs forcing their passage through a constantly warring mass of two-way traffic in a lane intended for only one. I stood stock still in an archway; behind me an ironmonger had baited hooks with pans and tin bowls to catch customers. I dislodged for scrutiny aluminium, enamel and, yes, plastic utensils so much lighter for women to balance on their heads. My head ached with the effects of India on my senses: rhythms of colour, shrillions of schoolgirls in a battered, honking bus, syllables of spice (coriander, peppers, tarragon, thyme) shaping into sentences of aroma: garlic, curry, and steaming piles of shit.

One shock after another was driving me pitilessly towards emotional fatigue. India, like the sea, is a concatenation of present participles: it is yelling, clashing, running, haggling. Eastbourne, St. Tropez, Hawaii, Pattaya, the Serengeti: these are simplicities I can manage. But India is glistening with the fragility of a lotus-pool splashing with monsoon rain, stinking with the helpless tyranny of slums, gleaming with the grace of an exquisite Maharani. The death of old men happens quickly, suddenly and ubiquitously, while new life is burgeoning uncontrollably beyond 800 million like an express train that warning signals are powerless to stop. Who is to say how soon it may crash?

The road back from Meherangarh will bring you to the Jaswant Thada Cenotaph of 1899, all previous rulers having been cremated at Mandore. The main cenotaph is built like a temple, its marble coming (like that of Agra) from quarries near the village of Makrana, not far from Jaipur. Jaswant Singh has been credited with miraculous healing powers as a demi-god; believers (among whom during my visit was a wizened old lady, muttering under her breath, with her eyes closed most of the time in a semi-trance) put money across votive strips on the floor. The marble walls are so thin (at some points barely six inches) that light can penetrate into the temple-tomb despite the absence of windows. A small reservoir can be found nearby, because ritual bathing after cremation is a religious duty. If you cannot deposit the ashes in the Ganges, then you have to visit another holy place, such as – in Rajasthan – the lake of Pushkar, near Ajmer.

Mandore
Mid to late afternoon is the best time to visit Mandore, with its sense of lost kings and kingdoms, preening peacocks and darting chipmunks, crows and sparrows. Parrots fizzed their rainbow colours among tamarind trees; langur monkeys crouched and swung in the banyans. Mandore is the English spelling of this cool, shady paradise: before the founding of Jodhpur by Rao Jodha it was for many centuries (from the sixth to the fourteenth) the capital of Marwar under the name of Mandavyapur. The rulers then were Parihar Rajputs. An unsteady langur finding it difficult to stand upright may well have been really drunk, for that is the effect of eating the fermented fruit of the *jamun* tree common at Mandore. Rao Chanda of the Rathore clan married a Parihar princess and settled at Mandore. The old city lies ruined all around you, above all on rocks above Mandore, where you can find an 8th-century Gupta temple and a monument to Rao Nahur, last of the Parihar rulers.

Two laughing urchins sprang and leapt, with a kite bobbing and feinting like a shadow-boxer in the gym. How different the scene of noise and scrimmage from the aristocratic scene of a Girl Flying a Kite in a Jodhpuri gouache of the 1760s which can be seen in London's Victoria and Albert Museum! A pale damsel in a flowing cream full-length robe raises her right hand gracefully against a reddish-brown background, the kite artfully filling the top left-hand corner with cream-and-brown stripes mimicking the distant folds of her dress.

A similar sense of height and motion arises from contemplation of the six ascending *chhatris* of Rathore, from the *dewals* of Rao Maldeo and Udai Singh (16th century), to those of Sur Singh (between them, so out of order), and Gaj Singh and Jaswant Singh I (all of the 17th century), culminating in the imposing, graceful Shivaite pyramidal temple of Ajit Singh (18th century), sullied with the blood of sixty-four wives. The ecumenism of Rajasthan is nowhere better understood than here at Mandore, where Hindu Rajputs of the Rathore clan created architecture in a mingling of Shivaite and Buddhist styles, with Jain carving in the earthy brown stone, and the Bheru temple is dedicated to a pre-Aryan god symbolised by a dog, which is why Indians even now do not kill dogs. A single low shrine to Shiva dateable to the first of the shrines or even earlier, near a sacred banyan, is adorned with Shiva's lingam and a Nandi bull. The gardens all around are restless with life and colour: half wilderness, half tended paradise, everywhere rampant with thrusting life. Even the stones themselves seem to heave with a pregnancy peculiar to fertile India. One of these enormous rocks has been carved out into a sculpture gallery which I found vapid and crude. It is the so-called 'Hall of the 300 Million Gods' with hyperbole typical

Mandore. Chhatris

of Hinduism. Actually, the figure is given as '30 crore' because the crore is what everyone outside India thinks of as ten million, just as the lakh is a Hindi number corresponding to foreign 'one hundred thousand', and very economical it is too.

Mandore's heroes and deities are somewhat mixed up in stone as in legend, local saints such as Mehaji, Gogaji (repainted very recently) and Harbuji seeming to take a situation somewhat above themselves in the exalted company of Shiva, Krishna, Rama (with Sita, Hanuman and Lakshman), Surya and Brahma. The style is folk art, with naive shaping and colouring, and the ambience is chauvinistic, pressing forward for attention the Rathore guru Goswamiji (here known colloquially as 'Gusainji'), and Chamunda, tutelary goddess of the Rathores, and another incarnation of Durga. The period is round about the time of Ajit Singh (1707-24), and the gaudy vulgarity of the so-called shrine reminded me of the hand-painted movie posters, like that in Jodhpur then advertising *Mardon Wali Boot*, a Bombay film of ritualised glamour, stylised dance movement, dubbed songs of vacuous sentimentality, mindless brutality, and a simpering love-story ending in empty bliss, in other words (like the Hollywood *Dallas* or *Knots Landing*) divorced from all semblance of human complexity.

I headed back for my hotel in the dusk. You could stay at Ghumar Tourist Bungalow, excellent value for its moderate price; the new Ratanada International near the airport if you wanted somewhere away from the town; or at Ajit Bhawan, near the Circuit House, a former royal palace from which you can arrange an unforgettable day trip to Bishoi villages. The Raika Bagh Palace Hotel near the Circuit House is another possibility, as is Karni Bhawan on Defence Laboratory Road in Ratanada district. But I determined to stay at the Umaid Bhawan Palace, with its 7 suites and 59 other majestic rooms. Interestingly, I did not feel as if I were staying in a palace at all, for the multiplicity of corridors and stairs gives the air of an officers' barracks. Every palatial hotel in Rajasthan differs from the rest, but the Umaid Bhawan Palace strives to create an oasis of opulence out of the human scale and, if you feel uncomfortable loafing about like an ant in a cathedral, you might prefer such noisy but authentically Indian hostelries as Adarsh Niwas (near the railway station) or Arun Hotel or Galaxy House, centrally located near Sojati Gate, for a tenth of the price you would pay at Umaid Bhawan Palace. But wherever you stay you can for a small payment use the underground swimming pool at the Umaid Bhawan, wander in its gardens, and enjoy its fantastic museum: both the regular daily sightseeing tours arranged from the Ghumar Tourist Bungalow include the monstrosity. It was created by H.V. Lanchester, twice Vice-President of the Royal Institute of British Architects, who should have known much better, for its position on Chittar Hill necessitated the transport of half a million donkey-loads of earth merely to fill in the foundations. There was no water supply, and a 19-km rail link had to be specially built to bring the reddish sandstone from Sur Sagar quarry. Altogether, over four thousand labourers toiled from 1929 to 1944 to provide the royal family with a pink elephant that not surprisingly, since Lanchester had worked with Lutyens, resembled the Viceregal Lodge in Delhi. According to Shobha Kanwar Balji who, as a member of the royal family, ought to know, Maharajah Umaid Singh moved in with his five sons, one daughter and retinue in 1943, and at his Christmas Party in the new palace that year invited a thousand men of the R.A.F., U.S.A.F., and Australian Air Force. Umaid Singh laid down a large airport which served as an international landing point up to 1939, a staging post for K.L.M., B.O.A.C., Air France and other companies. Balji, as she likes to be called, is the granddaughter of Pratap Singh (1845-1922) who was thrice regent. She detested restrictions of life in purdah after her father had insisted she be educated in England, as he had been. Her father had been brought up in a vicar's family in Sussex, and Balji was given an Italian governess. She stayed in Switzerland with a weakly brother for seven years and there she learned French, Italian, and some German. She believes she was the first aristocratic lady in Rajasthan to receive an education, so she found it even more galling to return to the old familiar purdah. She has become reconciled to her lot, as a significant go-between in the Umaid Bhawan Hotel, interpreting India to the rest of the uncomprehending world, for whom purdah is not a matter of pride, but either shame or ridicule. Balji expresses herself entirely content with her life in Jodhpur, where she is respected for what she is as much as for what she does. She would not choose to live elsewhere.

Balji showed me the extraordinary museum, with a durbar hall painted with peeling murals from Indian legend by an itinerant European painter of no great ability called S. Norblin. Two leopards in the next courtyard have been stuffed in mid-snarl. The library sports such familiar titles as Stella Kramrisch's *A Survey of Painting in the Deccan*, Kinsey's *Sexual Behaviour in the Human Male, Mr. Punch in Mayfair*, and Hervey's *Cameos of Indian Crime*. Of course, everything is locked and nobody actually *uses* the library, but it is revealing to note the headings over the bookcases: Biography-Literature-Travel, Sports, Animals, and Shikar, that is to say big-game hunting. Over all the trapped tomes heads of captured animals seem to threaten more in death than they did in life: a lion, a ferocious black bear. The sumptuous collection of clocks and watches, many presented to Umaid Singhji, has been the subject of a separate catalogue. Another room of glass and ceramics surrounds a portrait of Major His Highness Raj Rajeshwar Maharaj Dhiraj Shri Sir Umaid Singhji Sahib Bahadur, G.C.I.E.,

K.C.V.O., Ruler of Marwar State. The Diwan-i-Am displays the Ruler's selection of rifles, daggers, flintlocks and matchlocks. Rajput paintings on the walls include gentle Jodhpuri works with flat green and yellow backgrounds. On the table you can see likenesses of Gaja Singh, the present Maharajah, his father Hanwant (1947-52), his grandfather Umaid (1918-47), and Gaja Singh at his coronation. I visited the gents' toilet and was astonished to see 'tasteful' 'Thirties photographs of nude women on the walls: I was assured by ladies staying at the hotel that their toilet held no such delights. I chatted with Shiv Hazari, the hotel's general manager, to the strains of 'Vienna Woods' from a hidden loudspeaker. The slightly dejected open-air tennis court lacked its net, but was sharply floodlit, while the badminton court, with net, lacked floodlighting. Employees were leaping maladroitly on the volleyball court, losing points rather than winning them. A crow on the watered lawns was tearing out a pigeon's entrails. The croquet lawn, groomed for action, looked lonely, and a crowd of merrymakers descended on a huge buffet table at the entrance to the open-air theatre. Shri Hazari showed me the health club (open 6-10, 4-8) and the basement swimming-pool, with peeling blue-green frescoes so relaxing after the ardours of heat and dust. Rivalry between Jodhpur and Jaipur (not to mention Udaipur) remains so keen that I was reminded by three different individuals, without bringing up the subject, that the High Court of Rajasthan meets not in the capital of Jaipur but in Jodhpur.

I took dinner with Mr. Hazari in the Marwar Hall, where musicians were playing the *vina* and drum under a canopy. Foreigners were ignoring the *raga*, and speaking very loudly to make themselves heard over each other. I murmured that the evening *raga* was played with great beauty, and Mr. Hazari screwed up his eyes in pleasure and nodded in agreement. The beautiful durbar hall is vaulted, and the space below reminds you of a London rail terminal: St. Pancras or Euston. Soup was brought to the table by retainers of the former royal family, then we were able to choose from European or Indian-style buffets, finishing with dessert from a table at the opposite side of the hall, and tea or coffee brought by a retainer. Above the two musicians, the heads and front legs of two tigers had been mounted, ready to pounce on the unwary. They face two buffalo heads at the other end of the hall, near the lobby. The screech of peacocks on the lawns penetrated even this conversazione musicale: the grounds cover fifteen acres and peacocks seem to have colonised every last square metre. Altogether, it is alleged that up to a million square feet of marble can be counted in this immense palace. I was shown the extraordinary art-deco-style Maharani Suite, with a bathtub in the centre carved from a single block of pink marble. My own room was 403 (with a telephone numbered 402), its bath still slightly dirty from the last resident, and two tiny prints on the walls its only decoration. I paid $50.00 a night, which is very low by current American standards, whereas the most expensive royal suite would have cost me $154. You can book an exclusive trip to Jaisalmer in one or two royal railway carriages: one accommodates up to six persons, and the other up to 14. The former has three compartments, a bathroom, a lounge, and a kitchenette; the latter seven compartments with wash-basins and two bathrooms. You can arrange with Nahar Singh at the Umaid Bhawan Palace to travel to Jaisalmer (by night, that is the snag) in the Mahajarah's carriages (cables: SALOONS, phone 22316, telex 0352-022). Your itinerary is fixed as follows. On the first day, you leave Jodhpur railway station at 9.15 p.m., arriving at Jaisalmer by 7.15 a.m. on the second day. Breakfast, lunch, tea and dinner are all served in the dining saloon of the train kept permanently at Jaisalmer. Morning and afternoon excursions are arranged by camel, camel-cart, or jeep. Mr. Hazari told me that up to 65 % of Jodhpur state revenues came from the railways.

Next morning peacocks under my window woke me up and I gazed across early mist from the lionesque tawny hill to endless distances over dry plains. The air of Rajasthan seems to me, however unfoundedly, to be thick with the human spirit, its strength and its resignation, its searingly hot days, and its nights until seven years ago beating with monsoon rains. It seems to have endured more history and legend than it could reasonably be asked to bear, and to pant with exhaustion at the thought of more. Of recent years the failure of seven successive monsoons has weighed down the spirit with even more heat, drought, and apprehension of worse to come. When morning, afternoon, evening and night are against you, tired black eyes screwed up against the blinding midday sun seem to be appealing for mercy from Surya, the sun-god who has elbowed his way back into reckoning above the wiles of Shiva, Vishnu, Brahma and Indra. In Rajasthan there is no mother Ganges to worship; we can only plead for mercy to Surya that he shall not take away our lives as well as our crops.

After a hearty breakfast, I was whirled in ten minutes by a noisy auto-rickshaw to the Clock Tower of 1912, and the Sardar Bazaar. The population of Jodhpur is reckoned close to 320,000, and I felt most of them were running, shouting, sitting, shopping or selling in Sardar Bazaar, despite the absence of cars. Near Sojati Gate, amid cacophonies of eardrum-shattering intensity, I stood for a minute or two entranced by a cross-legged shopkeeper whose depth of immobility cannot be explained to people brought up with Bruce Forsyth and pocket calculators. Before entering by Sojati Gate, I swung up by rope-ladder to the first-floor bookshop above Rupan Jewellers: Rajasthani Granthagar, specialising in books about Rajasthan. I bought their own publication by Jagdish Singh Gahlot, *Rajasthan before Second World*

Jodhpur. Jewellers and bookshop

War (1986), Dinesh Chandra Shukla's *Early History of Rajasthan* (Bharatiya Vidya Prakashan, Delhi, 1978), Hirlal Maheshwari's *History of Rajasthani Literature* (Sahitya Akademi, Delhi, 1980), and Ramdev P. Kathuria's *Life in the Courts of Rajasthan during the 18th Century* (S. Chand, Delhi, 1987). I wanted to see the Talaiti Mahal, which according to Giles Tillotson 'appears to be the oldest surviving palace in Jodhpur: some of its *jarokhas* have temple columns – a feature not found in any surviving part of the *garh* palace.' It is therefore considered a building of the early 17th century, with additions such as the pseudo-Ionic capitals by Ajit Singh. A third palace for royal concubines in its day, it is now a women's hospital and can be reached on foot from the Juni Dhan Mandi, if you ask for the Hewson Dispensary. I revelled in the authentic

India of tumult and startling colours, greetings in Marwari and Rajasthani, a dog in a basket, a goat tethered up temptingly near a biscuit shop, scooters parping, fruit-laden carts, carpenters making and lacquering wooden boxes, 'welcome' boards gaudy with tinsel and tinfoil on plywood on sale for Rs 5 to Rs 25. I stopped by a slipper shop to quench my thirst with a Limca drink, but resolutely avoided the delicious-looking ice-cream and *lassi*. A charcoal cart rumbled past me, as I watched a glass-bangle maker and a turbanned man painting a wooden horse. Puppets are a thriving craft in Jodhpur, and you should see the range of tie-and-dye (*bandhana*) fabrics created by Muslim women still in purdah near Jalori Gate. Avoid as many cowpats as possible.

For the shop that shows 'everything' under one roof, take a rickshaw to Lalji's Emporium, fourteen rooms stuffed with all manner of Rajasthani handicrafts on Umaid Bhawan Palace Road, especially good on wall-hangings and silver.

But I suppose the best way to spend a day in Jodhpur (after the majestic fort and the extravagant palace) will always be to wander in alleyways, losing yourself as in any oriental dream, leaving your watch at home, and concentrating on scent as much as on sight, hearing, taste and touch. Try the spices, and buy little paper-screws of as many as you fancy, for the outlay is minimal and strong or subtle flavours of eastern aroma will beguile you long after your return. A maze of little awnings and balconies, telegraph posts and inexplicable poles, hoardings in Hindi and English, windswept hanging cottons and muslins, piles of grain, suitcases, popcorn and sweets. A procession of Hindu women and girls moving in single file with undulating, ululating grace bears on its many heads wedding gifts of cloth. Round another corner I was drawn insistently into a crowd of smiling, squatting Muslim men whose womenfolk were veiled and segregated. A master of ceremonies all in white, his black hair slicked gleaming black with cream, was displaying gifts of cloth to the assembled friends and family, full in the side of the street: presumably their home had no space to accommodate all their well-wishers. Everywhere, cows meandered.

If you find yourself puzzled by Hindu worship of the cow in India, cast your mind back to the early centuries of Christianity when the symbol of a fish for Jesus Christ would have confused pagans into thinking that Christians worshipped fish. In later centuries Christian iconography more widely identified the Saviour with a haloed lamb, which the astute Hindu observer might well relate to Christian worship of holy sheep. By contrast, the cow to a Hindu represents much that is indispensable: a symbol of divine gifts to man that he might be given to eat, to drink, and to see in his daily life, in backyards and in public streets, the blessing of Gods capable of creating, preserving and destroying. Like Buddhism,

Hinduism is intrinsically tolerant, for it does not accept converts. A Brahmin to whom I spoke in Jodhpur justified the thousands of aspects of God in cheap prints and poetic legends by explaining that religious understanding in Hinduism varies as much as the rate of literacy in India. You do not give an illiterate farmer *Rigveda* but an A.B.C. Equally, you cannot expect a Hindu caretaker of limited understanding to envisage (much less experience) the ineffable presence of God which Brahmins believe inheres in every atom of the universe. As always, looking, listening, thinking and feeling in India brings one even closer to an illusory belief in one's growing maturity. Illusory because of one's ignorance and fallibility: the pleasure is in the search, the journey to the heart of the lotus.

Imagine these streets as they were four centuries ago, or three, when Jodhpur lay on that trade axis between Delhi, and Gujarat, and Marwari merchants made swift and shrewd fortunes from camel caravans loaded with gold and ivory, sandalwood and spices, opium and silk.

This period, and many other phases in the long history of Rajathan, is readily evoked in the Sardar Museum erected in 1935, which you can find behind the Tourist Bungalow in Umaid Park. A Natural History Gallery displays hyenas and deer by diorama; very few wolves are left in Rajasthan. An Arms & Armour Gallery, uncaptioned or badly captioned, also includes model ships and 'planes. A Handicrafts Gallery features ivory bangles, rock-salt bowls, vases, cups and saucers, kites (very popular during Rajasthani spring festival celebrations), and papier-machê. I regretted that the museum catalogue had been allowed to vanish out of print because some of the sculptures are very fine, and deserve better: say a caption. Here are a ninth-century Vishnu and Lakshmi from Osiyan, a large 10th-century head of sleeping Vishnu from Agolai, exquisitely small 10th-century dancing girls from Harsor (Nagaur), and a marvellous stone 12th-century Vishnu from Kiradu (Barmer). A tenth-century stone Jivantaswami from Khimsar (Nagaur) has been well preserved. Wonders include part of a meteorite which landed on 29 December 1937 with a boom heard sixty kilometres away. Here are camelhide vases from Bikaner decorated with gold, brassware, and iron locks. A room of miniatures and portraits of maharajas includes images of Hanwant Singh, who inherited the title at 28 when his father Umaid Singh died in 1947 while hunting on Mount Abu. Hanwant himself loved flying and was killed when he flew into telegraph wires in 1952. Gaj Singh II was crowned at the age of four.

Three seated Jain *tirthankaras* dominate the main hall: a Mahavira of 1422, an Adinath of 1467, and a Chandraprabha of 1488.

I advise against touring the Umaid Park zoo: the black bears, for example are neither given proper food nor is their cage adequately cleaned. Only the walk-in aviary can be recommended.

On the way to Mandore, tell your rickshaw-driver to stop off at Maha Mandir ('Great Temple'), northeast of Jodhpur. Man Singh (1804-43) founded Maha Mandir in 1812 for his guru Deva Nathji, and to glorify Shiva, god of the Nath sect. Not far from Mandore you can find the charming artificial lake of Balsamand of the 12th century, with a summer palace and garden. Kailana is another lake about 10 km to the west of Jodhpur, much larger than Balsamand, and created for the purpose of supplying the city with drinking water.

Sardar Samand is a lake 55 km south of Jodhpur which you reach by crossing the countryside of the Bishnoi people, and their villages such as Jhalamand and Gura. Bishnoi men dress solely in white, but their women are brightly-dressed, often with bangles along their whole arms. Their burial customs differ from those of orthodox Hindus: a bishnoi is buried in the sitting posture, and belives he will be reincarnated as a deer, as were his ancestors. From the lakeside palace you might spot, depending on the season, egrets, ibis, flamingoes, and pelicans.

My bus took me from Jodhpur south to Pali and Ranakpur, but not before two hours' delay, caused by the overturning of a petrol tanker across the road. Although anyone could have driven parallel to the road, on hard desert sand to both left and right, nobody already driving on the road could descend, because the asphalt surface had been built up so far that no communication was possible. A petrol tanker painted 'Highly Inflammable' had in fact, using its driver's ebullient belief in his juggernaut's great size and power, just got stuck halfway up to the tarmac from the sand below. Luckily, oil was leaking from the overturned monster in the *other* direction! But in the increasing heat of the morning, many lives were at risk, and there was no shortage of drivers and passengers pouring out from cars and buses, standing and staring. A bus carrying German tourists to Mount Abu risked the downward spiral from asphalt to hard sand, and broke its back axle. Our driver, the Sikh Kuldeep Singh, turned the bus round and headed for the next village along the tarmac. A vast tortoise-slow fodder lorry taking the crown of the road forced Kuldeep on the side and there he became sanded in, just outside Dingana. I took the chance to play football with young lads from Dingana school in their mid-morning break; at home they speak Marwari, but they learn Hindi and English at school.

8: UDAIPUR

Ranakpur — Kumbhalgarh — Nathdwara — Eklingji — Ahar — Udaipur — Chittor — Bundi — Kota — Mount Abu

The approach to Udaipur from the northwest leads through Pali, baking in mid-morning heat like a chapati over charcoal. 'Nothing to say about it', howled a large hoarding for Forcast Televisions, 'everything to trust about it'. A pyramid of clay pots quaked as lorries crashed past in fumes of pollution. A cow sniffed at a foetid pool then, disillusioned, ambled away to pick over garbage below fruit and vegetable stalls by the side of the road. Trees flowered in the central reservation separating hubbubs of traffic. 'Bigston Black and White TV', 'Royal Remans Tailors', 'The Oriental Insurance Co. Ltd.' so remarkable in a country where fatalism reigns supreme. Bullock carts creaked between bikes and scooters, and the occasional roaring jeep. The driver of a Delhi-Bikaner lorry (some way off course) chewed betel beside a giant rear tyre. The first cinema showing of the day, at 11.30, was about to start. Women dyed cotton in the river, staining it a sensational saffron. The Collector's office on the right, then the Muslim cemetery.

Parched, and long behind schedule due to wreckage on the road, we stopped at a wayside drinks stall in Gundoj. I took tea with Kuldeep Singh, my friend Birendra, and the bus-boy Kesar. The name of this shack was Hotal Rajasthan. Its hoarding proclaimed 'Oll Modern Facility: Most Wel-Come'. The local alcoholic drink, *daroo*, is made from the acacia, virtually the only ubiquitous plant round Gundoj, and one or two inhabitants seemed to be taking full advantage of the modern facility in question, namely the dirt floor. There was no toilet, no bed, and indeed we could find no evidence of any food. But a straw awning, and a cool dark place to lie on the floor struck me as a *sadhu*'s 'modern facility', and I sipped my hot, sweet milky tea as if it had been the nectar of Arcadia.

And not far from here the landscape changed from arid plain to fertile foothills, as we branched off from the main road to Sirohi at Falna, with its memorable signs 'Earnest Gases Pvt Ltd.' and 'House of Life Seving Medicine'. To this day I cannot make up my mind whether the misprint replaces 'Saving' or 'Serving'.

Ranakpur

The Aravali Hills lured us gently higher past Kot towards Ranakpur, dried-up riverbeds mutely imploring rains that had been seven years absent. Bougainvillea enticed us into the Maharani Bagh Orchard Retreat, which reminded me of a garden restaurant in the Callejón de Huaylas of Peru's alpine region. But the similarity ended there, for this mirage offered neither food or drink. We continued to Shilpi Tourist Bungalow, offering an air-cooled single room for Rs 100 (UK£5) and a double for Rs 130. Minatory signs showed that we found ourselves in a religious district: 'Use of liquor and non-veg not allowed'; and 'Cooking washing not allowed', 'No guarantee for electricity and water' further dampened our expectations. No food at all was available, but eventually we drummed up glasses of hot sweet tea, without milk. Birds flew around the hotel rooms as if through a coppice, not particularly puzzled by the absence of crumbs, but just checking anyway. A sparrow cocked his chirpy head up at me as I examined paintings by the local artist and teacher S.M. Yunus, who had brought them from his village of Ghanerao, on the off-chance that his *karma* would include a meeting with a collector. Some work was crude and summary, the collapse of a dying convention, but he sold me two wondrous traditional paintings glowing with vitality. One, Capturing an Elephant, shows hills, fields and a pool of elephants cavorting in the wild, with a central image of two elephant-catchers, themselves mounted between them, horsemen scampering out of the way in fear of being trampled. The second is as magically serene and remote as the first is agitated and immediate. The snake-goddess Manasa, sister to the serpent-king Sesha and wife of the sage Jaratkaru, holds a cobra in her left hand, while other snakes approach the red rock on which she sits, some drawn to her and others to the music of Jaratkaru seated on the grass below his wife, a cobra rising from its basket on a patch which leads below them both to a lotus-pool, where a pair of herons survey the scene. The upper half of the miniature evokes a riot of paradisiac greens, from which emerge a myriad blossoms, and four birds in profile. We are needless to say not in India at all, but in the Ideal Heaven, where flowers never die, and lotus-pools never dry.

Such a utopia is visible not far away, in lyrical white marble, at a wooded shrine sacred to the Jains: Ranakpur. Start off at the 13th-century Sun Temple, to the Hindu God of the sun Surya, absorbed from prior animist worship by Brahmanical priests. Surya is one of the three major deities of the Vedic scriptures, the others being Agni (who will enter Latin as *ignis*, 'fire', and English as 'ignition') and Indra, the rain-god. His polygonal temple here, with a *sikhara* restored in the 15th century, is decorated with a frieze showing Surya in his 'chariot of the sun' drawn by seven horses.

Ranakpur. Jain temple interior

The Jain temples may be visited from midday to five in the evening, but photographing the idols is prohibited, as is the wearing or carrying of any leather object, such as sandals or belt. The atmosphere of quiet devotion is augmented by the absence of visitors (in Delhi or Agra these temples would be swamped with noise and motion), by the gleaming white of marble within and without, and by the proximity of gentle pigeons, as they flutter and coo singly and in pairs throughout the vast open play of light and shadow. The 15th-century temples to Neminatha (the 22nd *tirthankara*) and Parshvanatha (the 23rd) are overshadowed by the large but lightly-sprung rather than massive temple of Adinatha, the first *tirthankara*. Designed in 1439 by an architect called Dipak for a donor called Dharanki, the shrine reveals in stone the Jain view of the universe, and shows at the centre the quadruple face of Adinatha (the temple is popularly known as 'Chaumukh' or quadruple), facing each of the cardinal points of the compass. Four prayer-halls are carved with a multiplicity of erotic sculptures reminiscent of the much earlier Khajuraho. The ground plan seems entirely symmetrical, and the clustered *sikhara* almost conventional to those who know the *sikhara* of Khajuraho's Kandariya temple. But a closer look will dispel any slight sense of disillusion, for all is originality and movement, three-dimensional lithe bodies of dancing girls, *apsaras* and *devatas*. Three storeys beckon upward, and we can see details of carving on the *sikhara* which leap and carouse. On the balcony I found two great drums and marble elephants. And whereas in a Western cathedral you close the door behind you, at Ranakpur there are no doors to close, for paradoxically the shrine is placed there in a quiet valley to *look out from*, as well as to look into. Under a wooden ledge in the floor you can visit one or more of the eighty-four underground chambers which preserved idols from destruction during periods of Muslim fanaticism. On the roof again, I found my perception of steps towards the infinite grazed by little bells tied there, jingling in the perpetual mountain winds, reminding me of the ephemeral body in a universe that the Jains consider a human figure, the goal of liberated souls being the topmost part of the head of this universe-body. The soul possesses an inherent upward motion, and its bondage or liberation in the body is not thought by Jains to be a mere spiritual concept, as it is by Hindus, but at least in some degree a degrading or uplifting physical fact of each person. Lose yourself here, in an ocean of sculptures, elegant, refined, passionate, seemingly repeated in hall after hall, and storey after storey, but in fact each unique in its playful grace. It is possible to stay in the *dharamsala* inside the temple complex overnight (make a donation) and to eat simply (for another donation). I thoroughly recommend this if you can spare the time, for these valleys offer the greatest of all Indian luxuries: privacy and solitude, which you cannot find in Bombay or Calcutta without great effort and expense.

'You like to sit in rotten chair?' enquired a young man, clearly thinking that I looked much too decrepit to remain aloft for much longer without support. 'Thank you,' I replied politely. He brought me a rattan chair silently, and we continued to watch the sun go down together, over the Aravali peaks.

Kumbhalgarh

You can't drive your own car in India, as a foreign tourist, but you can charter a chauffeured car by the day; this is clearly a good idea in the Udaipur region, for many places are off the beaten track, and Kumbhalgarh falls into that category. The fort is a Mewar stronghold constructed at the behest of Rana Kumbha, the great 15th-century warrior who never lost a battle. Within its derelict walls, on the site of a Jain fort of the 2nd century, you can find places, temples and fields, several splendid temples and cenotaphs. Seven gates defend the ramparts from attack, and a series of messengers relayed information by a code of flashing mirrors from the forward gate to the summit. The *chhatris* are those of Rana Kumbha himself (murdered by his own son) and Prithviraj, brother of Rana Sanga). The temples are those of Kumbhaswami, Mahadeo and Nilkanth. Surveying the wooded hill, a thousand metres above sea level, stands Cloud Palace, Badal Mahal, erected by Rana Fateh Singh in the late 19th century. Kumbhalgarh Nature Reserve also encompasses Ranakpur, and can be seen at its lush and colourful best in October, though you will not easily glimpse the Indian wolf, which is bred successfully there, or the gentle four-horned antelope.

Rajsamand is a lake east of Kumbhalgarh created by Rana Raj Singh I in 1660. At the small town of Kankroli you can visit the Temple of Dwarkadhish, an incarnation of Vishnu, founded by Raj Singh I in 1676. A late 19th-century palace on the water's edge at Rajsamand is surrounded to landward by fine gardens. The white marble steps down to the lake date from the 17th century, when Maharani Charumati commissioned them in gratitude to her Hindu husband Raj Singh I. He had married her to forestall an offer from Shah Aurangzeb, who would have forced her to convert to Islam.

Nathdwara

The road through the Aravalis winds southward to Nathdwara, with its temple to Shri Nathji, one of the leading pilgrimage sites in Rajasthan for Hindus. Non-Hindus may not enter the temple. Nath is another incarnation of Vishnu, who was threatened by Aurangzeb's hatred of idolatry; the image was brought here from Mathura in 1669. As a non-Hindu I could not view beyond massive silver doors leading to the temple; an armed guard eyed me warily but kindly when I showed no signs of contriving illicit entry by bribery or bravado.

The temple itself looks modest enough, in brick and limestone, but the image of Nath (or Krishna) appears resplendent six times a day to throngs of visitors, first as a child, then as a shepherd playing his flute in the forest of Brindaban, then playing with *gopis*, as a god-king, and as a god-sage, and at last as Shri Nath, adorned with important jewels selected from the temple's treasury. The temple also stores food, and milk from the twenty thousand cows belonging to the temple given to worshippers who come from far and wide. Villagers of Nathdwara sell sweets to visitors, who have them blessed in the temple before sending them to distant relatives and friends. But the most celebrated export of Nathdwara is the cloth hanging known as *pichhwai* ('behind') deriving its name from its position behind the image of the deity in Vaishnavite temples of the Pushti Marga sect devoted to the child Krishna, Shah Aurangzeb proscribed the worship of Krishna, and Shri Vallabhacharya (1479-1531) escaped with his fellow-worshippers and followers to safety in the kingdom of Udaipur. The purpose of the *pichhwai* was to depict Krishna stories for the illiterate, and the painted *pichhwai* of Nathdwara became greatly cherished for its artistry and provenance. Devotional rather than creative, the hangings have their own appeal to a wide variety of worshippers, the artisans tending to show an idealized verdant Rajasthan with fertile fields and green hills well stocked with game, and cumulus clouds presaging quick, abundant rains. Early *pichhwais* have become very scarce, because they are eagerly sought and were made slowly and lovingly with vegetable colours such as indigo and mineral colours such as lapis lazuli which have been replaced in recent years by commercial colours.

Eklingji

Eklingji Temple (and we are now fast approaching the astonishing Udaipur) consists of numerous temples inside high walls beside a lake in the village of Kailashpuri. Momentous in the history of Mewar and its early rulers, Kailashpuri was originally a holy site dedicated to Shiva at least as far back as 734. Bappa Rawal, founder of the Mewar dynasty in the 8th century, became a pupil of the guru Harit and he convinced himself that prayers to Harit's *lingam* image had been responsible for overcoming the stronghold of Chittor. The Shivaite temple built to celebrate the victory has been superseded by structures designed for Rana Raimal (1473-1509).

The name 'Eklingji' means literally 'single-phallus lord', a reference to Shiva, who in his phallic manifestation is the dynastic deity of the Ranas of Udaipur. D.R. Bhandarkar, in the *Journal of the Bombay Branch of the Royal Asiatic Society*, records an inscription of 971 found in the Eklingji temple, in the form of a dedication to Lakulisa, a club-bearing form of Shiva, and noting the existence of a Shivaite sect called Lakulisa-Pasapatas known only from Eklingji. A certain king, Shri Bappaka (according to Tod without doubt the founder of the Mewar dynasty Bappa) then reigned at a place called Nagahvada, which can easily be identified with the modern Nagda, the ruins of which survive to this day at the foot of the hill on which Eklingji stands. The Ranas of Mewar acted as priest-kings in a manner familiar elsewhere in Rajasthan, a fact notably neglected by those civilian administrators who assumed that, because they were withdrawing privy purses from the princes, they would thereby derogate all authority from the ruling families. This never looked likely and in fact has proved impossible, especially in areas such as Bikaner where radical social improvements were set in hand by successive rulers.

Non-Hindus are welcome to explore the Eklingji complex, though not to photograph it. Opening hours (if one excludes the early morning up to 7.30!) are 10.30 to 1.30 and 5.30 to 7.30, though as always these hours are subject to change at the slightest whim of one or more of the guardians. A huge bronze statue and another of black marble depict Nandi, Shiva's bull. Inside the shrine, a four-faced image of Shiva in black marble receives the bows and whispered prayers of one line of female worshippers, and another of males.

At one time it was thought that Mira Bai, a Mewari princess, commissioned the temple to Vishnu, with 16th-century sculptures regrettably damaged and an eagle-headed garuda half-man, half-bird, on which Vishnu rides. But in the view of R.C. Agarawala ('Unpublished temples of Rajasthan', in *Arts Asiatiques*, vol.9, fasc. 2, 1965), the temple has no connection with Mira Bai at all. The 10th- or 11th-century sculpture on the exterior of the sanctum portrays a flying Kicaka or bracket-figure playing a flute, and not Krishna, as was hitherto believed. Partly out of a sense of duty, and partly to offset the Hindu ambience, my Sikh driver was reciting over and over the Mul mantra: 'There is one God. His name is Truth. He is the Creator, without fear or enmity. He was unborn and will not die, but is self-existent. Through the guru's grace you will attain Him', which sounds like this: 'Ik Onkar. Satnam. Karta purakh. Nirbhau, nirvair. Akal murat. Ajuni saibhang gurprasad.' Sikhism, which arose from a compound of Hindu reformism (in the manner of Kabir) and Islam, was founded by Guru Nanak (1469-1538). Though mainly found in Punjab, Sikhs have spread throughout India, being respected for their mechanical and engineering aptitude, and military prowess consonant with their proud bearing. Someone once remarked to me pensively that he had never seen a small, thin Sikh, and for the most part that generalisation stands up to criticism. The tenth guru, Gobind Singh, on his deathbed conferred guru status on the holy book, or *Adi Granth*, a compilation of songs in praise of God which also assists Sikhs to cross the world ocean, obtain salvation, and merge with God on the other side. Most Sikhs are born thus, but conversion is possible, after a profession of faith, statement of a catechism, and baptism. Guru Gobind Singh also founded the Khalsa, or Sikh military fellowship, which now aims to proclaim 'Khalistan', an independent nation-state for Sikhs, and it was he who nominated the five outward symbols of Sikhism: the five 'k's. The *kachera*, for modesty and free movement; the *kes* or uncut hair, for holiness; the *kangha* or comb in the hair-knot, for bodily purity and cleanliness; the *kirpan*, a knife worn on the left hip in a holster, for spiritual defence and dignity; and the *kara*, an iron bangle on the right wrist, for purity of action. Some ten million Sikhs outnumber Jains, for example, five to one. It may seem remarkable to try to reconcile the monotheism of Islam with the polytheism and 'idolatry' of Hinduism, but India has a habit of reconciling most differences with explanations that are often more confusing than the facts.

Nagda is the site of a 7th-century Mewar capital, with temples called Sas Bahu ('mother-in-law and daughter-in-law') dedicated in the 10th or 11th century to Vishnu, and a Jain temple to Adbhutji ('The Peculiar One') named for the strange idol within. You can find even earlier temples, of the 4th century, and fascinating prehistoric shrines created by ancestors of the Bhils, but the city was crushed by the Muslims in the 13th century.

Ahar

Before entering modern Udaipur, take the road to the left (eastward) which brings you out in 3 km to the prehistoric site of Ahar, where pottery sherds and animal remains dated to 4000 B.C. can be seen in a small museum summarising the finds from the Harappan site of Tambawati Nagari. Ahar not only preceded Chittor as the Mewar capital, but whenever Chittor was in danger, the dynasty fell back on Ahar until the creation of modern Udaipur. This accounts for the existence at Ahar of nineteen cenotaphs to commemorate nineteen Maharanas, each *chhatri* containing an image of Shiva and a stone portraying the ruler and his wives who committed *sati* with him, the most recent being for Swarup Singh in 1861. The necessary water was supplied by the reservoir known as Gangabhar Kund, near which you will find Hindu and Jain temples.

Roads surrounding Udaipur generally are subject to an ingenious ransom on the part of Bhil men and women tantamount to a road toll, though methods vary from time to time and place to place. Mountainous roads are subject to natural rockfalls, and Aravali roads are no exception. However, in certain areas populated by Bhils (once nomadic

Ahar. Chhatris

but in good times lured to harvest) mysterious rockfalls occur at regular intervals of two or three hundred metres, with boulders that just prevent passage but can easily be rolled away by one or two women or teenage boys. For a payment of a few rupees, a driver can stay in his car and pass over bank notes to one confederate while two or three helpfully roll back the offending rocks to the side of the road, awaiting the next vehicle. One suggestion would be to form an unobtrusive convoy behind a police or army truck, before which such obstacles vanish like snowflakes in August. Another suggestion would be to pay up with a smile. Resistance is hardly advisable, for punctures and broken windscreens not only have to be paid for by the passenger; it is he too who suffers from delay. However much you may detest blackmail, I cannot think of a preferable solution against the combined wiles of Robin Hood and Dick Turpin at their colourful best.

Furthermore, you can make friends with these artful brigands by inspecting their small dry-walled plots, and their wells worked by Persian wheels each whirling with little earthenware pots filling with water and emptying into a channel at the top. An old man stiffly drove on two yoked oxen, round and round like a perpetual calendar, amid fields of mustard, wheat and grass. Women laundered clothes, sang and laughed in the freshly risen water, cool and glittering in afternoon sun bold as brass and thrice as shining.

Three little lads clung to my hands and arms, comically whining for bakshish then running off unabashed when brusquely barked away by a near-naked farmer burnished brown except for his red betel-stained teeth. In these green fields dotting the Aravali hills it is hard to believe current estimates that 300 million of India's 800 million and more cannot afford to buy sufficient food. The old urban-rural dichotomy that is swelling Tokyo and Mexico City, Cairo and Dhaka, must be exacerbated in times like the present when insufficient rains fall to permit the rural population (still eighty per cent of the total) to remain on the land, when up to fifteen million farm labourers have lost their wages because there was so little to harvest.

Udaipur

I guiltily forgot such compassionate thoughts in the visual fascination of Udaipur. Would the drought have dried up Lake Pichhola, so that the palace on Jag Niwas could not be reflected in water? Should I find my reservation in the Lake Palace Hotel, or would it be necessary to view the glistening white summer palace from the shore? I need not have fretted: my room 208 faced the clifftop City Palace across the blue expanse of lake and sky. For hours I could not leave my picture window but sat there in a ferment of joy as daylight imperceptibly dimmed, electric lights gradually filled the middle distance (on the shore), and lanterns sparked Canaletto cream on little ferry-boats between the shore at Bhansi Ghat and Jag Niwas. The Lake Palace Hotel covers the whole of Jag Niwas island nowadays, over the original 18th-century structures first laid down for Maharana Jagat Singh II (1734-51). If the water-level permits, you can take a boat-ride around Lake Pichhola, looking at Mohan Mandir built in the northeast corner of the lake by Jagat Singh I (1628-52), and landing for half an hour or so at Jag Mandir, with a charming abandoned palace designed for Karan Singh (1620-28) and completed under Jagat Singh I. The heavy hand of history touched Jag Mandir in 1623, when Karan Singh gave sanctuary there to Prince Khurram, rebellious son of Shah Jahangir. Khurram became emperor as Shah Jahan in 1627 and you can be sure that he never forgot the service of the Mewar dynasty to the Mughal throne he personified. Jag Mandir still flowers with yew bushes and jasmine, blue larkspur, nasturtiums, verbena and moss rose. At the top of Gul Mahal I found a room lined with white marble and inlaid with coloured stones, roughly contemporary with the first recorded use of such a scheme in a Mughal building: the I'timad ad-Daula tomb at Agra of 1626. Like the room below, it is round, a shape uncommon in Rajput architecture, yet repeated in three pavilions at the western side of Jag Mandir

Udaipur. Jag Niwas

commissioned by Sangram Singh II earlier than 1720: round behind and rectangular in front.

Statues of eight elephants face Jag Niwas from Jag Mandir, and the empty island, congregating around the earliest palace known as Gul Mahal, echoes with sounds of the past, such as the flutter and warble of pigeons and the call of water-birds that I took to be cormorants, philosophically enjoying each others' company in tiny clusters. The boatman pointed over to a small fortress-like building on the shore near a wall at right angles to the lake, like Rumeli Hisar on the Bosphorus. 'It's a filter house', he explained, 'for purifying the water'. Returning by a little boat to Jag Niwas, I was just in time to transfer to the ferry for Bhansi Ghat and the Shiv Niwas Palace, where I was due to dine, after another marionette show typical of Rajasthan. The former royal guest apartments of Shiv Niwas Palace are now available for visitors: these are probably the most exclusive suites in India. Rooms are only Rs 600 (US$50), which must be the greatest bargain in the world today, but the eight super de luxe suites are Rs 1,800 (US$150) each, the five historic suites Rs 2,500 (US$205), the two royal suites Rs 4,000 (US$330) and the imperial suite Rs 5,000 (US$410); in the latter cases the prior approval of the management is required. For comparison, the Lake

Palace Hotel rates are Rs 1,000 (US$85) for a single, Rs 1,125 for a double, rising to Rs 3,000 (US$250) for a historic suite. The gardens of Shiv Niwas are even more green and cool than the lotus pool and mango-shaded courtyards of the Lake Palace. I confess that I fainted with excitement in the gardens of Shiv Niwas, and the solicitous staff laid me down to rest on dark lawns, where I revived amid the calls of cicadas and peacocks. A graceful receptionist ushered forward to this recumbent Englishman a quietly-spoken doctor called D.K. Babel, of 117 Lion Den, Hiran Magri Sector 13, Udaipur. He provided medicine against vertigo, stress and over-exertion but, as he so neatly expressed it, 'I am not giving you anything to stop your imagination, because we are not having any remedy for poetry'. Just rest, solitude, and a good long dose of prose.

But Udaipur is not like that. It ranks with Machu Picchu, Peking's Forbidden City, Lhasa, Chartres Cathedral and walled Dubrovnik as one of the heart-stopping experiences that no traveller, no matter how blasé, ill or tired, can ever dismiss as ordinary. It cannot be compared with other lakeside towns such as Geneva or Puno: it is suitably unique, as befits the latest hill-defended fortress city of the Mewar dynasty, the leading salute state of the former Rajputana Agency. It is all bougainvilleas in green gardens and lake views amid the sandy brown desolation of the desert.

The origins of the Sisodia family of Rajputs are, as usual, deliberately lost in that legend which ensures them reference back to Rama, the seventh incarnation of Vishnu, and thus to the solar race of Rajputs.

Early one morning I sat basking in the fresh breeze over the lake, in the pale sun, and from the terrace saw women of the town washing their saris and their own bodies at the same time, modestly dipping themselves into the waters fully dressed, and rising to reveal their slender, supple bodies. They rinsed their shoulders with elegant hands, singing or chatting with their neighbours, garnet studs in their noses. What a pity that a large modern statue of such a woman, gracelessly staring, faces the Lake Palace and diminishes the natural beauty of the lake, with its thousands of birds, endlessly fascinating shapes and colours of rising shoreline buildings, and high above and in the distance the fortress of Sajjangarh.

Around these stagnant tanks, mosquitoes breed with the kind of felicitous fecundity I have found elsewhere only in the Amazon. Fonte Boa on the Upper Amazon was known to the naturalist H.W. Bates as 'the headquarters' of mosquitoes, and I thought of Fonte Boa while smiting the denizens of Pichhola. Bates recorded, with great good humour and fortitude, how a cloud of mosquitoes would hover around his head, humming so loudly that they drowned the birdsong! If this story does not help you to remember your daily pills against malaria, nothing will.

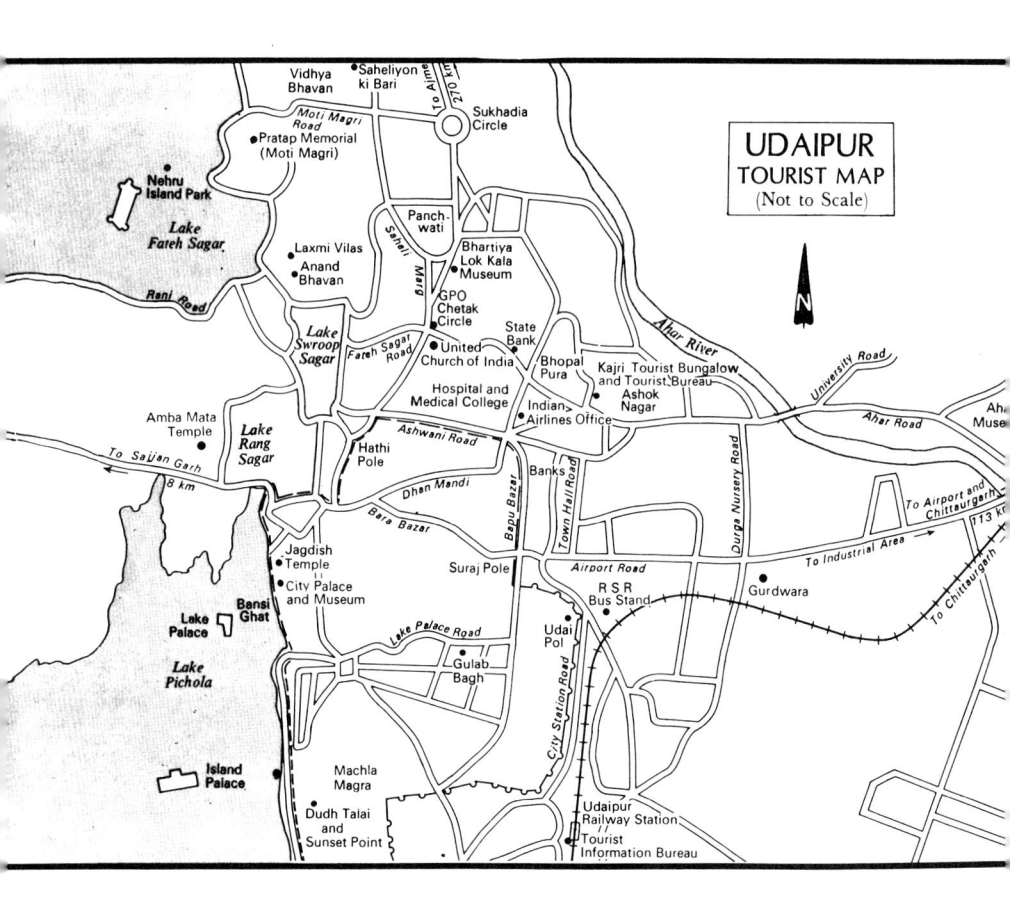

The equestrian statue to Maharana Pratap Singh astride his steed Chetak on Moti Magri is a notable landmark and this will help you to orientate. On this hill a few derelict walls, in the style of Chittor's walls, prove the whereabouts of the first fortress in Udaipur, abandoned probably because there was no room for expansion. The ruling family moved southward to the eastern bank of Lake Pichhola, and began the fortress palace now known as the City Palace around 1567 with the large *sabha* or audience hall at the south end of the *mardana* or men's quarters; the Sileh Khana and above it the Rajya Angan courtyard, and the rooms flanking this courtyard. Badal Mahal, part of the women's quarters, dates from 1567-72.

But the principal building phase was the seventeenth century, when most of the four great palaces and more lesser buildings were

Udaipur. City Palace. East front

constructed. From the Lake Palace the ensemble looks like a massive fort, but the impression within is quite different: intricate, multifarious, varied, even playful and intimate. The palace faces east, appropriately for a palace made for a sun dynasty. The first daily duty of the Maharana ('Great Warrior', not the Maharaja or 'Great Ruler' of most other Rajput states) is to pray to the sun, even before he takes breakfast. The shield on the *mardana* depicts a Bhil, the sun, Chittor Fort and a Rajput, with a saying from the *Gita* which can be translated 'God helps those who do their duty'. Pigeons fluttered and flapped in a plebeian fuss on the Bara Chowk or Great Courtyard between the main palace and the ranges of guardrooms and stables nowadays fitted out as shops and cafés. At the northern end of the terrace Hathi Pol (Elephant Gate) leads to the Tripolia (1725), or triple gate of marble arches, below a

Jaipur-like Hawa Mahal where court ladies could watch processions without being seen. Suraj Pol (Sun Gate) leads off eastward from the guardrooms, but to gain access to the palace you enter Toran Pol. Below the sun emblem is a platform where visitors descended from elephants, or from horses, replaced in recent years by Rolls Royces. Inside the small gate called Ganesh Deorhi I found tiles made in Japan in 1927 showing such deities as Krishna and Ganesha understandably enough with Japanese eyes.

Ganesh Deorhi was formed by enclosing the stairway access to Rajya Angan courtyard from 1614, a period when Chandra Mahal was added above the temple Nau Choki Dhuni Mata, and Dilkushal Mahal was added above the treasury. The shrine of Dhuni Mata, the earliest part of the palace, is illustrated by pictures of the four greatest divinities of the Mewar dynasty: Shri Nathji, Shri Eklingji, Shri Charbhujaji and Amba Mata. Much of the palace is now a museum, and Rajya Angan courtyard leads to rooms of this museum devoted to Rana Pratap, his arms and armour, and paintings depicting his life and times. Pratap Singh (1572-97) resisted the mighty Mughal armies which had defeated his father Udai Singh II at Chittor. He lost to the Mughals at the field of Haldighati, 27 km north of Udaipur, and surrendered one after another all the strongholds of Mewar, including Kumbhalgarh. Strategically, historians compare the pass of Haldighati with that of Thermopylae, and the tenacity of the Rajputs, allied with Bhil infantry, troops from Gwalior, and Pathans from the north-west, proved in summer 1576 every bit as courageous as the tenacity of the Greeks holding Thermopylae in 480 B.C. against the vastly superior forces of the Persians under Xerxes. Like the ruler of Bundi, Rana Pratap never compromised with Akbar, and it says much for the sagacity and tolerance of Akbar that the Hindu rebel of Udaipur was permitted to rule in relative peace.

Ascending to Chandra Mahal ('Moon Palace'), I was immediately struck by the elegant cusped arches in this relatively small room, with its numerous columns, open sides and irregular plan. The marble throne on the platform was used for the coronation of rulers up to that of Sangram Singh II in 1710. The monolithic marble basin in the centre, apparently intended for water, was in reality filled with gold on royal birthdays, and the pieces then distributed to the poor.

Dilkushal Mahal consists of a suite of four 17th-century rooms, including Kanch-ki Burj, with late 19th-century grey and red mirrors, and Chitram-ki Burj with 18th-century murals portraying scenes of life in Udaipur during the time of Jawan Singh (1728-38) when crocodiles in Lake Pichhola discouraged citizens from approaching the summer palaces on Jag Niwas and Jag Mandir. An exquisite *Bear Shoot* (1900) is signed 'M. Fateh Singh'.

You now take a staircase to Bari Mahal ('Great Palace') also known as the Garden Palace, intriguingly, for the garden here is laid out on a natural hill 27 metres above the rest of the palace, making ground-floor rooms around it seem fourth-floor rooms. The swimming pool here played a part in the annual Holi celebrations, and charming views can be enjoyed over both the lake and the city. A narrow passage brings you to a hall where miniatures of the 18th and 19th centuries are displayed. Fascinating Mewari-style paintings reveal Jag Mandir as it was in the 18th century, a view of the temple to Vishnu, a painting of this very courtyard, and an elephant fight over a wall. Elephants fought after being fed opium (used with other drugs by virtually all Rajput warriors too, and by Muslims, if we remember that the derivation of 'assassins' is from 'hashish') and the last recorded elephant fight in Udaipur was held as recently as 1955.

My guide pointed out an electric lift, and farther on a 'lift' for women which he encouraged a German lady to enter, but the 'door' was painted on the wall, so cleverly that we were all neatly taken in. Here is the antique wheelchair of the former ruler Bhopal Singh (1930-47) who was paralysed at the age of 16. A family consisting of an old man and three beautiful daughters stared at me in the familiar Indian manner showing respectful curiosity; they would consider it as rude to pay no attention to a stranger as we think it to stare. Most Indian guides speak and think a kind of English which is not infected by current reading of English authors, but relies on recollection of English textbooks of their youth, translating Hindi phrases and words into their often inaccurate English counterparts, and oddments picked up by half-listening to American or Australian visitors often themselves confused by what they see and hear. Thus it is that you may be told what is visibly wrong, and be offered dates or names that clash with recent scholarly research. Guides frequently spend all their lives in one place, so have no comparative knowledge even of relatively close Indian towns and cities, and make no stylistic comparisons which enable you to understand development of art, architecture or crafts. So you should prepare for Udaipur (and elsewhere in Rajasthan) by reading James Tod's classic *Annals and Antiquities of Rajasthan* (last reprinted 1972) and Giles Tillotson's architectural guide, *The Rajput Palaces* (1987). Indeed,

> For those who read of Rajasthan
> Giles Tillotson and Tod
> occupy the rôles in Christianity
> of Christ and God.

Maharawal Lakshman Singh of Dungarpur was once told by Sir George Ogilvie of the Indian Political Service, 'for political officers Tod's *Annals* is what the *Gita* is to you. It's the political officer's bible.

No political officer can come up to me and say he hasn't read Tod's *Annals*. If he does, I tell him, "You fool, go and read it and then come back to me".' Ogilvie's daughter Vere, later Lady Birdwood, arrived at the British Residency in Udaipur as a seventeen-year-old in 1926. In that converted 17th-century palace, she writes, 'I could hardly have had a more glamorous beginning to life in India, because apart from a few cars there couldn't have been any change in the way of life there for the last several hundred years.' For most of the year they were the only Westerners in Udaipur, although for part of the time an Indian Medical Service doctor and his wife lived there, as did a couple of Scottish missionaries whose total haul in thirty years was one convert. 'It was rather like sending a Hindu mission to the Vatican'.

An Indish notice, intelligible but wrong as usual, warns the visitor 'Please mind for head' in the tradition of G.V. Desani's novel *All About Mr. Hatterr*. I possess E.M. Forster's copy of one of the most amusing books that almost entered the English language but stuck in the doorway and has stayed there, half in and half out, since its publication in 1948. One can view it either as a funny story in an imitable style littered with catch-phrases like any comedian's ('old feller') or as a linguistic artefact. Between the uncertain covers of a single book you marvel at oracular Johnsonisms like 'By the acknowledged Indian and Greek aesthetic tenets, she is not at all beautiful', English Edwardian slang including mild oaths like 'damme', and a half-English mashed up by a B.A. in English Calcutta (failed) with a mastery of mostly inappropriate Shakespearean saws amounting to genius. Such was the way of our guide round Udaipur City Palace, whose floral explanation was: 'They have this small small plants are there', an idiom I tried to transmute dramatically in a radio play after my return. The Pearl Palace glitters with mirrors and coloured glass, then I descended again to the Sun Gallery, or Surya Gokhra, from which the Rana greeted his ancestor the sun at dawn each day. The 17th-century Mor Chowk, or Peacock Courtyard, was created on the roof of the *sabha* as a new durbar area, with throne rooms to the north and south, respectively Manak Mahal ('Ruby Palace') and Surya Chopar. The punishment for killing a peacock in Rajasthan is six months in jail and a fine of Rs 500, which will explain why these birds roam unharmed throughout the territory, and why they festoon (in mosaic relief) the Mor Chowk.

Manak Mahal contains a fine display of porcelain and glass, featuring notable specimens of Chinese porcelain.

Leaving the men's quarters for the women's, the *mardana* for the *zenana*, used up to 1973, we pass a cage in the centre of the courtyard once occupied by a tiger, and the Maharana of Mewar Research Institute. The Zenana Mahal's courtyard displays a cart used to bring mail between Udaipur and Chittor up to 1899, pony-traps and landaus,

Udaipur. City Palace. Mor Chowk

a Rolls Royce of 1920 used for the crippled Rana Bhopal Singh, and silver caskets for carrying messages from state to princely state. A lovely view over Lake Pichhola distracted me from examining traditional Mewari costume fitted on a dummy, and old cannon, a tiger-shoot painting and large wooden boxes for carrying jewellery on camels and elephants. On the first floor I found miniatures of the hunt in that extraordinary Mewari style which manages to view the same scene from various angles simultaneously in a manner presaging (though naively) the discoveries of Cubism. Daily life in the court of Udaipur is the main theme, and what could be more interesting to the modern visitor? A fascinating source-book I recommend wherever you go in Rajasthan is Ramdev P. Kathuria's *Life in the Courts of Rajasthan during the 18th Century* (S. Chand, Delhi, 1987), superbly evocative of manners and customs in Udaipur. Photographs and memorabilia of British Residents and Viceroys are led by a display devoted to the great Tod, Resident Representative here from 1818 to 1822. We have already seen his Mewari portrait in the *mardana*, painted when he was first received by Rana Bhim Singh.

Painting in Mewar state began with the angular blue-and-red Jain manuscript paintings from the twelfth century, and changed with the arrival of an unnamed Muslim artist from Jaunpur in the late 16th century; subsequently schools are known to have existed at Chawand (capital of Mewar from 1576 to 1615), Chittor, and Udaipur, characterised by glowing colours, strong simplification and flowing rhythm. Two series of *Ramayana* illustrations were produced; one of them dated 1649 by a named artist, the Hindu Manohar, can be seen in the Prince of Wales Museum, Bombay. These themes and sensibilities were maintained through the regions of Raj Singh (1652-81) and Jai Singh (1681-1700), but thereafter the rulers and their lives at court or on journeys began to dominate artistic life in Udaipur, and copies of earlier work revealed a steadily fading inspiration.

While travelling in the realms of Mewar, and exploring palaces now for the greater part deserted, resounding only to your soft footfalls and hushed voice, you will wonder how a Rana might have spent his days when not out on campaign, and luckily the Sanskrit *Amarsar* of Pandit Jiwadhar survives as MS 709 in Saraswati Bhandar Library, Udaipur. Dated 1685, the MS was written in 1628, in the last year of the reign of Karan Singh, but refers to the reign of his predecessor Amar Singh I (1597-1620), the son and successor to the celebrated Pratap Singh. Drummers would wake the Maharana, who would then participate in the morning hymns. He moved from his golden bed to attend the calls of nature and to take a bath, accompanied by maids and menservants. His first act after completing his toilet was to proceed to the temple of Shiva to worship, then listen to guru Shripati Vyas reciting the Puranas. He

Udaipur. City Palace. Zenana

would next bestow charity in the form of gold coins and cows to the Brahmanas, pay his respects to his mother and receive her blessings, and begin the day's durbar, which would be concluded with the drummers announcing lunch.

This midday meal would be taken with the royal princes and nobles (though without any women, of course), following which a rest-hour would intervene. The afternoon would be spent in military matters, such as an inspection of infantry and cavalry at the barracks within the fort or watching manoeuvres, or at the hunt. An evening durbar in the private audience hall would be confined to court officials and the nobility. The maharana would then spend some time in the *zenana* with one or more of his wives and concubines, often leaving them and returning to sleep in his own chambers. During times of peace, as for example under Jagat Singh II (1734-51), new feasts and festivals were appointed to display the maharana's power and splendour, but the routine typical of Amar Singh corresponds quite closely to the precepts considered princely and statesmanlike in the *Artha Shastra* (*c*. 300 A.D.), a manual of statecraft wrongly attributed to Kautilya (*c*. 322-298 B.C.).

The ground floor of the *zenana* is occupied by rooms of jewellery in gold and silver and treasures of the state, such as shrines to Krishna and a Mewari princess called Mira Bai, poetess, saint, and daughter-in-law of a ruler called Sangram Singh, or Rana Sanga, who suffered a massacre at Khanwa in 1527.

Next to the *zenana* is the latest addition to the city palace, Fateh Prakash, closed to visitors because it is the residence of the present Maharana Mahendra Singh, who succeeded Bhagwant Singh in 1984. Neither can one see these days the mid-19th century Shambu Niwas, next to the Durbar Hall founded by Fateh Singh (1884-1930); nor the apartments of the saint Kanwarji Bhai where services are still held. But you can visit (and indeed stay in) the opulent royal guest house, Shiv Niwas: even if you do not stay there, at least you can take luncheon or dinner in a restaurant or garden.

There is so much to see within the City Palace that you really need a meal to restore your energies and stillness to calm your beating heart. Once revived, explore the city bazaars, for fine marionettes, silver, copper, tie-and-dye textiles, and *pichhwai* paintings, or traditional wooden toys, birds and animals.

If you want a bookshop in Udaipur, try Suresh Book Service, near the General Hospital which was constructed by the former royal family and is now operated by the Government. I wandered around the University (one of five in Rajasthan) and watched flying foxes and vultures competing for tree-space in the Rang Niwas Hotel Garden.

Once in a while it happened that the proverbial good manners of Indians to Westerners would be contradicted by an old man spitting in my direction, or a young woman calling out an insult she could not have expected me to understand. (She could not have known I had spent a year studying Hindi at evening classes). Then barefoot waifs, artful dodgers in the pay of absent Fagins, would try to catch me off guard, rifling a hip pocket, where I kept only a cheap comb. But in Udaipur I felt cheerful, adventurous, always on the brink of sensuous discoveries, hot and sweaty, festive. The pungent smells of the bazaar drew me into dark and unswept passageways where pi dogs sniffed passionately then slipped guiltily past, as thin as shovels, to paw like a starving beggar at a stall of steaming chapatis. What we recall as a Dickensian hubbub, a kind of historical fairground with street cries and sleeping babes in cardboard boxes beside mothers who sell vegetables or firewood, is in present Udaipur a wholly rounded actuality, Eastern cries and startling colours reducing our memories of sepia photographs to dull anonymity. I could never imagine any of these streets or alleys still or quiet. At whatever time of day or night you pass, lights are on, children in rags are being scolded, and men gaze through tiny open windows into the half-light of eternity's monsoon breath.

Bara Bazaar ('Great Bazaar') runs from Delhi Pol to the Jagdish Temple: here you can be dazzled by the sights and overcome by the scents that rise from shops and stalls. Jagdish Temple itself is a Vaishnavite temple constructed in the last years of the reign of Jagat Singh I (1628-52) and adds little to architectural history, evolving almost without effort from the mediaeval Khajuraho temples or those of the 15th century at Chittor. One ascends by a steep staircase that reminded me of Besakih on Bali. A pavilion opposite the entrance covers a fine bronze figure of Garuda, Vishnu's mount, and the god himself, a black effigy enthroned, reigns in his incarnation as the four-armed Lord of the Universe of Jagat Nath. A Sikh gurdwara can be found near the junction of the Airport Road with Durga Nursery Road. The leading Jain sanctuary in Udaipur is the 16th-century Adinath Mandir, on the opposite side of the Clock Tower from Jagdish Mandir, on the southern side of Bara Bazaar. Also within the old city walls you can discover the delights of Sajjan Niwas Bagh, with its Gulab Bagh, or rose garden, the Victoria Hall (1890) now a library known as Saraswati Bhawan, and a small zoological garden. Try to take an auto-rickshaw or taxi round Lake Pichhola, Rang Sagar, Swarup Sagar, and Fateh Sagar, passing Moti Magri and the monument to Rana Pratap Singh.

You will see the lakes from a new perspective: on one side the rising storeys of white Udaipur; on the other the rising slopes, undulating towards the horizon, of the Aravali Hills. Pichhola was the first of these man-made lakes, created by a merchant in the 15th century when he built a dyke and causeway for his caravan to cross the Ahar river and dammed it for his own convenience. A century later Udai Singh

Udaipur. Bazaar

strengthened the dam and enlarged Pichhola Lake, named for the village of Pichholi on its shore. In the 17th century, Jai Singh excavated a new lake, Fateh Sagar, which drowned the ladies' garden Sahelion-ki Bari and so was altered in the late 19th century by Fateh Singh. In 1937, work was started on a water palace on the island in Fateh Sagar now known as Nehru, but the palace was understandably abandoned during the turmoil of war and partition and the island transformed into a public park accessible by a boat from the municipal garden.

I had almost stopped wondering what Indians thought about the Raj that had suddenly been withdrawn at midnight some forty years before. The wondering should be irrelevant, and there can be no real agreement in the kaleidoscopic opinions of the millions with an opinion to express, but... But then again, so many of the older generation, like one of the grizzled caretakers of this museum, strike up conversations in game English, idiosyncratic rather than idiomatic, like Robinson Crusoe rescued by a crew of Latin-speaking dons, capable of making himself understood in the half-familiar phrases of a school long left. He showed me colourful terra cotta steles from Molela, silver *phul* used as amulets, and small portable wooden altars known as *kawad*. Another room illustrates Rajasthani traditions in photographs, and a third deals with tribes from other parts of India. Other rooms are devoted to local musical instruments and marionettes, with the possibility of attending a show at certain times.

On the road north to Sahelion-ki Bari I passed Bhil tribeswomen bringing wooden logs from the hills to sell for fuel, and gardens with guava trees netted against thieving birds. The 'Maids of Honour Garden', one way to translate 'Sahelion-ki Bari', was created in the early 18th century by Maharana Sangram Singh II as a summer palace where he could be entertained behind three successive walls by his favourite concubines. The waters of Fateh Sagar ran into elegant pools and fountains, though the five fountains playing now came from England in 1889. Orange-saried gardeners, who must have one of the most enviable outdoor jobs in the Orient, pointed out a darting cuckoo in the mango trees, and a red-whiskered bulbul always associated with the loved one in Mughal poetry. A bathing-pool with four marble elephants, a painted metal fountain with four lions; trailing hibiscus and darting chipmunks: how could one fail to be enchanted by this retreat? Very few, if the hundreds of names and initials carved on palm trunks are valid testimony.

I caught a bus back to the Lake Palace; it charged through red lights like an angry bull, past a wayside stall reading 'Mukesh Eggs Centre' and a hoarding announcing 'Parle Biscuits of Bombay'. Across the five-minute ferry I discerned flights and roostings of tufted ducks and coots, terns and great egrets, though none of the kingfishers for which

Pichhola is renowned. Back on Jag Niwas Island, I dipped into Pierre Loti's romanticised *India* (1903), written when the Maharana lived in the Lake Palace. 'He possesses both charm and grace', noted Loti of Fateh Singhji, 'together with an exquisite courtesy that is tinged with a certain shyness, the kind of timidity that I have sometimes noticed in the very greatest aristocrats'. The Maharana's interpreter glided in silently and placed himself behind the princely chair. Each time that the interpreter spoke he held a napkin of white silk in front of his mouth so that his breath might not annoy his lord – 'a useless precaution, however, for his teeth are white and his breath is sweet'.

The former ruling family have now left their Lake Palace to the daydreams of visitors from all over the world who vie for the best rooms, an idle contest for every room has its own pleasures. Of the five suites, Sajjan Niwas offers a lovely view from its private terrace, and Rajasthani miniatures within; Sarvaritu opens on to the pool; Khush Mahal filters sun through its stained glass; Udai Prakash possesses a particularly ample terrace; and Kamal Mahal is distinguished by charming glass inlay in lotus patterns. Beside a lotus pool I sipped orange juice and offered fragments of chapati to a pigeon that was waggling its head at me in a mixture of anxiety and approval. Far above lake, palaces and city soared the eyrie of Sajjangarh, a hunting palace overlooking a Safari Deer Park protected since the time of Bhagwat Singhji. The palace of Sajjangarh was built by Sajjan Singh in the late 18th century, and one can easily imagine its hazy magic during the monsoon season, 750 metres above sea level. The views are amply worth the fixed price of Rs 150 (one tout tried to charge me Rs 500) by taxi from the shore near Shiv Niwas, especially as it is situated only about six km from the city. The drive takes you around Lake Pichhola, with views ever more dizzy as you ascend, past an inquisitive mongoose, and finally riding above a rapacious eagle as it drifts deceptively gently on the air currents. Sajjangarh is now a police post and entry is not permitted except by administering a slight injection of bakshish to the duty guard. The place has the sadness of any derelict pleasure palace, and presents little architectural distinction to detain you. The revelation is rather in the series of views outward in every direction: beyond the Aravali hills, down to the scintillating blue waters of the lake, across to the white-housed town shimmering in afternoon heat. Sajjan Singh's enterprise is planning a nine-storey observatory up here was cut short to one by his early death at 25, but I cannot regret its incompletion, because it would have looked nine times as forlorn today.

On the way back to Udaipur, my driver Kalu Singh turned off the road towards the hunting lodge or Shikarbadi also known by the name Khas Odi (private shooting box), a locality familiar to those who have taken pleasure in Mewari miniatures. Imagine the pit in the centre still filled with fighting tigers or boars as they were in less enlightened times! If you wish to spend the night at the lodge for a contrast, it may be possible by arrangement with the management at the Lake Palace Hotel.

Where else could one stay in Udaipur? The choice is comfortably wide, from the former royal palace of Laxmi Vilas overlooking the eastern shore of Fateh Sagar, and next door to Rajasthan State Hotel. In that area you might try at the middle of the price range the Hilltop Hotel, Amba Mata Marg 5, and the Lake End Hotel. The Kajri Tourist Bungalow (with tourist information and restaurant) is one of a number of inns on Shastri Circle, a roundabout on Ashoka Marg, such as the Prince, the Alka, and the Ashok. As usual there are several places to stay near the railway station south of the walled city, including the Payal, the Tourist and the International. The railway station itself offers cheap retiring rooms, and dormitory beds at even lower rates. Rang Niwas Hotel is a quiet retreat near Sajjan Niwas Gardens, with the same wide price range as the Keerti on Saraswati Marg. The Keerti group includes Pratap Country Inn at Titadha, a village seven km outside the city, and they can arrange for you to be taken there for a taste of village life. If you stay at one of the hotels near Chetak Circle, like the Lake View or the Chetna, you will find there the best choice of local restaurants for eating out.

North of Chetak Circle (the name of Rana Pratap's stallion is also given to the rail express linking Delhi with Udaipur) you will find Bhartiya Lok Kala Mandal, a museum for Rajasthani folk art, crafts and music, particularly strong on marionettes, textiles, and music. Founded in 1952, it is open daily from 9 to 6. The hallway shows examples of *pichhwai* from Nathdwara and a great *phad* with a *bhopa* and *bhopi* in dummy-form showing how these traditional textiles were used to tell the stories of the hero Pabuji.

Since the daily express from Delhi via Jaipur and Ajmer takes over twenty hours to reach Udaipur, you may prefer to fly one way. Dabok Airport lies 24 km to the east, and your flight may stop at Jodhpur and Jaipur en route. From Udaipur there are connections to Aurangabad and Bombay. Buses, as usual in Rajasthan, are your obvious way to get around from Udaipur to local cities such as Chittorgarh (roughly six times daily), Bundi and Kota (three or four times a day), and less frequent departures for Mount Abu, Ajmer and Jodhpur. You can enjoy a splendid country bus ride for fifty km to Jaisamand, from its great size also called a 'sea', Jaisamudra! The lake was created by Maharana Jai Singh in 1691, when he walked around its shore and presented his own weight in gold to the poor. Jai Singh's summer palaces Hawa Mahal and Ruthi-ka Mahal are set in foothills overlooking Jaisamand, where you can stay overnight at a tourist bungalow administered by Rajasthan Tourist Development Corporation. Jai Singh's damming of the Gomti river was reinforced in 1875 when Maharana Sajjan Singh completed another dam. There is a temple to Shiva amid six *chhatris* decorated with carvings of elephants. A boat will take you to islands where Bhils scour a scanty living from fishing in the lake. Beware crocodiles, who also live off the lake's plenty! A nature reserve, the Jaisamand Sanctuary, protects graceful chinkara, chital, abundant birds, and wild boar. It is said that a few leopards roam Jaisamand, but these you are unlikely to glimpse from the road.

Chittor

If you prefer to spend your time in the historical dimension of Rajasthan rather than in its natural beauties, instead of taking the road southeast to Jaisamand (also known as Lake Dhebar) you could take the bus or train eastward towards Bundi and Kota, stopping for at least half a day in Chittor, familiar too by the name of its great Mewar stronghold Chittorgarh. It takes three hours by bus, and you can find tourist information near the railway station at Janta Tourist Bungalow. You could stay there or at Panna Tourist Bungalow on the Udaipur Road, where you can take a reliable, detailed standard tour starting at eight in the morning or half-past two. The bus station is situated near the Gambheri river, between the railway line and the ascent to Chittorgarh itself. In legend and history alike it would be impossible to overstate Chittor's position. We are looking for the clan that sprang from one Guhil, 'cave-born' in the sixth century to Princess Pushpavati whose family was massacred in Gujarat by savage invaders. Guhil's descendants eventually settled in Dhulkot near the village of Ahar, close to Udaipur, and later at Nagda. More secure than either was Chittor. The rock commanding Chittor is 5 km long and rises 170 metres above the monotonous plain. For eight hundred years it was the key to unlock Rajputana, which is why it was so bitterly contested. It was taken by Bappa Rawal of the Guhilots now called the Sisodia dynasty, in 728 if you credit Louis Rousselet's *India and its Native Princes* (1876) or 734 if you prefer the date suggested by Hugh Davenport in *The Trials and Triumphs of the Mewar Kingdom* (Udaipur, 1975). Like the hilltop fortress of Jaisalmer, Chittor rock accommodated – until 1568 – townspeople as well as rulers. So there is a great deal to see on the orange-brown plateau, where dusty bushes and trees relieve deserted temple forecourts. The first plundering of Chittor, known as a *shaka* or sacrifice, occurred in 1303 when the Pathan Ala-ud-Din Khilji, Delhi's Sultan, attacked on the pretext of winning Padmini, Rani of Chittor and queen to Rawal Ratan Singh. Ala-ud-Din, at the head of his armies, demanded to meet Padmini, guaranteeing he would then spare the city.

The Sultan was permitted to see her reflection in a lotus pool, and escorted down to his army by Bhim Singhji, uncle to the young prince Lakshman. At the outer gate, Bhim Singh was taken hostage by soldiers of the Sultan. Padmini then used the Trojan horse device, promising by messenger that she would come down to Ala-ud-Din accompanied by her serving-ladies in palanquins. Every palanquin concealed Mewari warriors, and each palanquin-bearer bore arms, so the destruction was terrible and astonishing on both sides. It is said that 7,000 Rajputs died in the fighting and, though one has to allow for exaggeration, Chittor's defences were almost certain to fall that day. The women sent their children into hiding with their servants and prepared for mass ritual suicide in their wedding finery. Their remaining menfolk watched the flames leaping higher in their 'great subterranean retreat' as it consumed the clothes and flesh of their wives, then covered their foreheads with ashes from the pyre, exchanged their clothes for sacred saffron, and rushed out of the gates to die in combat. Architecturally, nothing survives from that period, though the lake palace of Padmini and the lakeside palace of Bhim Singh were rebuilt about 1880 on the site of their late 13th-century predecessors. The first authentically historic buildings date from the time of Rana Kumbha (1433-68), reached through the great Bari Pol and the smaller Tripolia, three bays deep, leading to the army parade ground and a council chamber or sabha. To reach this high point we have passed through seven gates altogether, each guarded by a watch-tower and defended by doors with iron spikes to repel elephant charges. Kumbha is reputed to have built more than thirty fortresses over the Mewar kingdom, but none more impressive than this, with its ramp leading up to seven gates: the Padan Pol or Buffalo Gate, the Bhairon Gate named for a Rajput warrior killed on this spot, Hanuman Pol dedicated to the monkey-god of the Hindus, Ganesh Pol named for a small nearby altar, Jorla Pol or 'Joined Gate' since it is connected with Lakshman Pol, dedicated to Rama's half-brother, and Rama Pol with its neighbouring temple to Rama, seventh incarnation of Vishnu.

We have met Rana Kumbha at Kumbhalgarh and we shall meet him again on Mount Abu as the founder of the temple Kumbha Sham near Achalgarh; he was a poet and great warrior as well as a builder, and may have married Mira Bai, a poetess and mystic. But we cannot be sure on that point, for Har Bilas Sarda states that she was married to Bhojraj, son of Rana Singh of Merta.

Rana Kumbha's own palace is deserted and ruinous, but from the sabha you can easily make out the stables, the *zenana*, and to the south-west parts of the former palace of the heir apparent, or Kanwar Pade-ka Mahal. The *zenana's* incorporation into the main part of Rana Kumbha's palace can be proved from a sentry box and *jali* screens.

Chittor. Rana Kumbha's Palace

Kumbha was assassinated by his own son Udai Singh I (1468-73), who ruled only five years and is known in Mewari annals not by his name but by the epithet of 'murderer', or Hatyara. Hated by his subjects and reviled by rulers of other princely states, Hatyara finally sought sanction for his authority from the Sultan in Delhi but on leaving the Sultan's diwan it is recorded by Tod that he was struck by a flash of lightning, 'whence he never arose'. Hatyara was succeeded by Rana Raimal (1473-1509), Rana Sanga (1509-28), and Rana Ratan Singh II (1528-31). Ratan Singh built for himself at the north of the slope a new palace evenly rectangular and with a single high wall, with six massive defensive towers, octagonal at their base. It too has been remodelled, the southern part becoming a *zenana*. Shortly after this palace was completed, the second great siege of Chittor took place in 1535, four years after the teenage prince Vikramaditya had ascended the throne of Mewar. This time the threat came from the south, as Sultan Bahadur of Gujarat sought to avenge the insulted memory of Muzaffar, who had been defeated and captured as a hostage by Raimal. The young prince Udai was escorted to safety and his mother Karnavati led the women of Chittor to another great *jauhar* or mass immolation of (the record tells us) thirteen thousand women. The men of Chittor, led by Baghji of Deolia, then rushed forth to kill as many of their enemies as possible before being outnumbered and slain, but not taken alive.

Sultan Humayun, when begged to protect the rights of the infant Udai Singh from invaders, sent troops to recover Chittor from Bahadur of Gujarat and, when they achieved victory, replaced the sword of Vikramaditya in the citadel of Chittor. The advisers of the insolent and vindictive young Vikramaditya took offence when the *maleducato* struck the aged and loyal Karamchand, and 'arranged' for Banbir, illegitimate son of the hero Prithviraj, to take over at the expense of the liquidated Vikramaditya. Banbir then tried to remove Udai Singh in the same way, but the infant's noble, selfless and resourceful nurse allowed her own baby to be murdered in place of Udai, whom she sent to safety. He succeeded in 1541, but lacked the true Rajput qualities of perseverance, courage and nobility. In 1567 the Mughal Shah Akbar attacked Chittor, and conquered it after a siege lasting more than four months, during which he raised a hillock called Mohar Magri or 'Hill of Gold Coins' because its building was so dangerous that he paid one gold coin for every basketful of earth added to its height. From Mohar Magri, at the southern end of the fort, Akbar's cannons fired into the fort and finally won the day. Though Rajputs were to regain Chittorgarh, the Mewar capital removed to Udaipur for good, and ironically the architectural monuments of Chittorgarh have remained almost intact as a result, for they have – with a few exceptions – never been built over, razed, or robbed for new palaces. The golden gates from Padmini's water palace were transported by Akbar's men and set up in his fort at Agra.

The 20th-century palace called Fateh Prakash after Fateh Singh, who died in 1930, has been converted into a museum, interesting largely for sculptures rescued from various sites within the fort. Nearby is a Jain temple to Adinath, first of the *tirthankaras*, restored in 1946 but originally dating probably to the 12th century like the Kirti Stambh, ('Tower of Fame') which is sculptured with naked figures of the *tirthankaras*, and consequently is a monument of the Digambara ('Sky-clad') sect within Jainism, whose monks practise asceticism including nudity within their temple precincts. The other sect, clothed and less puritanical, are the Shvetambara. The relationship of tower to temple in scale and distance struck me as more harmonious than the more awkward nine-storey Jai or Vijay Stambh ('Tower of Victory'), a Hindu work of 1440-8 (restored in 1906) according to Coomaraswamy intended to commemorate the consecration in 1440 of the Kumbhasvami Vaishnava temple. (The local travel brochure says it was built to celebrate the military victory of Rana Kumbha over Mahmud of Mandu, but Mahmud also built a Victory Tower, at Mandu!) You can climb the 157 steps to the top of the 37-metre tower, enjoying wonderful views on all sides.

Though Udai failed his people, two young men in their mid-teens deserved more of posterity. Patta from Kelwa and Jaimal from Badnur are commemorated in their secular palaces of about 1560 on the west side of the fort south of the reservoir called Gaumukh Kund and next to Jaimal Tank. Patta's palace resembles, possibly as a subtle compliment, the *zenana* of Rana Kumbha's palace with a stepped wall concealing a stairway; that of Jaimal is an almost pure cube, with a roof terrace on the upper storey between two equal rooms accessible by internal enclosed stairs at the front.

A red-winged bush lark swept up, a glint of scarlet, from Maha Sati, the great suicide square which saw the immense *jauhar* of Karnavati in 1535, attested by a thick layer of ash found during excavation. Immediately to the south rises the Samideshwara Temple to Shiva reconstructed in 1428 by Rana Mokal on the site of a 9th-century temple traditionally ascribed to Bhoj, a ruler of Malwa. Shiva's bull Nandi protects the entrance, and within a three-headed figure of Shiva is the object of worship. Southward you find the tanks of Gaumukh and Hathi, then past the mansions of Patta and Jaimal you come once more to the old Surya Temple, possibly as early as 8th-century in its original form but during the zenith of Chittorgarh's fame and prosperity it became a temple of Kali and was several times restored. The so-called summer palace of Padmini close by probably has nothing to do with her at all, especially since the larger part is clearly a *mardana* or men's quarter, while the *zenana* nestled in the centre of the artificial lake.

On your way out you will come to another Shivaite temple, called Jata Shankar, and the Vaishnavite temple called Kumbha Shyam, rebuilt in 1448, protected by Vishnu's bird Garuda at the entrance. Beyond Kumbha's palace, a reconstruction of an early 14th-century palace built by Rana Hamir, we pass a charming 15th-century Jain temple called Shantinath Mandir, near an unfinished wall started by Banbir in a vain attempt to divide the fort area, the more efficiently to rule. A round edifice called 'Nine Hundred Thousand' or Nau Lakha once guarded the treasure of Chittor. The last building before regaining Rama Pol, the seventh gate, is a temple called Tulja paid for by Banbir during his short reign.

There is nothing monumental to see in the town of Chittorgarh, but as always you will enjoy wandering in noisy, bright and bustling streets with their munching bovine divinities and the kind of restless energy that tires you out while you watch it from your haunches, or from an old rickety chair that allows you to rest legs apparently made out of sweating cotton wool. During my visit to the fort I found no restaurant, so my advice is to eat before you start, and to start at 8 a.m., because the afternoon tour, though shorter, becomes much more tiring in the merciless sun. And keep your *hat* on, or you will suffer.

Bundi

I took a bus to Bundi, 120 km to the east, a small town still comically underprepared for visitors. Bundi has a high reputation among art connoisseurs far beyond its small size for exquisite miniatures especially of the 18th century, and murals in the palace's Chitra Shali (1748-70), in particular a range of panels glorifying Krishna, with Radha and the *gopis*. You can stay at the Circuit House in Bundi, at a pinch in the Jain Dharamsala near the bus station or the very basic Dak Bungalow, but generally speaking it is advisable to reach Bundi in the morning and leave before nightfall, for it has to be confessed that Bundi cannot believe how beautiful, unspoilt and desirable it is: a veritable virgin among Rajput cities. Sometimes one can stay in Ranjit Niwas, the former ruler's guest-house, but a New Zealand friend who had cabled there was assured on arrival that her reservation had never been received and there was no room. The 20th-century palace of Phul Sagur 10 km to the west was begun in 1945 and decorated by Italian prisoners-of-war. But that is where the former ruler lives, so permission to visit parts of it must be sought in advance and in writing from the private secretary to His Highness. A small pavilion was built in 1603 and the lake or *sagar* was added during the time of Maharao Ram Singh (1821-89). Bundi's name derives from a *bindo* or cleft in the Aravali hills into which it fits like a glacier of white and brown flat-roofed houses trapped in a valley. Tongas are plentiful if you cannot walk easily or for long, but there is no better way to explore Bundi than on foot, for its variety of elegant step-wells or *baolis*, some dating from as early as the 16th century (Raniji-ki Baoli) and others rather later such as Jaipuria Kund.

The hilly Bundi Palace has been adapted to the site, like an Italian hill town, and does not impose itself on the landscape as does, for instance, Amber Palace. The main gate of Hathia Pol is reached through Hazari Pol, or gate for the barracks guard. Ratan Singh's Hathia Pol is dramatically contended by two stone elephants locked in frozen battle high above the entrance. A crowded courtyard within is flanked by former royal stables, and the atmosphere is martial, masculine, Rajput. This is a place where a Rajput and his attendants lived a life more spartan than that we have seen in larger courts such as Jaipur heavily influenced by Mughal taste and fashion. If you climb the steps you come to the Public Audience Hall or Diwan-i-Am constructed by Rao Raja Ratan Singh (1607-31) with its plain marble throne; it is small because only the favoured few sat inside, the generality viewing the ruler (who viewed them) from the courtyard. Ratan Singh's successor, Maharao

Bundi. Fort Palace

Chattar Sal (1631-58), built a new palace, the Chattar Mahal, whose courtyard has remnants of decorations which might be Muslim in their geometrical designs. Chattar Mahal's western hall, the so-called Hathi Sala, beguiles you with its quartet of small elephants on each column; its eastern hall is a delight of duodecagonal columns though which you pass to the private rooms of Chattar Sal, a long central chamber and two smaller rooms. In the long room little elephants and horses act as inspired clothes pegs for a ruler constantly on the move to protect his dominions and to take pleasure in the hunt. The southern room is decorated with fine murals depicting life in the circumscribed world of 17th-century Bundi.

Bundi painting developed much later than at Udaipur, whose style is evidently influential, with yellow margins and red surrounds. Bundi miniatures can be recognised by an emphasis on feminine shapeliness, passionate colourism, romantic passion echoed by symbolic courtship between birds, and an ardent devotion to Krishna, rising to new levels under Raja Ajit Singh (1771-1804).

Bundi's finest murals are those of the Chitra Shali, a square courtyard we owe to Rao Raja Umaid Singh (1739-70), a ruler who retired from his high office to become an ascetic and monk. The paintings on the walls of Chitra Shali reflect the devotion of Bundi's royal dynasty to the Vallabha sect, one of whose tenets says that one can be saved through meditation on the loves of Krishna for Radha and the *gopis*. These walls are almost as varied as a Diego Rivera mural, with fighting elephants, fantastic floral scenes, the Bundi palace and life within it and without, including processions.

Umaid Singhji was also responsible for the large tank of Nawal Sagar with its temple to Varuna in the centre. At the hilltop a 14th-century Star Fort, known in Hindi as Taragarh, offers wonderful views over the plains, and on a clear day you can even make out the city of Kota. On the northeast you can see below you the reservoir of Jait Sagar with the summer palace of Sukh Mahal ('Palace of Happiness') created in 1773. Rudyard Kipling found it uncomfortable to spend the night there because the pavilion at that time (not today) was 'open to the winds of heaven and the pigeons of the Raj; but the latter had polluted more than the first could purify'. His essays, published as *From Sea to Sea* (1889), were written when he was 22. You could well open *Kim* for an hour in this quiet spot, but try too to find time for the place of cenotaphs at the other side of Jait Sagar: the *mahasati* called Sar Bagh, with 66 royal cenotaphs. As in life, the rulers are accompanied in death by elephants, sculptures that you will find echoed at Kota.

Your tonga could then take you out to the hunting tower (Shikar Burj), where Umaid Singhji lived after his retirement; the Hanuman Chhatri, and the Temple of Kedhareshwar Mahadeo.

I took a late tea in the K.N. Singh Restaurant, where two young raven-haired graduates of Udaipur were eager to get into conversation. What did I think of Bundi, their home town? Did I know about corruption at all levels of Indian society? One of them, nervously drumming his shapely fingers on the table as I gratefully drank down another long cold drink, expressed his concern at Western misconceptions about caste. The other answered my questions about child brides in Rajasthan. Thousands of little children are married off in mass ceremonies performed by village priests at Akha Tij, the harvest festival. Some of these children are so young that their parents recite the marriage vows, encircling the sacred fire seven times with their innocent victims in their arms. The infants are immediately separated, and the bride goes to live with her unknown 'husband' at the age of sixteen. Infant mortality is terribly high in jrajasthan, especially during the recent years of drought and, if the boy dies before the bride reaches sixteen, she faces life as a widow and cannot remarry, despite the fact that her earlier marriage was illegal by the Child Marriages Restraint Act (1939) which forbade marriage below 18 for girls and 21 for boys, a law honoured more in the breach than in the observance. The best that can happen to the widowed girls is that their family will continue to look after them; the worst is disgrace, destitution, and a life of unhappiness. Some 80% of Indians live in villages where the approval of one's immediate family, one's caste, and the 'neighbours' play a much greater part in a woman's life than any laws emanating from the Government.

Kota

It is a short 35-km bus-ride from Bundi to Kota, also an important historic centre for miniature painting but in recent years a highly-developed industrial town with seven times the population of Bundi (roughly 350,000 against 50,000), with an atomic plant, chemical industries including the largest fertilizer factory in Asia, and a station on the broad-gauge line from Delhi to Bombay. Bundi was intimately related to Kota because the Hara Chauhan clan of the Agnikula or fire dynasty Rajputs (whose Deora Chauhan also took Sirohi) seized Bundi from the Minas in about 1341 and Kota in about 1364. Kota originally formed part of Bundi state, becoming autonomous about 1624 when Ratan Singh of Bundi gave it to his son Madho Singh, and from Kota state Jhalawar became autonomous in 1838.

One leading factor in Kota's importance has been its situation on the east bank of the river Chambal, which flows into the Yamuna in the direction of Agra. The Aravali hills and neighbouring plains, once rich in wildlife, have been mercilessly plundered by official and unofficial hunting and shooting parties, and your only chance of seeing wild animals will be within sanctuaries such as Mukunddarrah, about 80 km to the south, called 'Mukund Pass' after Rao Mukund Singh of Kota, where he and other scions of the ruling dynasty of Kota enjoyed hunting with their retainers from the 18th century until 1955. Rhinoceros and wild buffalo once roamed these forests and clearings, but the species have been greatly reduced over the years and now you will be lucky to see spotted deer, panthers, wild boars and tigers while cruising along jungle roads by jeep or spotting them from watchtowers. There is a resthouse at Mukunddarrah, known to the locals as 'Darrah' for short. The best season there is from October to March.

But your best reason for staying in Kota will probably be to visit the historic city, the City Palace, and the Chambal Gardens (once home to hundreds of crocodiles) next to a pleasure-palace called Amar Niwas. Approaching the palace you will recognise from Bundi's Hathia Pol the linked trunks of two elephants on this Hathia Pol, which was built later, has no side towers, and must be a good deal smaller too. Indeed the whole Rajput *garh* of Kota reminds you of its predecessor at Bundi, from Arjuna Mahal (with its elephant-columns similar to the ones we have seen in Bundi's Hathi Sala) to the slight asymmetry, clearly calculated, in Raj Mahal (similar to Bundi's Chitra Shali). Kota City Palace belongs to the mature Rajput style, like those of Jaisalmer and

Kota. Fort Palace

Udaipur, being situated in a fort, the fort within a city, and a bazaar leading through the city to a fort gate, as at Jodhpur.

Dates are hard to come by and approximate, relying on local traditions, but it seems likely that much of the earlier phases of the palace were due to Rao Madho Singh (1625-48), who certainly erected Hathia Pol, the great audience hall or Raj Mahal, Lakshmi Bandar Tribari and above it a hall called Baradari, which strictly means an open-columned hall. Maharao Bhim Singh (1707-20), who added the elephants to Hathia Pol, was responsible for a new wing of the *mardana* or men's quarters, consisting of Bhim Mahal and Bara Mahal, the former a fine durbar hall and the later enlivened by excellent murals. Durgan Sal (1723-56) added the Akhade-ka Mahal, intended as a wrestling hall but rebuilt by Umaid Singh (1888-1940). At the east you will be enchanted by an elegant, modest Hawa Mahal (1864), which refers respectfully to the 18th-century model at Jaipur but to my eye seems more in scale with its surroundings than its flamboyant and much more ostentatious antecedent. Umaid Singh finally decided to add two identical *zenanas*, one for each of his two wives, and while these may not win anyone's award for fine buildings, they have a certain confident integrity as part of that tradition which we have come to recognise in Rajputana of the Rajputs: indefatigable independence of spirit, preferring variety to orthodoxy, and personal idiosyncrasy to unthinking symmetry.

Internally, the elegant palace provides us with an absorbing museum of weapons, regalia, flags, historic photographs, early stone idols, and interesting architectural fragments from city and state. Raj Mahal displays a throne on which successive rulers of Kota were anointed and where they sat during durbar. Its walls are painted with Krishna themes, as at Bundi, hunting scenes, and portraits of rulers and other notables. Bara Mahal is decorated with some of the earliest of all Kota school miniatures, dating to about 1680. Arjuna Mahal's murals are of the 19th century. Kota painting developed to its highest point after 1780, with the movement of artists from Bundi, but Kota's style is much more naive in treatment, familiar in the West from such endearing artists as Henri Rousseau, whose poetic imagination and eccentricity make up for deficiencies of technique. We can see Ram Singh (1828-66) massacring tigers and lions in a fairy-tale setting. After that in the City Palace, the best collection of Kota miniatures is the Gayer-Anderson Gift in London's Victoria and Albert Museum.

Close to the City Palace is an artificial lake called Kishor Sagar (1346), with its island palace built by Maharani Brij Kanwar about 1740. Do not miss Chattar Vilas Gardens and Brij Vilas Palace with the royal cenotaphs in Sar Bagh.

Wandering about the town of Kota you will find tombs of Kesar Khan and Dokhar Khan, Pathan brothers who held Kota from 1531 until their overthrow in 1551 by Rao Surjan. Nearby you can explore the aromatic, noisy and bustling vegetable market.

Once the British Political Residency (about 1840), Brij Raj Bhawan Mahal became a state guest house in 1900, and is now a tourist hotel for the isolated groups who have the insight to plan a night in Kota. Sir Swinton Jacob, an architect we remember from Jaipur and Bikaner, also designed Umaid Bhawan Palace here in Kota, built in 1905.

Do not miss Chambal Gardens, and Amar Niwas, a charming pleasure palace. If you arrive by bus, the most convenient accommodation is in Chambal Tourist Bungalow; those coming by train may use the railway retiring rooms, and I recommend breaking your journey between Delhi and Bombay here. If you have a car, on the other hand, I suggest continuing to Jhalawar in the Mukunddarrah hills to the south.

Mount Abu
Two overwhelming reasons may persuade you to travel westward from Udaipur to Mount Abu. One is to escape the searing heat of the plains

in favour of cool, green hills on a granite dome 1220 m high. Another is to rejoice in some of the most marvellous religious sculpture anywhere in the world, in glorious Jain temples generously opened to non-Jains. A third good reason would be to see a great range of animals and birds in their natural surroundings, though for this you would need patience and adequate time to explore off the beaten track. There is no airport for Mount Abu closer than Udaipur, so you would take the bus from Udaipur (184 km) or the train to Abu Road on the Delhi-Jaipur-Ahmedabad line with a bus connection for the 26 km drive to the hill station. You can stay at the Mount Hotel on Dilwara Road, Abu International or the Shikar Tourist Bungalow near the Polo Ground, or Bikaner Palace Hotel. Auto-rickshaws or taxis will take you around, but note that there are regular buses to Dilwara (10 km) and you will want to walk in Mount Abu itself for ever-changing views and Raj Bhawan Art Gallery and State Museum opposite the Post Office on Raj Bhawan Road. The best times of year for Mount Abu are from late February to late June, and from late August to late November. Between early December and late February be sure to wear heavy waterproof clothing, such as an anorak. The tourist bureau is situated on Rajendra Road opposite the bus terminus. On the lower slopes you can see fleet-footed chinkara, and the sub-tropical forest is radiant with pink oleander, flame-of-the-forest, and jacaranda, and botanists can enjoy several gardens in Mount Abu itself: Terrace Garden, Gandhi Park, Ashok Vatika, Shaitan Singh Park and the municipal gardens. Two five-hour daily sightseeing trips offered by Rajasthan Tourism Development Corporation (one starting at 8 a.m. and the other at 2 p.m.) will suit those without transport of their own: they cover Dilwara, Achalgarh, Guru Shikhar (at 1,725 m the highest point in Rajasthan), Nakki Lake, Sunset Point, and the rock temple of Arbuda Devi, also called Adhar Devi.

I started by trekking past a Hanuman Temple some 5 km to the Temple of Gaumukh, named for a spring gushing through the mouth of a marble cow. A shrine to Vishnu shows him as both **Rama** and **Krishna**. The place is at once sacred and historic, for here – so the legend goes at least – near the ashram of Vashishtha, the four dynasties of *agnikula* or fire-born Rajputs were created by an ordeal of purification. These Kshatriyas were the Chauhans (who went on to found Sirohi in 1426, the state in which Mount Abu is situated, Bundi and Kota); the Paramars, whose temples are the pride of Madhya Pradesh; the Pratiharas; and the Solankis, kings of Gujarat.

On the south bank of Nakki Lake you can visit the Hindu temple of Shri Raghunathji, and on the road leading from there via the bazaar to the Mount Hotel the Christian Church of S. Lawrence stood quiet and deserted.

But if you have time for only one day in Mount Abu, the plan will be to see the glorious complex of Jain temples near the village of Dilwara. From Mount Abu in 4 km you arrive at a *dharamsala* on the right-hand side of the road; on the left rises a white world of architecture deriving from the same mines of Makrana that gave Agra its Taj Mahal. But whereas that mighty Mughal landmark stands out for its large-scale grandeur, here at Dilwara the Jain temples are resplendent in countless tiny details, both figurative and abstract. They are open daily from noon to six. The earliest of these temples, dedicated to Adinath the first *tirthankara*, was commissioned about 1032 by Vimal Shah, Jain prime minister of Bhim Deva, the first Solanki king of Gujarat. As H. Cousens notes in *The Architectural Antiquities of Western India* (1926), 'the amount of beautiful ornamental detail spread over these temples in the minutely carved decoration of ceilings, pillars, doorways, panels and niches is simply marvellous; the crisp, thin, translucent shell-like treatment of the marble surpasses anything seen elsewhere, and some of the designs are veritable dreams of beauty. The work is so delicate that ordinary chiselling would have been disastrous.' Cousens infers that much of the detail was produced by scraping the marble away, in that infinity of patience which the modern world finds impossible to contemplate, a technique more like ivory-carving than sculpture.

Before entering the temple to Adinath, look at the pavilion of donors, with ten stone elephants mounted by donors, the victim of iconoclasm. Even the least whisper would be sacrilegious in the extraordinary white and shadowed eternity of the domed temple, its portico of forty-eight columns leading us inexorably to the *mandapa*. The *makara toranas* or scrolled archways lift the spirits which are further enchanted with nymphs and musicians sinuous yet rounded, ravishing in their beauty yet ethereal in their schematic realization. We see no person, no individual, no character, but a visualisation of the immanent, as in the graphic works of the greatest Western abstract artists: Mark Tobey or André Masson. The dome comprises eleven concentric rings, of which the five lowest contain sixteen stelliform *mandalas*, and the six above them whirl and heave with elephants, horses, and dancers. What a contrast then to encounter the central meditative idol of Adinath, looking inward to the heart! Explore the cloisters, their pillars carved to the point of ecstasy and their fifty-two niches filled with images of the *tirthankaras*. Photography is permitted (for a small fee) and one delight of Dilwara is that one might create a photographic archive of a hundred of the most beautiful Jain marble carvings.

Very close to the Adinath Temple is the Neminath Temple (1230), dedicated to the twenty-second *tirthankara* and financed by two brothers (Tejpal and Vastupal) who were ministers to a Solanki ruler of Gujarat. They were also responsible for a temple at Girnar in

MOUNT ABU
TOURIST MAP
(Not to scale)

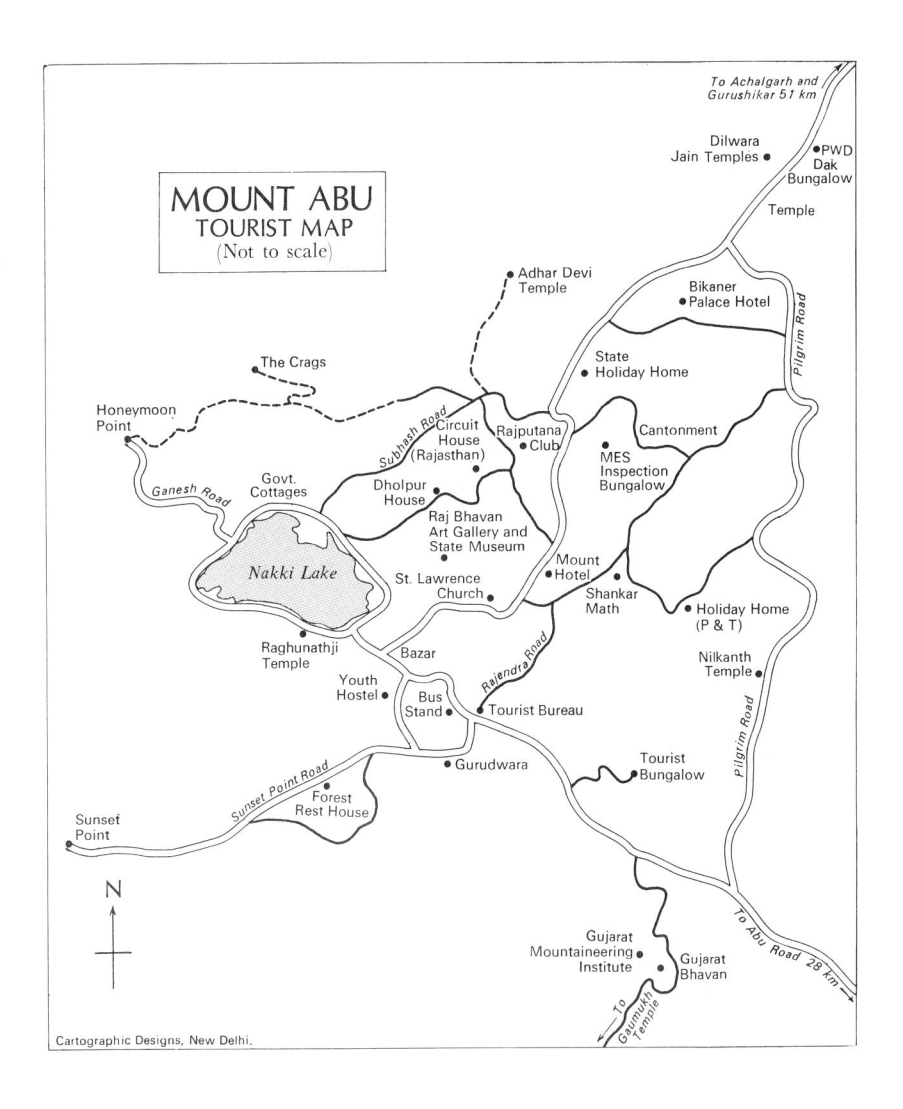

Kathiawar. Again, the hall of donors and elephants is of great interest, and can be found in this instance behind the central shrine. The quality of the carving seems, were it possible, even more refined, voluptuous and prolific than in the earlier temple, and one might well spend hours entering the mental world of these craftsmen, these *silavats*, before whom the expanse of marble must have contradicted their ingrained and inherited theories of cyclical time. It is hard, and finite though so abundant, for it will not grow again like the mangoes in the grove outside. But no, I am wrong for they would argue that whatever they did showed merely the superficial face of the eternal, which was indeed cyclical, aeons beyond aeons, and their ancestors had carved such shrines before and their descendants would carve such shrines again. It is a great privilege to stand in the Neminath Temple in Dilwara, and move clockwise through its infinite variety, observing the apotheosis of white, grey and black as the shadows lengthen throughout the afternoon. Paradoxically, I have never been so keenly aware of my temporal existence at this moment when infinity spreads like a cloud around the microcosm of the tiniest hair on the head of a dancer, and up into the macrocosm of the shrine and the universe of which it forms a mere dot.

It is almost an anticlimax to continue to another of the forts built by the Rana Kumbha of Mewar: Achalgarh, dating to 1452, found off a right turning on the road to Guru Shikhar. But the effort is worth it because of the remarkable views, and there is something appropriate about rising to the highest point in the whole of Rajasthan, and observing *sadhus* at their devotions in caves all around. At one moment you are swept by a cold wind under a bright sun, hungry, uncomfortable, far indeed from any city, isolated and forlorn. At the next moment you are exhilarated by the presence of the numinous, an inner reality, a verdict of the just, that you were right to have come thus far, and right to return home. Can it really be only a matter of a few weeks ago that you arrived in Delhi on a passage to India, unaware of Udaipur, unfamiliar with Ranakpur, with only a hazy idea of Jaisalmer, ignorant concerning Dilwara and the repeal of time?

Useful Information

When to Come
The best months for Delhi are February, March and April, and the same is true for Agra. May and June are generally oppressively hot and dusty, July and August sodden with monsoon rains, then the climate begins to recover a little equipoise with September, and October and November seem pleasant. December and January can be quite cold, for Delhi's buildings are not warm enough for the winter.

December and February are the best months for visiting Rajasthan, except that the hill station at Mount Abu, too cold then, can be found at its best in April-June and September-October. Bikaner and Jaisalmer should be avoided in June, July and August.

Here are the temperatures (maximum and minimum) and the average rainfall in millimetres recorded for Delhi over the year, and Agra will be roughly similar. Jaipur and area works out marginally warmer between December and May and a degree or so cooler from June to November. Jodhpur is two to four degrees hotter, but the rainfall is very similar.

J	F	M	A	M	J	J	A	S	O	N	D	
21	24	30	35	40	40	35	34	35	34	29	23	Max. °C
7	10	15	21	27	29	28	26	25	19	13	8	Min. °C
25	22	16	7	8	64	210	174	152	31	1	5	Rain (mm)

How to Come
Air connections to Rajasthan can be made from either Delhi or Bombay. Indian Airlines fly more than once a day between those international airports, by way of Ahmedabad-Jodhpur-Jaipur (and vice versa) and by way of Aurangabad-Udaipur-Jodhpur-Jaipur (and vice versa). Agra is linked by air with both Delhi and Jaipur. Occasional Vayudoot flights link Kota with Jaipur and Bikaner and Jaisalmer with Jaipur-Jodhpur, but these arrangements should be checked locally. Frankly, there is not much to recommend travelling by air in Rajasthan, because the landscapes and people seen close to must be one of the most powerful of motives for visiting India in the first place: it is not a country where speed aids appreciation.

Rail travel in Rajasthan can be divided roughly into two categories: broad-gauge lines (in which the rails are 1.676 m apart) and metre-gauge lines, such as that from Jodhpur southwest to Barmer and northwest to Jaisalmer. Broad-gauge lines are comfortable and generally faster, and you should try the Taj Express from Delhi to Agra one way, returning the other way by road.

Delhi to Jaipur on the metre-gauge runs via Alwar, and Agra to Jaipur via Bharatpur. By rail you can also travel from Jaipur to Bikaner (via Sikar and Fatehpur Shekhavati), Abu Road (for Mount Abu), Jodhpur, Ajmer (for Pushkar), Sawai Madhopur and Udaipur.

The daily Shekhavati Express links Delhi and Jaipur via Jhunjhunu, Mukundgarh and Sikar.

Bikaner is connected with Delhi (via Hanumangarh), Jaipur and Jodhpur. Jaisalmer is connected by night and day trains with Jodhpur. The 'Palace on Wheels' (described in the chapter on Jodhpur) is available by prior booking (at your travel agent or direct through the Umaid Bhawan Palace, Jodhpur) to transport you from Jodhpur to Jaisalmer: it is actually not a separate train, but private de luxe accommodation attached to the regular trains.

Jodhpur may be reached by a very fast night train from Delhi, and by slower trains from Jaipur, Ajmer, Abu Road, Bikaner, Jaisalmer and Barmer.

Udaipur is connected with Delhi by the daily Chetak Express via Jaipur and Ajmer. Mount Abu is accessible by Delhi trains to Ahmedabad (via Jaipur and Ajmer) stopping at Abu Road, then the regular buses leaving from Abu Road station 27 km to the hill-station. By train you can get to Chittorgarh on the Delhi-Ratlam line as far as Chittor station, then a bus 6 km to the fortress. Kota is on the broad-gauge Delhi-Bombay line via Bharatpur and Sawai Madhopur.

Do you need an Indrail pass? Yes, you do if you are travelling everywhere by rail over, say, 15 days, currently costing £120 for air-conditioned class, £60 for first-class/a.c. chair class, and £30 for second class. Second class is hopelessly crowded and uncomfortable, but first-class may be converted during the day to air-conditioned coaches, space permitting as it nearly always does, at no extra charge. You can vary the period of the ticket, which includes sleeper berths on overnight journeys, but you may pay for the pass only with hard currency overseas, at a 'gateway' airport such as Delhi, or at reservation offices in the main Indian cities. Given the delays and confusion in India, my advice is *always* to buy it overseas, in the U.K. from S.D.E.L., 21 York House, Empire Way, Wembley, Mddx. Despite all appearances to the contrary, Indian trains are almost always on time, which is significant if you have a 'plane to catch at the other end.

It must be emphasised that trains themselves, their passengers, and the countryside through which they travel, form an integral part of the Indian experience, and should not be missed on any account, even if you have to confine yourself, through lack of time, to one short stretch. In Rajasthan, buses are not only more frequent and much faster, but they get to many places (in Shekhavati, for instance) where no train goes, such as Ranakpur or Mandawa.

You can take organised bus tours through Rajasthan (with Agra) from any one of a number of agencies in Delhi, and this method is very much cheaper than buying tours abroad, because you cut out the foreign middleman. They are also very competitive, and if you put on your best haggling voice and gestures, you should be able to strike an excellent bargain. Public buses are much more crowded, but much cheaper, and if you have time to spare this – like the railways only more so – connects you effortlessly to the real India and Indians travelling for their own varied motives. I especially recommend the efficient air-conditioned express bus from Delhi to Agra, and Haryana Roadways from Delhi to Jaipur. Rajasthan Roadways will take you from Jaipur's Sindhi Camp bus station almost anywhere in the state, including Ajmer, Shekhavati, Alwar, Bharatpur. The air-conditioned bus from Jaipur to Bikaner is a boon during the hot season; Delhi to Bikaner is served by a bus stopping in Jhunjhunu, Churu and Ratangarh, and the service to Jaisalmer continues through Phalodi and Pokaran. From Jaisalmer you can reach Barmer by a bone-shaker, and a better bus to Jodhpur through Pokaran, and Decchu. Udaipur offers frequent connections with Chittorgarh, Mount Abu, Ajmer, Bundi and Kota, and of course with Jaipur and Jodhpur.

There is no possibility at present to hire a self-drive car in India, but cars with drivers can be hired by the hour, day or week at relatively low cost, compared with what you would pay in Europe or North America. Such an arrangement is perfect for the many little villages and larger towns of Shekhavati, but within bigger cities such as Agra or Jodhpur you are better off hiring local rickshaws and, haggling with them, negotiating a price higher than they expect but lower than they demand. In hilly places like Mount Abu you will use auto rickshaws, in flat places like Bikaner you will use tongas, and elsewhere you may prefer cycle rickshaws. Walking may suit those with a great deal of time, but exploration of castles and palaces is too hard on the aching feet for you to pass up the chance of transport when it is offered: remember you are contributing to the local economy by employing rickshaw-wallahs, without depriving yourself of all the sights and sounds of streetlife and bazaars. Always settle on a price *before* starting.

Accommodation
Throughout the text I have indicated places to stay in Rajasthan. There is often a stark choice between a royal palace and a Dak bungalow or tourist hotel near the bus or rail station, with no intermediate

price-range. My suggestion is to experience all types of acccommodation, because even the expensive palaces are reasonably priced by western standards, with discounts discreetly available most of the year, and nobody should be deprived of staying in a rowdy, sweaty 'Indian' hotel at least once in their life. Try a youth hostel one day, and a mansion the next.

Delhi is different, with abundant hotels to suit every pocket, from Chanakyapuri hotels such as the expensive Maurya Sheraton and Taj Mahal to the middle-range places near Connaught Place such as the Alka or the Marina, and the cheap but convenient lodgings on Janpath Lane such as Mr Jain's or Mrs Colaco's. The Y.M.C.A. Tourist Hotel can be found on Jai Singh Road, and the Y.W.C.A. at 10 Parliament Street. Youth hostels in Chanakyapuri include one at 5 Nyaya Marg and the International Youth Centre behind the Chinese Embassy: you can ask your rickshaw-wallah for Chanakyapuri Police Station, which is quite close.

For Mathura, where I suggest you spend a night, there is little choice: try the railway retiring rooms at Mathura Junction or the Agra Hotel on Bengali Ghat.

Agra has opulent hotels such as Clark's Shiraz, the Mughal Sheraton at Tajganj, or the Taj View, formerly the Holiday Inn. If you prefer a mid-range place with a choice of air-conditioning, I can recommend Laurie's on Gandhi Marg for those with a sense of nostalgia for the Raj, but be prepared for less than five-star comfort and service! At the cheaper end of the market, Agra Fort rail station has convenient retiring rooms, Agra Hotel on Metcalfe Road in the Cantonment has a view of the Taj, and on Fatehabad Road you can find Mayur Tourist Complex, the Mughal and the Galaxy. Since the Fort is closer to the heart of Old Agra, you may care to explore for typical little hotels between Agra Fort station and Agra City station. Human life teems and yells with a vociferousness that comes from trying to assert one's identity in an environment more suited to the crowd. You can always restore your equilibrium in the privacy of your own room.

Passports and Visas
Visitors to India must possess a current valid passport with a visa for India and special permits for any restricted areas that you plan to visit. Do *not* try to obtain these permits after arrival, because conditions may change and no permits may be issued for given districts, so that if you discover that fact in advance you can change your route without loss of time or money. Permits are not currently needed for any sector of Rajasthan, though the actual border with Pakistan (not covered in this guide) is closed and therefore no access is available by road. Allow two weeks for your visa, obtaining the visa form beforehand from your

nearest Indian embassy or consulate. In Britain, visas and permits are obtainable from the travel agents with whom you book (for an extra fee) or direct from the High Commission for India, India House, Aldwych, London WC2. In the U.S.A., the Embassy is at 2107 Massachusetts Avenue, N.W., Washington, D.C. 20008, and there is a Consul-General at 3 East 64th St., New York, N.Y. 10021. In France, the Indian Embassy can be found at 15 rue Alfred Dehodencq, 75016 Paris.

Customs and Currency

It is prohibited to carry Indian currency into or out of India, and it is very time-consuming to change money at banks, so you can risk taking a credit card (easily lost or stolen), but I recommend travellers' cheques in either sterling or U.S. dollars. These may be changed on arrival at the airport, or at your hotel. Banks should be avoided, because of long delays. If you have no money belt, you can buy (or make) a pouch to hang around your neck, or sew an inside pocket on your skirt, trousers or jeans for high denomination notes, and count out for your bag or outside pocket whatever money you allocate for each day, replenishing at night when you set your alarm and take your malaria pills.

The unit of currency throughout India is the rupee, divided into one hundred paisa. Coins are minted in 1, 2, 3, 5, 10, 20, 25 and 50 paisa, and banknotes are printed in 1, 2, 5, 10, 20, 50, 100 and 500 rupees.

Tipping in small denominations greases the machinery of travel all over India, and nobody is exempted from this golden rule.

The idea is to avoid giving money to beggars, but to produce one- or two-paisa notes for services actually rendered, like a small boy's showing you *havelis* in the back streets of Nawalgarh, or a station porter's finding you a seat in the train at Sawai Madhopur when congestion seemed to involve squashing all limbs like a compulsory mass wrestling match lasting three hours or two submissions.

The golden rule is to cash money to avoid running out at embarrassing moments, like paying for a bus ride to Jaisalmer or lodgings on Mount Abu. Indians are very sensitive about being given damaged banknotes and may well refuse to accept any notes torn at the edges: you can give any such away in tips, but try to avoid accepting them in the first place. Small change is very hard to come by, and you should take every opportunity to change large notes into smaller denominations.

Health

Visitors are rightly preoccupied about health and hygiene when travelling in India, and some Westerners refuse to go there because of concerns on this count. This resembles objecting to flying over the English Channel because the aircraft might drop in the water. You simply take precautions. For one thing, try to follow a diet as close as possible to what you would eat at home. This is increasingly feasible in the bigger cities like Delhi, and in places where tourists roam as thick on the ground as fleas in a dog's tail, like Agra or Jaipur. Failing familiar ingredients, you can always find bland food: bread, rice, potatoes, omelettes, and believe it or not Indian restaurants are very much aware of the sensitivities of Western palates and stomachs, and routinely reduce the amount of chili or curry when serving Westerners. Buffets are usually divided into Indian-style and Western-style counters.

Toilets abound in areas frequented by tourists, such as major sights, palaces, forts and museums. You may have to use a squatting-type, but more and more lavatories are being at least partly converted to Western use. Hotels and Western-style restaurants are normally the best places to frequent, and you do not have to stay in a hotel to use the facilities.

Injections needed for India will vary from time to time and must be checked with your local doctor, or in London at British Airways, 65-75 Regent Street, London W1, but it is safe to assume that you will need protection against hepatitis, polio, tetanus and typhoid.

Current suggestions among doctors in the U.K. to combat malaria include both Maloprim and Paludrine and, as both courses must be begun well before departure, you should consult your family doctor in good time. Sunstroke, dehydration and exposure can become quite a hazard in hot, dry Rajasthan, so make sure your face and neck, especially lips and nose, are well protected with your usual lotions. *Take everything with you*, because while some chemists stock some preparations, coverage is patchy and hunting for pharmacies and drug-stores may prove frustrating and will certainly waste time. It is virtually impossible to prevent stomach problems, but the golden rule will be to try to eat and drink as much as you do at home as far as possible. To cure the problem, take with you Streptotriad pills (unless you are sensitive to sulphonamide) for which you may need a prescription. Avoid eating anything at all for twenty-four hours after being struck down, rest as much as possible, and keep taking soft drinks and weak tea to avoid dehydration. Imodium works well, but may take a day to work. *Never* drink the water, even if you are assured it has been boiled, without Sterotabs or a similar sterilizing pill in the strengths prescribed. Mosquito coils, lit before you go to bed, generally last long enough to remain effective till morning. During the daytime you can rub over your exposed body one of the anti-mosquito preparations recommended by leading chemists. I even take my own shampoo sachets, toothpaste and shaving kit, hand-towel, soap in a soapdish, and a roll of high-quality toilet paper, which also helps in sundry other ways. A bath plug of the kind needed for the U.S.S.R. will be a blessing, but do *remember* to take it away again when you dry yourself; in the absence of a plug, I find that toilet-paper saturated and stuffed into the hole will retain the water as long as necessary. One final suggestion: antiseptic cream and a choice of three or four dressings will quickly solve those minor accidents and prevent their becoming major.

Clothing

Take as little as possible, but remember that nights can be cold and if you intend to travel by night an anorak can double as a pillow. For long daytime journeys by bus or train I wear a 'sleepover' or similar airfilled cushion on my shoulders to take the weight off my head and reduce the wear and tear on my neck muscles caused by bumping and jerking. Indians dress modestly and are offended by the sight of many immodest Western men and women in shorts and short skirts, so it is sensitive to wear long trousers or long skirts. Even the best hotels do not insist on formal wear, so you can be relaxed except at formal dinners with dignitaries who will themselves take enormous trouble. You should *always* have a hat, and if men want to use hotel swimming-pools they must use swimming trunks; women should cover up in what might be considered 'old-fashioned ways'. You can buy excellent, very cheap sandals in India; it is distinctly desirable to wear such simple footwear if visiting mosques, temples or shrines. Cotton socks will be needed against hot red sandstone: bare feet quickly burn. Hotel laundries can be trusted to return clothes but there is a heavy surcharge for urgent work, damage to clothes is not unknown, and if you have running water in your room you can handwash clothes quickly and leave them to dry in a couple of hours. Handy sachets of *Travel Wash* or a similar detergent are convenient.

Speaking the Languages

Readers who know my previous travel guides will be familiar with my proposition that learning one or more of the local languages will repay the effort in proportion to the effort. Sadly, this does not apply to India, where you stand a grave risk of offending somebody by trying to speak in a regional language or in the lingua franca, Hindi. It is assumed that, by avoiding English, you consider that your new acquaintance is ignorant, uneducated, stupid, or from a lower class, and this assumption is offensive. I am afraid I committed the solecism too often to be mistaken.

Undaunted, I still feel that it is a good idea to be able to read street signs, shop signs and notices (though even many of these are in English or bilingual), to offer courteous greetings, and to know the numbers. Just as Bengali is the lingua franca of the east, and Telugu and Tamil in parts of the south, so Hindi has taken over much of the north, and Rajasthani is closely related to Hindi. Sitaram Lalas has produced a 9-volume Rajasthani-Hindi dictionary entitled *Rajasthani Sabad Kos*

(1962-79) containing some 200,000 Rajasthani words, idioms and proverbs. Rajasthani has been recognised as a modern literary language by the National Academy of Letters (Sahitya Akademi, New Delhi) and the University of Jodhpur has set up a Department of Rajasthani.

The all-purpose greeting in Hindi, your palms and fingers touching at or near your forehead, is *Namasteh*, meaning 'hullo!' and 'good morning' but valid for any time of day. Inferiors may often greet superiors with the respectful *Namaskar*.

R.S. McGregor's *Outline of Hindi Grammar* (2nd ed., 1977) is an ideal 'teach yourself' grammar and textbook, with a key to the exercises, but you will need a tape to familiarise yourself with pronunciation. Avoid like diphtheria such efforts as *Learn Hindi in 30 Days* very commonly found in Indian bookshops, for their helpfulness is limited to such observations as 'There are two ears in the head' and, somewhat less accurately, 'There are two legs both sides of the stomach' when a neutral observer might have expected two altogether. You may also do without 'Kya tumhare dada dadi nahim haim?' for it means 'Are you not having your peternal (sic) grand father and grand mother?'). Having surmounted these hurdles, you are confronted with: 'We smear with our nose', 'Stand from the floor', 'There are two hands both sides of the neck', and 'I take rice, What are there for rice?' to which the prescribed retort is 'Sir, sambar, chatny and potato are there'. Some Hindi phrases which may be useful are listed below.

What is this?	Yah kya hai?
Excuse me!	Sunie!
What is this in Hindi?	Hindi mem isko kya kahte haim?
Yes	Han (nasal)
No	Nahim (nasal)
How are you?	Apko kaise hai?
Fine	Maim thik hu
What is your name?	Apka nam kya hai?
My name is John	Mera nam John hai
What time is it?	Kitne bajje haim?
Thank you (Urdu)	Shukria
Thank you (Hindi)	Dhanyavad
Is this the way to Udaipur?	Ye Udaipur ki taraf hai?
Where do you come from?	Kaham se a rahai hai?
I'm going to Agra	Maim Agra tak ja raha hum
I live in Jaisalmer	Maim Jaisalmer mem rahta hum
I have no time	Mere pas vaqt nahim hai
I can speak Hindi	Mujhe Hindi ati hai
There's no water in the room	Kamar mem pani nahim hai
Give me the bill, please	Bil dijiega

Go! Let's go!   Chalo!
On the left; on the right   Baem; daem
Straight on   Sidhe
In the morning; evening   Subah (ko); sham (ko)
Today; yesterday *and* tomorrow   Aj; kal
Last week   Pichle hafte
Next month   Agle mahine
Next year   Agle sal
Cheap; expensive   Sasta; mahanga
Clean, dirty   Saf, maila
Black, white   Kala, safed
Large, small   Bara, chhota
Beautiful   Sundar
Very, many; few   Bahut; kam
Red, blue   Lal, nila
Green, yellow   Hara, pila
Quickly, slowly   Jaldi, dhire
Water, tea   Pani, chai

Numbers and Days of the Week

The numerals, like words in Hindi, are written in Devanagari, but you will find them also in the form familiar to you. To recognise how the numbers sound, and to be able to use them yourself, here is their transliteration into English, though compounds are not easily worked out, and must be memorised. The number 1-10 can be recognised from Greek, Latin, Italian, French and so on, because Sanskrit (from which Hindi derives) is an earlier language of the same Indo-European family to which English and most other European and Western Asiatic languages (except Arabic and Basque) belong.

1 ek 2 do 3 tin 4 char 5 panch 6 chah 7 sat 8 ath 9 nau 10 das 11 gyarah 12 barah 13 terah 14 chaudah 15 pandrah 16 solah 17 satrah 18 atharah 19 unnis 20 bis 21 ikkis 22 bais ... 30 tis 31 ikattis 32 battis ... 40 chalis 50 pachas 60 sath 70 sattar 80 assi 90 navve 100 sau 101 ek sau ek 200 do sau 1,000 ek hazar 100,000 ek lakh 10,000,000 ek karor (written crore). You will find the number 29,148,756 split up in Indian newspapers and books as 2,91,48,756 and written as 2 crores, 91 lakhs, 48 thousand, seven hundred and fifty six.

Monday   somvar
Tuesday   mangalvar
Wednesday   budhvar
Thursday   guruvar
Friday   shukravar
Saturday   shanivar
Sunday   itvar

Holidays and Festivals

Hindu festivals are fixed in accordance with the Vikramaditya calendar based on lunar months which begin with the full moon, and intercalate a thirteenth month of the year every thirty months to ensure the months stay consonant with the seasons. Years of the Vikramaditya era are often cited on monuments or in books, and you need to remember that these years are 57 or 58 years *ahead* of the Christian calendar. The Indian Government has officially sanctioned a third era (Shak) which is 77 or 78 years *behind* the Christian era.

You are never far in time or place from a festival in India: it is almost impossible to weave your way around them. So make the best of them and try to immerse yourself into what happens.

Delhi can be relied on to provide an almost year-long festival, from Republic Day (26 January) and the Folk Dance Festival immediately afterwards to the December Chrysanthemum Show and Christmas Day. In odd-numbered years, Delhi holds an international film festival in January. February sees music and dance festivals and during February and March the social season reaches a crescendo with polo, the Horse Show, the Flower Show and the Golf Championship. Muslim festivals move through the lunar calendar, so you can check with your nearest mosque or reference library when the end of Ramadan is due that year (the Id-ul-Fitr is celebrated at the end of it), and the dates of the first of Muharram, Id-ul-Adha, and the Urs or death-feast of Nizam-ud-Din in Delhi. Holi in Delhi can be violent (March). April 13 is a public holiday to celebrate the official New Year. Good Friday is also an Indian holiday. August 15 is Indian Independence Day, and thus a national holiday. Dussehra (September-October) has much to celebrate, including ten days of music, dance and drama, with processions through Old Delhi, culminating on the tenth day in a great fireworks display and procession at Ram Lila Square. Diwali comes three to four weeks after Dussehra and for about ten days thereafter you can visit fairs and welcome in the new financial year with offerings to Lakshmi, goddess of wealth.

Rajasthani festivals occur throughout the year, and you would be dramatically unlucky to miss them all. The most exhilarating fair is at Pushkar near Ajmer about mid-November (in 1989 the dates were 10-13 November), roughly the same time as the Bikaner Festival, with its great cattle fair. In November-December the Rani Sati Festival at Jhunjhunu in Shekhavati commemorates the first of the thirteen *satis* of the Jalan family. In January you can see the Saraswati festival known as Vasant Panchami, when pens and books are laid in front of an image of the goddess of learning. In February the Hadoti Festival at Kota celebrates the regional arts of Jhalawar, Bundi and Kota; the Desert Festival is held at Jaisalmer. In March the Holi ceremony takes place throughout Rajasthan, with especial splendour at Jaipur's Elephant Festival and the Brij Festival at Bharatpur. In April the Gangaur traditions are re-enacted throughout Rajasthan, with particular interest at Deshnok, Udaipur and Jaipur. The tribes celebrate Gangaur at Gogunda, near Udaipur. Mount Abu's Summer Festival occurs in early June, and Nag Panchami (in honour of the Serpent King) at Jodhpur in July. Early in August comes the Tij Festival at Jaipur, when the anticipated arrival of the monsoon coincides with celebrations of Parvati's reunion with Shiva; twelve days later the festival of Rakhi throughout Rajasthan is the time when young women select a 'brother'. In September (especially in Jaipur) the ceremony of Janma Ashtami commemorates Krishna's birth. At Ramdevra (east of Jaisalmer), an ecumenical gathering pays homage to Baba Ramdev, a local saint. All Rajasthan at the same honours the birth of Ganesha in the ceremony called Ganesh Chaturthi. Dussehra is especially splendid at Kota, and Diwali at Jaipur and Udaipur. Jodhpur's Marwar Festival is held in mid-October.

Books and Maps

Two basic reference books will answer most of your questions about the history and architecture of Rajasthan. The first is Lt.-Col. James Tod's indispensable *Annals and Antiquities of Rajasthan* (3 vols., 1920), inconveniently reproduced in India as two volumes on poor-quality paper in too large a format for reference while travelling. The original 2-volume edition (1829-32) costs about £1,000, but the Oxford University Press reprint cited above can be found second-hand for less than £50 the set. The second is Dr. G.H.R. Tillotson's magisterial *The Rajput Palaces* (Yale University Press, 1987), with its comprehensive and up-to-date bibliography and 245 illustrations. There is no such comprehensive work on the art, music, literature, folklore or social costumes of Rajasthan, though Aman Nath and Francis Wacziarg have collaborated in a comprehensive guide to *Arts and Crafts of Rajasthan* (Mapin International, New York and Ahmedabad, 1987). Handbooks and monographs on each of the towns and cities of Rajasthan are mentioned throughout this book, though all are difficult to obtain in Rajasthan itself, and you should try to read in advance such authorities as Judamati Sarkar (*A History of Jaipur*, Longmans, 1984), Hermann Goetz (*The Art and Architecture of Bikaner State*, Bruno Cassirer, Oxford, 1950), Om Prakash Gupta (*Mount Abu*, Ajmer, 1960), and R.A. Agarawala (*History, Art and Architecture of Jaisalmer*, Agam Kala Prakashan, 1979).

One of the best maps is Bartholomew's World Travel Map no. 15 (*The Indian Subcontinent*), though I used the *Rajasthan* map (scale 1:120,000) in the 'Discover India' series, which is much cheaper, published by TT Maps of Madras, who also produce city maps to Delhi, Agra and Jaipur. In Delhi I used *Know thy Delhi Road Map and Guide*, but -I always recommend checking at any good map shop before departure to check whether something more up-to-date has appeared, and then double-checking on arrival in Delhi and in each town you visit. You can prepare for a study of Indian art, with especial reference to Rajput and Mughal painting, at the National Art Library in London's Victoria and Albert Museum. 'Books from India' at 45 Museum St., London WC1 is situated near the British Museum: its excellent stock of language and literature, travel, maps and guides is perennially replenished from Indian suppliers. Take along to India more films than you think you will need, a second camera in case your good one packs up, and plenty of exercise books and pencils for the notes ahead, because you will want to remember every detail of your days in India as they lengthen into weeks. Have I persuaded you to visit Delhi, Agra, and Rajasthan?

Appendix

Salute States of Rajasthan in Local Order of Precedence (1931)

State	Area in sq.m.	Title, Race, Religion of the Ruler	Guns in Salute
1. Udaipur	12,915	Maharana, Sisodia, Rajput, Hindu	19
2. Jaipur	16,682	Maharajah, Kachhwaha, Rajput, Hindu	17
3. Jodhpur	35,066	Maharajah, Rathore, Rajput, Hindu	17
4. Bundi	2,220	Maharao Rajah, Hara, Rajput, Hindu	17
5. Bikaner	23,315	Maharajah, Rathore, Rajput, Hindu	17
6. Kota	5,684	Maharajah, Hara, Rajput, Hindu	17
7. Karauli	1,242	Maharajah, Jadon, Rajput, Hindu	17
8. Bharatpur	1,982	Maharajah, Jat, Hindu	17
9. Kishangarh	858	Maharajah, Rathore, Rajput, Hindu	15
10. Jaisalmer	16,062	Maharawal, Jadon, Rajput, Hindu	15
11. Alwar	3,213	Maharajah, Naruka, Rajput, Hindu	15
12. Tonk	2,586	Nawab, Pathan, Muslim	15
13. Dholpur	1,200	Maharaj Rana, Jat, Hindu	15
14. Sirohi	1,964	Maharao, Deora, Rajput, Hindu	15
15. Dungarpur	1,447	Maharawal, Sisodia, Rajput, Hindu	15
16. Pratapgarh	886	Maharawal, Sisodia, Rajput, Hindu	15
17. Banswara	1,606	Maharawal, Sisodia, Rajput, Hindu	15
18. Jhalawar	810	Maharaj Rana, Jhala, Rajput, Hindu	13
19. Shahpura	405	Rajah, Sisodia, Rajput, Hindu	9

N.B. The only rulers of Indian states entitled to a 21-gun salute at that time were Hyderabad, Mysore, Baroda, Jammu & Kashmir, and Gwalior, in that order of precedence.

Index

Abhai Singh, 164, 168
accommodation, 38, 40-1, 68, 72, 92, 95, 97, 100, 103, 107, 127, 143, 151-2, 174, 183, 185, 192-3, 205-8, 213, 218-9, 225-6
Adilabad, 11
Afdhal Khan Shukrullah, 54
Agarawala, R.C., 188
Agolai, 159-60, 180
Agra, 26, 40-57, 211, 224-6
agriculture, 102-3
Ahar, 189-90
air travel, 223-4
Ajit Singh (Bundi), 214
Ajit Singh (Jodhpur), 163, 165-6, 173-4, 178
Ajmer, 5, 195-9, 207, 224-5, 232
Akbar, 1, 8-9, 37-40, 44, 46, 58-64, 66, 94-8, 169, 196, 211
Akhai Singh, 141, 143, 156
Ala-ud-Din Khilji, 1-2, 4, 6, 14, 94, 208-9
Albert Hall (Jaipur), 78-82
Alwar, 32, 70-2, 235
Amar Singh (Jaisalmer), 141, 143, 153
Amar Singh (Udaipur), 200, 202
Amber, 69, 73-8, 84, 161
Amir Khusraw, 4, 9
Anup Singh, 123, 126
Aram Bagh (Agra), 53-4
Aravali Hills, 71, 183, 189, 191, 213, 216
Archer, Mildred, 29
Arjumand Banu Begum. *See* Mumtaz Mahal
arms and armour, 33, 84, 176
Ashoka, 32
Atga Khan, 9
Aurangzeb, 18, 20, 33, 37, 47, 51, 60, 66, 89, 100, 123, 166, 168, 186

Babel, D.K., 193
Babur and *Babur-Nama*, 32, 41, 46, 53-4, 58, 61
Badan Singh, 66-7
Bahadur Shah, 20
Baker, *Sir* Herbert, 27

Balban, 4-5, 15
Balji, Shobha Kanwar, 175
Ballabgarh, 35
Balsamand, 181
Banbir, 211-2
Banswara, 235
Bap, 137-8
Barmer, 224
Baroda House, Delhi, 30
bazaars (Agra), 48-9; (Ajmer), 96; (Bikaner), 124; (Delhi), 21-4; (Jaipur), 92-3; (Jaisalmer), 149-51; (Jodhpur), 170-1, 177-9; (Udaipur), 203
Benares, 25, 36
Bernier, François, 47-8
Bhadreśvar, 6
Bhagwant Singh, 202
Bharatpur, 39, 51, 66, 224-5, 235
Bhartiya Lok Kala Mandal, 207
Bhils, 189-90
Bhim Singh, 200, 208-9
Bhopal Singh, 197, 200
bhopis, 105
Bikaner, 32, 69, 98, 101, 116-35, 166, 180, 223-5, 232-3, 235
Birdwood, Vere, *Lady*, 198
Bishnoi, 157-8, 181
Black Mosque, Delhi, 9
Blomfield, C.G., 29
bookshops, 22, 82, 177-8, 202, 234
Brindaban, 37-8, 187
British Library and Museum, 30, 32-3
bronzes, 31
Brown, Percy, 161
Buddhists and Buddhism, 30-1, 36
Bundi, 32, 69, 125, 196, 207, 213-6, 232, 235
bus travel, 207

camels and camel-breeding, 129
canals and irrigation, 123-4, 138
Carstairs, G.M., 159
cattle, 138, 179-80
Chambal, 216

236

Chandni Chowk, Delhi, 4, 21-4
Chaudhury, J.S., 131
Chauhan dynasty, 1, 5, 31, 95, 216, 219
chhatris, 89, 156, 164, 172, 189, 215
child marriage, 215-6
Chini-ka Rauza, 54
Chirawa, 101, 113
Chishtiyyah order of mystics, 8, 44, 58, 63-4, 96
Chittor and Chittorgarh, 69, 75, 194-5, 198, 200, 207-13, 224
Chola art, 31
Chopra, Veena, vi
Churu, 101, 114, 225
City Palace (Udaipur), 191, 194-202
climate, 1, 223
clothing, 229
Communism, 29
Connaught Place, 24-5
costume, 168
cows, 138, 179-80
crafts, 24-5, 49, 92-3
currency, 227
customs, 227

dancing, 131
Daniell, Thomas *and* William, 29-30
Datia, 69
Daulatabad, 11
Davenport, Hugh, 208
Delhi, 1-34, 223-6, 232
Deora dynasty, 235
Desani, G.V., 198
Desert National Park, 156-8
Deshnok, 131-4, 233
Dholpur, 235
Dig, 66-70
Dilwara, 219-22
Dingana, 181
Diwali, 232
Dundlod, 101, 106-7, 119
Dungarpur, 69, 88, 235
Dussehra, 118, 232

education, 97-8
Eklingji, 187-8
embassies, 227

Fateh Singh (Udaipur), 205-6
Fatehpuri Mosque (Delhi), 22
Fatehpur Shekhavati, 101, 106, 113-4
Fatehpur Sikri, 38, 40-1, 57-64, 101
Ferozabad, 4, 11
festivals, 38, 82, 232-3

films, 16-17, 71
Fitch, Ralph, 59
food, 227-8
forts. *See* under the name of individual forts
fortune-telling, 93-4
Fossil Park (Jaisalmer), 156
Friday Mosque. *See* Jami Masjid
Gaj Singh I, 141, 144, 168
Gaj Singh II, 180
Gajner, 127-8
Galta, 89
Gandharan art, 31-2, 37
Gandhi, Indira, 29
Gandhi, Mohandas Karamchand, *Mahatma*, 4, 17, 27-9, 98
Gandhi, Rajiv, 29
Ganga Golden Jubilee Museum (Bikaner), 125-6
Ganga Singh, 118, 120, 122-3, 127, 135
gardens. *See* under the name of individual gardens
Gayatri Devi, *Maharani*, 83-4, 90
Ghalib, *Mirza* A.K., 8-9
Ghiyas-ud-Din Tughlaq, 4, 7, 11
Ghuri, Muhammad, 4-5, 95
Goenka *family*, 102, 106, 110-3
Goetz, Hermann, 133, 233
Government Museum (Ajmer), 96; (Mathura), 37
greetings, 230
Guhilot *dynasty*, 208
Gupta *dynasty*, 36
Gupta art, 31-2, 37, 96
Gwalior, 69

Haldighati, 196
Hanwant Singh, 180
Hara *dynasty*, 235
Hauz-i-Khas (Delhi), 14
havelis, 101-2, 106-7, 109-14, 124, 144, 149-53
Hawa Mahal (Jaipur), 78
Hazari, Shiv, 176
health, 227-9
Hindi, 1, 203, 229-31
Hindus and Hinduism, 28, 34, 36-8, 129-31, 136, 155-6, 160-1, 179-80, 186-7, 232-3
Holi festival, 104, 124, 129-31, 137, 139, 149, 197, 232-3
holidays, 232-3
horses, 21
Humayun, 4, 8-10, 61, 211

237

Ibn Battuta, M. ibn A., 7
Iltutmish, 5-6
Indian Army, 159
Indraprastha, 1, 11, 15
Indus Valley civilisations, 30, 154
Isa Khan, 4, 10-11
Islam and Muslims, 22-3, 28, 36-7, 57, 96-7, 138, 232. *See also* under the names of individual mosques and Muslims
I'timad ad-Daula, 55-6, 191
ivories, 32-3

Jacob, *Col. Sir* S. Swinton, 79, 120-1, 218
Jadon dynasty, 235
Jagat Singh (Jaipur), 62
Jagat Singh I (Udaipur), 191, 203
Jagat Singh II (Udaipur), 191, 202
Jahanara, 4, 9, 51, 97
Jahangir, 32, 38, 41, 46, 49, 55, 64, 75-6, 86, 97, 191
Jahanpanah, 4, 7, 11
Jai Singh (Jaipur), 25, 66, 75-6, 82, 86, 89
Jai Singh (Udaipur), 205, 207-8
Jaigarh, 73, 76-7
Jains and Jainism, 21, 97, 124-5, 141, 144, 146-7, 154-5, 160-1, 183-5, 203, 211, 220-2
Jaipur, 25, 27, 69, 78-95, 101, 223-5, 233, 235
Jaipur House (Delhi), 29-30
Jaisalmer, 69, 116, 123, 134-58, 216, 223-5, 232-3, 235
Jaisamand, 207-8
Jait Singh, 156
Jamali Mosque (Delhi), 15
Jami Masjid (Agra), 22-59; (Delhi), 22-3, 57; (Fatehpur Sikri), 58-64; (Mathura), 37
Jantar Mantar (Delhi), 4, 25; (Jaipur), 83
Jaswant Singh I, 141, 162, 166, 168, 173
Jaswant Singh II, 172
Jats, 66, 235
jauhar, 94, 144, 209-12
Jhalawar, 216, 232, 235
Jhunjhunu, 101, 106, 113, 224-5, 232
Jodha, 161, 165-6, 169, 172
Jodhpur, 69, 99, 116-7, 135, 159-81, 207, 217, 223, 233, 235
Junagarh (Bikaner), 116-21, 125

Kachchwaha *dynasty*, 73, 84, 101, 161, 235
Kailashpuri, 187

Kanoria *family*, 102
Kanwar Devi Singh, 107
Karan Singh (Bikaner), 124
Karan Singh (Udaipur), 191
Karauli, 235
Karni Mata, 133-4
Karni Singh, 123, 127
Kathuria, R.P., 200
Keoladeo National Park, 68-9
Keshava Deo, 37
Keshri Singh (Dundlod), 107
Keshri Singh (Mandawa), 107-9
Khan-i Khanan, 4
Khetri, 101-2
Khilji *dynasty*, 7-8, 11
Khurram, *Prince. See* Shah Jahan
Kishangarh, 99-100, 166, 235
Kota, 69, 98, 153, 207, 216-8, 224-5, 232, 235
Kumbha, *Rana*, 186, 209-10, 212, 222
Kumbhalgarh, 186, 196
Kushan art, 30, 37
Kushan *dynasty*, 36

Lachhmangarh, 102
Lahore, 52, 58, 86, 96
Lake Palace (Udaipur), 191-3, 205-7
Lakshmi Narayan Temple (Delhi), 4, 34
Lal, Ganeshi, 48-9, 51, 56
Lal, Nand, 125, 130
Lal Qila (Agra), 49-52
Lal Qila (Delhi), 4, 18-21
Lalkot, 7, 10-11, 15
Lallgarh Palace (Bikaner), 116, 120-3
Lanchester, H.V., 174-5
Lapierre, Dominique, vii
libraries, 147, 169-70, 175, 200, 203
Lodi *dynasty*, 14-15, 38, 41
Lodruva, 141, 147, 154-5
Loti, Pierre, 206
Lutyens, *Sir* Edwin, 27, 175

McGregor, R.S., 230
Madho Singh I, 84
Madho Singh II, 84, 88
Mahmud, *of Ghazni*, 5, 36
Maldeo, *Rao*, 164-5, 173
Man Singh I, 37, 75, 77
Man Singh II, 75-6, 86, 88, 92, 162
Mandawa, 101, 106-13
Mandore, 161-2, 172-4
Mandu, 211
manuscripts, 32, 71, 86, 147
maps, 233-4

Marathas, 19, 71
marionettes, 81
marriage, child, 215-6
Mathura, 5-6, 25, 31, 36-7, 186, 226
Mauryan art, 30
Mayo College, Ajmer, 97-8, 107
Meherangarh, 162-76
Mehta *family*, 141-2, 149
Mihr an-Nisa. *See* Nur Jahan
mirror palaces. *See shish mahals*
Modi, Raghuvir, 123
monsoons, 102
mosques. *See* under the name of individual mosques
Moth-ki Masjid, 15
Mount Abu, 207, 209, 218-22, 225, 233
Mubarak Shah, 4
Mughal *dynasty*, 86. *See also* under the names of individual Mughal rulers and queens
Mughal painting, 82
Muhammad Shah, 9, 26
Muin-ud-Din Chishti, 8, 96-7
Mukund Singh, 216
Mukundgarh, 224
Mumtaz Mahal (Arjumand Banu Begum) 44, 47, 51, 55
museums. *See* under the names of individual museums
music, 168

Nadir Shah, 19, 26
Nagda, 188-9
Nahargarh, 89
Naruka *dynasty*, 235
Nath, Aman, 93, 101, 109, 233
Nathdwara, 186-7, 207
Nathmal *family*, 150-1
National Gallery of Modern Art (Delhi), 29
National Museum (Delhi), 4, 30-4, 37
national parks (Desert National Park), 156-8; (Keoladeo), 68-9; (Kumbhalgarh), 186; (Mukunddarrah), 216; (Ranthambore), 72, 94-5; (Sariska), 72-3·
National Rose Garden (Delhi), 5
Nawalgarh, 101, 104-6
Nehru, Jawaharlal, *Pandit*, 17, 27-9, 138
Nehru Memorial Museum (Delhi), 27
New Delhi. *See* Delhi
Nizam-ud-Din Aulia, 4, 8, 232

Norblin, S., 175
numbers in Hindi, 231
Nur Jahan (Mihr an-Nisa), 55

Orchha, 69
Osiyan, 159-61, 180

pachisi, 59
Padmini (Chittor), 208-9, 211
painting, 29, 32, 82, 100-2, 200, 214, 218
Pali, 181-2
Pallava art, 31
Pallu, 31
Parasrampura, 102, 106
Parikh, *Dr* Indumati, 28
Parliament, 27
passports, 226
Patnaik, Naveen, 121
pichhwai, 187
Pokaran, 138-40, 159, 225
Pratap Singh (Alwar), 71-2
Pratap Singh (Udaipur), 194, 196-7
Pratapgarh, 235
prehistory, 30-1
princes, 91. *See also* under the names of individual princes
prisons, 165
Purana Qila, 1, 4, 15-17
purdah, 175
Pushkar, 99, 232

Qila-i Rai Pithaura, 5
Qutb Minar, 1, 4-7
Qutb-ud-Din Aibak, 5-6, 15, 95
Quwwat-al-Islam, 6, 9-10

rail travel, 107-8, 177, 223-5
Railway Museum (Delhi), 5
rainfall, 223
Raj Ghat, 4, 17
Raj Singh I, 186
Rajasthani language, 229-30
Rajgarh, 72
Rajput painting, 82
Rajsamand, 186
Ram Bagh, Agra. *See* Aram Bagh
Ranakpur, 183-6, 225
Ranthambore Tiger Reserve, 72, 94-5
Rashtrapati Bhawan, 27, 30
Ratan Singh, 213, 216
Ratangarh, 114-5, 225
Rathore *dynasty*, 118, 161, 165-6, 172-4, 235
Ray, Satyajit, 16-17, 144

Red Fort. *See* Lal Qila
Reynolds-Ball, Eustace, 118
Ringas, 103
Rousselet, Louis, 75, 208
Rupsi, 153

Sachcha *family*, 146
sacrifice of children, 35
sacrifice of women, 94, 144, 209-12
Sadul Singh, 129
Safdarjang, 4, 14, 25-6
Sahelion-ki Bari, 205
Sajjan Singh, 206
Sajjangarh, 89, 206
Samod, 103
Sanganer, 90
Sangram Singh II, 33, 192, 196, 205
Saraf *family*, 112
Sardar Museum (Jodhpur), 180
Sariska Tiger Reserve, 72-3
sati, 28, 165
Sawai Madhopur, 72, 94-5, 224
Sayyid *dynasty*, 14
Shah, Naseeruddin, 17
Shah Jahan, 9, 18, 20-2, 41, 44, 46, 48-9, 51, 97, 166, 168, 191
Shahjahanabad, 1, 11, 14, 18
Shahpura, 235
Sharma, Bijay Bhushan, 4-5, 23
Shekhawati, 101-15, 149, 224-5
Sher Shah Suri, 4, 9-10, 15-16
shikar, 175
shish mahals, 51, 88, 167-8
Shiv Niwas (Udaipur), 192
Shokoohy, Mehrdad, 6
shopping. *See* bazaars
Sikandar Lodi, 4, 9, 37-8, 41
Sikandra, 38-40
Sikar, 101-4, 224
Sikhs and Sikhism, 40, 56, 188-9, 203
Silk Roads, 33
Singh Tanwar, Birendra, vi, 129, 182
Singhania *family*, 102
Siri, 4, 7
Sirohi, 235
Sisodia *dynasty*, 193, 208, 235
State Archaeological Museum, Bharatpur, 67
Stern, Robert, 88
Subbamma, Malladi, 28
Sunga art, 6-7, 30

Tagore, Rabindranath, 17
Taj Mahal, 9-10, 40-1, 44-7, 51, 55, 58

Taragarh (Ajmer), 97
Taragarh (Bundi), 215
Tarain, 5
Tata *family*, 34
Tavernier, Jean-Baptiste, 21, 44, 47, 51
temples. *See* under the names of individual temples
terra cottas, 31-2
Thapar, Valmik, 94-5
Thar Desert, 116, 138, 140, 143, 156-8
tigers, 72-3, 94-5
Tilangani Mausoleum, 9
Tillotson, G.H.R., vi, ix-xi, 69, 75, 89, 144, 166, 178, 197, 233
Tod, James, 66, 140-1, 161, 170, 188, 197, 210, 233
toilets, 228
Tomar *dynasty*, 5
Tonk, 32, 90, 235
train travel, 107-8, 177, 223-5
Tughlaq *dynasty*, 4-6, 8, 11
Tughlaqabad, 4, 7, 11

Udai Singh (Jodhpur), 170
Udai Singh I (Udaipur), 210-2
Udai Singh II (Udaipur), 196
Udaipur, 69, 75, 89, 153, 182-207, 214, 217, 219, 223, 233, 235
Ujjain, 25
Umaid Bhawan Palace, 174-7
Umaid Singh (Bikaner), 175-6, 180
Umaid Singh (Bundi), 214-5

Victoria and Albert Museum (London), 32, 37, 61, 79, 172, 218, 234
visas, 226-7

Wacziarg, Francis, 93, 101, 109, 233
wages and salaries, 56-7
water, 228
weather, 1, 223
women, 28, 94, 165, 209-12

Yamuna, 15, 37, 40, 48, 53-4
Yunus, S.M., 183

Zahara Bagh (Agra), 53-4
Zoological Gardens (Bikaner), 129; (Delhi), 17; (Jaipur), 78; (Jodhpur), 180

ARABIA PAST AND PRESENT

ANNALS OF OMAN
Sirhan ibn Sirhan

ARABIA IN EARLY MAPS
G.R. Tibbetts

ARABIAN GULF INTELLIGENCE
comp. R.H. Thomas

ARABIAN PERSONALITIES OF THE
EARLY TWENTIETH CENTURY
introd. R.L. Bidwell

DIARY OF A JOURNEY ACROSS ARABIA
G.F. Sadleir

THE GOLD-MINES OF MIDIAN
Richard Burton

HA'IL: OASIS CITY OF SAUDI ARABIA
Philip Ward

HEJAZ BEFORE WORLD WAR I
D.G. Hogarth

HISTORY OF SEYD SAID
Vincenzo Maurizi

KING HUSAIN & THE KINGDOM OF HEJAZ
Randall Baker

THE LAND OF MIDIAN (REVISITED)
Richard Burton

MONUMENTS OF SOUTH ARABIA
Brian Doe

OMANI PROVERBS
A.S.G. Jayakar

SOJOURN WITH THE GRAND SHARIF OF MAKKAH
Charles Didier

TRAVELS IN ARABIA (1845 & 1848)
Yrjö Wallin

TRAVELS IN OMAN
Philip Ward

OLEANDER MODERN POETS

CONTEMPORARY GERMAN POETRY
comp. Ewald Osers

THE HIDDEN MUSIC
Östen Sjöstrand

A HOUSE ON FIRE
Philip Ward

IMPOSTORS & THEIR IMITATORS
Philip Ward

LOST SONGS
Philip Ward

ONCE OFF (Lenier poems)
Royal College of Art

RAIN FOLLOWING
Sue Lenier

THE SCANDALOUS LIFE OF CÉSAR MORO
César Moro

SWANSONGS
Sue Lenier

UNDERSEAS POSSESSIONS
Hans-Juergen Heise

OLEANDER LANGUAGE AND LITERATURE

THE ART & POETRY OF C.-F. RAMUZ
David Bevan

BIOGRAPHICAL MEMOIRS OF EXTRAORDINARY PAINTERS
William Beckford

CELTIC: A COMPARATIVE STUDY
D.B. Gregor

FRENCH KEY WORDS
Xavier-Yves Escande

FRIULAN: LANGUAGE & LITERATURE
D.B. Gregor

GREGUERÍAS: Wit and Wisdom of
R. Gómez de la Serna

INDONESIAN TRADITIONAL POETRY
Philip Ward

A LIFETIME'S READING
Philip Ward

MARVELL'S ALLEGORICAL POETRY
Bruce King

ROMAGNOL: LANGUAGE & LITERATURE
D.B. Gregor

ROMONTSCH: LANGUAGE & LITERATURE
D.B. Gregor

OLEANDER GAMES AND PASTIMES

CHRISTMAS GAMES FOR ADULTS
AND CHILDREN
Crispin DeFoyer

DARTS: 50 WAYS TO PLAY THE GAME
Jabez Gotobed

DICE GAMES NEW AND OLD
W.E. Tredd

ENLIGHTENMENT THROUGH THE ART
OF BASKETBALL
Hirohide Ogawa

ENNEAGRAMS: NINE-LETTER WORD GAME
Ian D. Graves

PUB GAMES OF ENGLAND
Timothy Finn

SUMMER GAMES FOR ADULTS
AND CHILDREN
Hereward Zigo